DISEASE X
AND MEDICAL MARTIAL LAW

DEFEATING THE GLOBALIST PLAN TO DEPOPULATE THE WORLD AND ENSLAVE THE REMNANT

TODD S. CALLENDER, J.D., JEROME R. CORSI, PH.D., AND CRAIG D. CAMPBELL, PH.D.

BOMBARDIER
B O O K S

Published by Bombardier Books
An Imprint of Post Hill Press
ISBN: 979-8-89565-422-4
ISBN (eBook): 979-8-89565-423-1

Disease X and Medical Martial Law:
Defeating the Globalist Plan to Depopulate the World and Enslave the Remnant
© 2025 by Todd S. Callender, J.D., Jerome R. Corsi, Ph.D.,
and Craig D. Campbell, Ph.D.
All Rights Reserved

Cover Design by Cody Corcoran

This book, as well as any other Bombardier Books publications, may be purchased in bulk quantities at a special discounted rate. Contact orders@bombardierbooks.com for more information.

BOMBARDIER BOOKS   Post Hill PRESS

Post Hill Press
New York • Nashville
posthillpress.com

Published in the United States of America
1 2 3 4 5 6 7 8 9 10

In the end, God always wins.
—Dr. Jerome Corsi

1 Peter 5:8–9 (ESV)

Be sober-minded; be watchful. Your adversary the devil prowls around like a roaring lion, seeking someone to devour. Resist him, firm in your faith, knowing that the same kinds of suffering are being experienced by your brotherhood throughout the world.

TABLE OF CONTENTS

ACKNOWLEDGMENTS

This experience of fighting for the survival of our species over the last four years has helped me understand that most every shivering highlight in my life was for the purpose of leading me to this moment in the history of humanity—the threshold decision in our hands just as it was for Pontius Pilate—do we follow God, or do we kneel before Satan?

Of most all the astounding souls I've met along the way, especially in the last four years where people openly proved their courageous faith by fighting evil totalitarianism, I came to find that, almost universally, we've either been dead or were close enough to see this life is very temporary.

The most amazing people, who I did not know exist, banded together across all manufactured barriers that were enforced by public shame and public perception carefully crafted by the "Owners." They are too numerous to list here, and I've struggled with the choice of writing many pages of credits or simply mentioning that I am nothing without them and nothing without God's remarkably kind and adept hand—but these people include my family especially, who have endured my absence, mentally and physically, while I spent most every waking hour doing everything in my power to stop the attack on humanity and restore God's Earthly kingdom to its rightful holding of his creations. Alexandra (love of my life for twenty-five years), Katelyn, and Cameron sacrificed every lost moment and opportunity for joy as a family because they understand the true landscape. We are in a do-or-die scenario, yet they "Meet the Challenge" (the slogan of my basic training company in the Army) with earnest determination to *live*—they *really live*!

I am only as capable as the people around me who have counseled, collaborated, and encouraged me to this place and at the twelfth hour. It's easier and more fair to name them by the formidable teams they form:

- my magnificent wife and family team who challenged and tempered me for the furnace we've endured and stood by me when I was a lonely voice;
- the whistleblowers (so many) who risked *everything* to do the right thing for our Republic and humanity's survival;
- the badges and guns (law enforcement) folks who I've had the inexplainable pleasure of working with and representing—those experiences allowed me an understanding of the true global power paradigm (thanks Brooks, et al);
- the Cotswold Group of Companies team for agreeing years ago on November 4 to double their efforts to afford me time for litigating and lawyering (Nick, you are exceptional in all respects);
- the Disabled Rights Advocates legal team, my battle buddies from the *Robert v. Austin* legal team, and the one hundred or so lawyers (globally) that collaborated, supported, and

rallied each other through the often fruitless and disheartening legal war, as well as the expert witnesses who gambled their reputations, relationships, remuneration, and careers on correcting the record and "science";

- the doctors and scientists who honored their oaths and conglomerated to heal and save our species, the CloutHub and Vaxxchoice teams who include victims and whistleblowers, and the whole of the alternative media and truther influencers who (gratefully) never stopped sharing their knowledge nor rested;

- the hero pro se litigants who papered the hell out of our governments and the masses of discerning and heartful souls who dared share a link, comment, or dinner discussion about *the truth*;

- the skeptical, faithful government workers who subverted the master plans with little disruptions and wins each day; and

- to the ever-righteous military (retired and uniform-wearing) men and women who followed their oaths of office and allegiances to our Republic, especially including the astounding courage and leadership of Dan Robert and Hollie Mulvihill (the plaintiffs in *Robert v. Austin*) for being the first to stand against the biggest, most lethal killing machine this world has ever known. The battle cries of our troops still ring in my head…"*Hold the line*!!" A special thanks is owed to our Department of Defense whistleblowers who applied the phrase and led this battle cry (Lt. Col./Dr. Theresa Long, Lt. Col./Dr. Pete Chambers, Maj./Dr. Sam Sigoloff, and Lt. Mark Bashaw).

I apologize in advance for missing anyone or group that made it possible for us to have this opportunity at *reclaiming and recovering our* world.

I'm honored to have stood with all of you, and I'm honored to tell *our* story in this book with two noble and seasoned Owner-slayers, Dr. Jerome Corsi and Dr. Craig Campbell. But for you and your encouragement, I would not have found the time to dare.

God bless you all.

—Todd S. Callender, J.D.

INTRODUCTION

THE "OWNERS" VERSUS HUMANITY
BY TODD CALLENDER

A dark, evil ideology has descended over the world. We are facing a many-tentacled global coup d'état that involves the United Nations 2030 Agenda, the World Health Organization, the World Bank, the International Monetary Fund, the European Central Bank, the US CIA/State Department/Defense Department globalist cabal, and the World Economic Forum.

I have labeled this evil conglomeration of elitist power mongers the "Owners," the world's self-appointed puppet masters.

These malevolent forces are willing to manipulate and lie about a "plandemic" that was a bad flu and a "vaccine" that does not prevent the disease while genetically modifying the DNA that God bestowed upon us.

Under the banner of "saving the planet," these Satanic forces are willing to deprive the modern industrial state of the available hydrocarbon energy needed to sustain the world's more than eight billion inhabitants. Willing to create wars, diseases, and

starvation, this globalist cult is, at its core, a democide ("extermi-
nationist") movement. The criminal handling of the plandemic
first and the green agenda later unequivocally demonstrates a
willingness to implement a plan to decimate the world's population, as theorized by the leading proponents and funders of the
"Great Reset."

As accurately declared by Archbishop Carlo Maria Viganò,
the former papal nuncio to the United States of America, in an
open letter to President Donald Trump in 2020:

> In recent months we have been witnessing the
> formation of two opposing sides that I would
> call *Biblical*: the children of light and the chil-
> dren of darkness. The children of light constitute
> the most conspicuous part of humanity, while
> the children of darkness represent an absolute
> minority. And yet the former are the object of a
> sort of discrimination which places them in a sit-
> uation of moral inferiority with respect to their
> adversaries, who often hold strategic positions
> in government, in politics, in the economy and
> in the media. In an apparently inexplicable way,
> the good are held hostage by the wicked and by
> those who help them either out of self-interest or
> fearfulness.[1]

---

[1] Archbishop Carlo Maria Vigano, "Archbishop Viganò's Powerful Letter to
President Trump: Eternal Struggle Between Good and Evil Playing Out Right
Now," Opinion, LifeSiteNews, June 6, 2020, https://www.lifesitenews.com/
opinion/archbishop-viganos-powerful-letter-to-president-trump-eternal-
struggle-between-good-and-evil-playing-out-right-now.

The peoples of nations that call themselves "democratic" are not consulted by their rulers but, on the contrary, are treated as servants and silenced or even subjected to censure and imprisonment if they express dissent.

At stake is the freedom of ourselves, our children, and our grandchildren should this transhumanist elite succeed in controlling the masses, the "useless eaters," with their fast-growing army of artificial intelligence-assisted robots and machines.

In the godless secular world in which we now live, self-appointed globalist deep-state actors are running naked to the finish line, imposing their totalitarian nightmare upon us. These self-appointed globalists hide deep within the intelligence bureaucracies, within our justice systems, our educational systems, our state and federal bureaucracies, and the editorial offices of our mainstream media. Now they are hiding in plain sight, unashamed of their malevolence and dark intentions.

Most of the world's nations are ruled by emissaries of supranational powers who obey their orders not only in violation of the constitutions they are sworn to defend but, above all, of the citizens, who have become victims and hostages of their political class.

In order to don a thin veil of protection, many of these supposed civil servants have not signed oaths of allegiance for the offices they hold. By not openly committing to obey the laws of the land, they broadcast their true dedication to the forces of darkness amassing against the very states they are to defend. Such duplicity does not go unnoticed.

Whether in the United States, Canada, Australia, European states, and China, the same darkness is in motion. All minions are following the same script going in one direction as dictated by the Owners. To believe that in our connected society the events in the other states have no correlation constitutes an unforgivable naiveté. Such a flawed notion is belied, first of all, by the facts themselves, their consistency and synchrony, and the lies that have been spread everywhere to cover up their almost infinite list of crimes.

The North Atlantic Treaty Organization, the United Nations, the World Health Organization, the European Union, the International Monetary Fund, the World Economic Forum, all self-described "philanthropic" foundations, and other private entities share a common trait. No one has elected them to represent us. No one has transferred our national sovereignty to them. They are making decisions that have a major impact on the world's population, without any mandate.

By their own admission, the Western world must be radically altered in its social, political, cultural, religious, economic, and health fabric through social engineering interventions. They proceed unhindered, with the cooperation of individual governments acting in a collectivist fashion.

In many cases, these interventions are being financed by the World Bank, the European Central Bank, and large investment fund entities such as BlackRock. Although believed by almost everyone to be "public" in nature, they are actually private enterprises under the control of the big families that control world finance, the Owners.

Conflicts of interest are to be ignored as long as the minions are dutiful operatives working to ensure that the plans of the Owners are realized. These minions are mere employees hired into supervisory bodies that are supposed to oversee the activities of their respective companies, and if at the end of their term they suited their purpose, they are hired again.

Nepotism is a primary factor enabling the scheme to succeed. Relatives of the directors of public bodies are called upon to supervise the work of their relatives. Companies engaged in publishing and media belong to investment groups, and the exchange of critical information benefits both. Accountability becomes impossible. Recent scandals in the pharmaceutical industry are but the tip of an iceberg that no one dares to denounce.

2020: The year the earth stood still and began to rotate backwards

The year 2020 ushered in a less than "great reset." It was not actually a reset; it represented the public launch of a multi-phased plan by the Owners. The unfolding plan represented the culmination of decades of evil visions and dark secrets coming together in an orchestrated attack on humanity itself.

Starting that March, the US government reengineered America with a mandate to supposedly protect lives. Such a mandate had not been experienced in the United States since the military mobilization of the nation required to defeat Nazi Germany and Imperial Japan.

Eight decades later, tyrannical government rules were issued by health authorities in the name of waging war against a wee but deadly virus. Government health authorities worldwide deceived the public, insisting COVID-19 was but a natural mutation passing between species by moving from bats to humans in the Huanan open seafood market in Wuhan, China (Communist China, our mortal enemy).

The virus was actually a bioweapon developed by an "Army of Darkness," with key players within US- and Communist-Chinese-government-funded laboratories, for the express purpose of depopulation.

Ominous as that might sound, the bioweapon turned out to be one of many weapons in a vast arsenal aimed at all of humanity. The Owners possess a vast quiver of various toxic arrows, all with one purpose: culling out the "useless eaters" among us, resulting in a remnant of human slaves.

Key players in this fight to the death are the World Health Organization, the United Nations and its 2030 Agenda, the World Economic Forum, transhumanism, artificial intelligence, nuclear war, and the invasion of Western nations, in particular the United States of America. The shadowy figure behind it all is Satan, as this is perhaps the final battle in the dark one's forever vendetta against God's creation.

Ephesians 6:12 (NLT)

For we are not fighting against flesh-and-blood enemies,
but against evil rulers and authorities of the unseen
world, against mighty powers in this dark world,
and against evil spirits in the heavenly places.

My background, experience, and relationships have placed me in a unique position. I have worked in the disability, health, and life insurance industry for more than twenty years and focused on the international convergence of biomedical, morbidity, and mortality risks in the global legal context. I currently serve as an executive board member of many multinational companies and was responsible for the completion of the Food and Drug Administration's registration process for a new medical device in the mass vaccination industry. As briefly stated before, my experience in the vaccine business made this all possible. I was at the table during formative and course-changing moments in the industry and world and could not knowingly watch our government poison (exterminate) our volunteer protectors (troops) and fellow humans in the preplanned military operation to eradicate or transform seven billion people. I knew the contents of the COVID-19 "vaccines" were deadly. There was a lot of talking about doing something to stop the secretary of defense from issuing the order, but very few lawyers were willing. I was the only lawyer in our small group licensed in the federal district courts (trial courts), so I filed the first federal lawsuit against our government to stop the liquid pathogens, a process that lasted over three years. Our mostly volunteer team took *Robert v. Austin* all the way to the Supreme Court of the United States. Taking it to the ultimate court could not have happened without the seasoned and able collaboration of my co-counsel and colleagues (lawyers and others).

I have developed a close relationship with Jerome Corsi, PhD. Dr. Corsi is a political commentator and author of over thirty books on politics and economics—best known for his *New York Times* bestsellers, *Unfit for Command: Swift Boat Veterans Speak Out Against John Kerry* (2004) and *The Obama Nation: Leftist Politics and the Cult of Personality* (2008), which presented critical views on Democratic presidential candidates. Corsi holds a PhD in political science from Harvard University and has written on a wide range of subjects, including politics and finance. His career has included roles such as the Washington, DC bureau chief for InfoWars, although he is no longer with the organization. In 2018, he was involved in the Robert Mueller special counsel investigation due to his alleged connections with WikiLeaks and former Trump adviser Roger Stone. His new book, *The Assassination of President John F. Kennedy: The Final Analysis* presents indisputable forensic evidence that two shots fired from the front and one shot fired from the rear killed the president in the Dealey Plaza crossfire—exposing a sixty-year cover-up by the CIA, the FBI, the Pentagon, and the Secret Service. Dr. Corsi's latest book, *The Anti-Globalist Manifesto: Ending the War on Humanity* is a call for action to reverse the totalitarian goals of the New World Order globalists.

I have also developed a relationship with Craig Campbell, PhD. Craig has a bachelor's degree in political science and history, master's degree in public administration, and PhD in administration and management. Craig has over thirty years of experience in several sectors as a human resources professional, including as senior vice president of human resources for a worldwide nonprofit organization. He has worked as a volunteer for Dr. Corsi for over six years, including as a broadcast producer, webmaster, editor, and writer.

We are following 1 Peter 4:10 (NLT): *God has given each of you a gift from his great variety of spiritual gifts. Use them well to serve one another.*

This book is an example of a faithful application of that biblical instruction. Dr. Corsi, Craig, and I have teamed together to combined our varied talents and knowledge to produce a work that will awaken the unaware to the truth, increase the understanding of all, and ultimately bring glory to God. May it be so.

PART I
A RUN THROUGH THE JUNGLE

CHAPTER 1

TODD CALLENDER'S CUBAN ADVENTURE BEGINS

March 1998

"**G**ood morning, Miami Center, November Eight-Five, One-Two Yankee is with you level ten thousand." The crackling of the radio in my headset and the drone of the two piston engines of the Piper Twin Comanche made me wonder if anyone was listening per the normal hand-off routine to a new controller.

It's not the ideal airplane to transport cargo, but it is reliable, speedy, and what Bahamian pilots call a "baby Aztec." The Aztec was also made by Piper at that time but built for lifting heavy loads of people and cargo. Still, the baby Aztec was reliable and up to the job.

The Caribbean islands were built on the backs of Douglas DC-3s (still in operation) and Piper Aztecs. That day, my baby

Aztec was performing flawlessly, which should have been an indicator that trouble lied ahead. In the military, people used to avoid going through airborne school by asking "who would jump out of a perfectly good airplane?" without knowing what all pilots know—there is no such thing as a *perfectly* good airplane. To have everything going right: weather, controllers, engines, systems, and an on-time departure is extraordinarily rare. And that day would prove this theorem as to the rarity of perfect flight operations.

Having just left Nassau and Bahamian airspace, I climbed to my filed-assigned altitude of ten thousand feet, and following protocol, I checked in with the new controllers to let them know I was on their frequency in order for us to communicate.

Miami Center responded, "Good morning Eight-Five, One-Two Yankee, Nassau altimeter is two-eight, nine-nine," confirming they saw me on their radar, were hearing my transmission, and I was to remain at my assigned altitude.

Having ascended more than four thousand feet above the level of the Bahamian airspace and according to the Instrument Flight Rules,[2] I was to be serviced and controlled by the US radar controllers, which is why I was then speaking to the Miami Center (controllers) even while still flying over the islands of and past Andros, the biggest island of the archipelago.

As I glanced skyward, at ten thousand feet, the clouds were dense but not too wet, considering how crappy the weather would become with a dropping barometer. I was flying in what pilots of all languages refer to as "soup." There are times when a pilot cannot see much of anything beyond the aircraft's wingtips, kind of like losing a spoon in a big bowl of chili. That day, I was a small

---

[2] Instrument Flight Rules, 14 C. F. R. § 91.167–91.199 (2024).

spoon in a big bowl of chili; I was essentially flying blind. In such times, pilots rely heavily on their sense of hearing, listening for different noises from the aircraft and the surroundings.

During my flight that day from the Bahamas to Cuba, the cadence of the engines sounded like a weird drum beat. I was soon locked into a sensorial battle between the audible engine noise and visual attraction of the electronic device on the instrument panel that transmits a four-digit code ("squawk code"). This device is normally dormant during most of a flight and only emits its orange light when it senses a radar signal from air traffic control (ATC). On that flight, the abnormal squawking became concerning.

Transponders enable ATC to identity the aircraft, its location, and its flight plan details. Thus, ATC is able to differentiate between aircraft and spot potential hazards. That day, the transponder was lighting up in a very regimented manner, indicating a radar system was "pinging" me at a regular interval. Was it an equipment malfunction at my end or Miami Tower, or was another interested party tracking me...and for what purpose? Friend or foe? I would soon find out.

Much of the Bahamas is very remote, and for safety reasons, controllers often inform pilots about hazards and anomalies they can't see and their radar can't reach. Although remoteness itself may pose certain problems for the ordinary flier, smugglers have enjoyed the quiet and relatively uncrowded airspace of the large seven-hundred-island nation to ply their illegal trade.

But my experience that day in March was considerably different and potentially more dangerous, as I was very clearly being "painted" by some unknown radar beacon, and the signal was strong and consistent. Pilots learn to stay calm under all circumstances, not overreacting to negative stimuli, but still staying on high alert in times of uncertainty. As the radar continued to blast at me from the transponder, the blips kept beating perfectly with my favorite in-flight music, the Creedence Clearwater Revival song "Run Through the Jungle," which I had cranked up upon takeoff.

There is something special about putting the throttles to "firewall forward" (pilot-speak for "going full power") on takeoff that goes well with Vietnam War–era vintage music. Again, I should have listened more carefully to the clues the tune bode about my soon-upcoming encounter with fate. Either way, I needed both entertainment and distraction as I not so blissfully continued on my mission: I had no choice but to physically transport through potentially hostile airspace an airplane full of medical supplies destined for the clinical field trials I was conducting. Placing concerns over airworthiness aside, my mind focused in on the blinking light and potential warning I was receiving courtesy of lyrics from John Fogerty's legendary rock and roll band and his admonition to run through the jungle when the Devil is on the loose.

Danger seemed far away, and my mind reflected on what all seemed surreal to finally get this field trial underway after spending the last year negotiating with the various organs of both the Cuban and American governments.

Leaving the United States with an airplane full of medical equipment destined for what was then classified as an enemy nation was, by itself, no small or innocuous feat. Aside from actually obtaining the required licenses from all the various regulatory and law enforcement agencies to receive approval for my plan and application, I also needed to comply with the very technical, strict, and punitive measures taken against any organization or individual providing support to an "enemy" nation, in this case Fidel Castro's Cuba. Most such restrictions are designed to prevent other threatening nations from obtaining technology that could afford them any integration or creation of weapons and "weapons of mass destruction" in particular.

At the last US port of disembarkation for that shipment (Melbourne, Florida), I had to clear the goods for transport with a US Customs agent (this was well before the creation of the Department of Homeland Security) and various government agencies, including the Department of Commerce. I was engaged in odd turf battles, all claiming jurisdiction over US–made technology and dual-use technology,[3] in particular. On the day I was clearing customs with the shipment, the customs lady (middle-aged, well-fed, Karen-like) was most unhappy being bothered to leave her little regulatory kingdom (a doughnut-rich office) to inspect an airplane full of "medical supplies." To add to the drama, these were not run-of-the-mill medical supplies routinely transported to a friendly neighboring country like Canada, but suspicious objects embarking on a maiden voyage to a verboten land. I'm sure the hair stood up on the back of her neck upon reading, "Destination: Cuba." This nearby enemy nation, ninety miles off her coast, and very nearly a launch platform for incoming missiles but a few decades prior. I don't know what was in the mind of Customs Lady, but I'm sure she was more than encouraged to hate that island because it existed as a potential threat in

---

[3] See Hannah Kelley, "Dual-Use Technology and U.S. Export Controls," Center for a New American Security, June 15, 2023, https://www.cnas.org/publications/reports/dual-use-technology-and-u-s-export-controls.

her mind, firmly implanted by our three-letter agencies and media propaganda machines. Haven't all of our minds been so warped? Anyway, she expressed her displeasure through tone and gesture during our entire encounter as she relentlessly rummaged through every box, pulling all of them baggage-handler-style out of the aircraft and spreading them out on the hot tarmac in a fashion she deemed appropriate (most likely based upon some barely remembered training exercise).

"Did you get Pfizer's permission to export this vaccine?" queried Customs Lady.

Her tone was accusatory, clearly meant to be—and even more clearly received as—a threat. She rattled off a series of accusatory questions/statements. Undaunted, I immediately displayed firm resolve, confident and composed, ready to prove complete compliance with all requirements.

I knew my paperwork was in order, and as a lawyer with experience in federal law enforcement while in law school, I knew the drill and the grill, fully able to answer her staccato questions supported by a ream of documents from the requisite thick three-ring binder. As part of the worst-case preparation for a dreaded moment such as this, my materials were meticulously arranged. And so my painstaking pre-customs work paid off, as all of the legal work came into play. Thank you, University of Denver. After all, it was to be expected; this was the very first export of *any* goods whatsoever to Cuba since the embargo and enemy nation declaration.

Looking back at that experience, God's hand was evident. Was it fortune or providence that I had worked in this very same area of law enforcement and developed personal friendships with, and received professional assistance from, two special agents? Those agents were my secret weapons (shield, helmet, and sword) and essential elements enabling defeat of the "bureau-beast." Customs Lady, eventually exhausted by the heat steaming from the asphalt tarmac and reluctantly satisfied that all of my documents were actually in order, relented. However, not before snarling a face-saving canard under her breath while stamping "CLEARED" on my outbound papers: "Next time you had better get your story straight!" My story was straight, true, and irrefutable, but apparently flawed in some minute way in her mind as a defense mechanism.

She headed back to her kingdom in a snit—surely a doughnut binge was to follow—and punctuated her displeasure in having come up dry in her rejection quest with a final angry glare. No matter, I had just completed the most intimidating and challenging part of the very long process of acquiring *all* of the many approvals necessary to make that flight—including the licensing of my aircraft as a temporary export. Yes, your eyes did not deceive you, my plane itself was considered a "temporary export." "How so?" you ask.

Well, even my middle-aged aircraft contained avionics or other components that were subject to the same restrictions that covered "weapons of mass destruction" parts going to Cuba, North Korea, or other "hostile" countries.

I was so filled with excitement and relief from having been cleared to proceed with my mission that I had forgot to remove one set of wheel chalks after starting up to taxi my plane—perhaps a harbinger of the cascading events that were about to unfold, events that usually resulted in downed planes and dead pilots.

"November Eight-Five, One-Two Yankee, confirm your destination is Mike-Uniform-Hotel-Alpha?" my radio crackled once again.

Requesting confirmation of destination was an unusual question as the flight plan clearly stated my destination.

"Roger that Miami, the destination is MUHA—Havana," I radioed back.

"Roger Eight-Five, One-Two Yankee, standby...uh...uh... do you have an authorization or some kind of permission to go there?" stuttered the controller.

The controller's hesitation was understandable considering the following history lesson:

According to the administrators at the Department of the Treasury (and the aforementioned agencies from which I had to obtain permission), I was the very first American to receive a license to travel to and engage in business with the Cuban government under the regime. Successfully securing the licensure of my airplane by the Commerce Department as a temporary export was also a result of the time I had spent working in this area of law.

Cuba had been completely economically sanctioned since the Cuban Revolution of 1958, prohibiting all access to US resources of any kind. Still, narrow exemptions had just appeared in the US regulatory code that prompted me to apply so we could conduct the US Food and Drug Administration–mandated clinical field trials for our then-unlicensed and clinically untested needle-less injector.[4] That revolutionary handheld device is capable

---

[4]   See Robert Steinway and John Bigham. Needle-less injector. US Patent 20080281261A1, filed May 3, 2005, and issued April 20, 2010. https://patents.google.com/patent/US20080281261A1/.

of delivering liquid medicine directly into the muscle or fat layers of a patient by quickly and efficiently forcing the medicinal fluid through a small (eight-micron) hole in the disposable plastic vial. The technology was an enormous breakthrough, and we just needed to prove it.

Cuba was the ideal place for this type of clinical trial as that country had already developed a vaccine, along with highly trained and extremely knowledgeable medical professionals.

Cuba is a poor nation today in large part due to the embargo in combination with the end of Soviet support.[5] In 1976, Cuba included in its constitution an obligation to provide health care and education to its citizens. Since prevention is less costly than treatment, the country invested heavily in prevention (vaccines) to avoid the expense of treatment. The eleven million people living there in isolation from the rest of the world provided an ideal patient population for our prepared protocol regarding the safety and efficacy of our injector.

The project and approach made perfect sense to me and obviously to the United States government as I received the proper permissions and exemptions from what otherwise would invoke punishment, including prison and even execution for violating the law. Considering the health benefits for all of mankind that could be attained and the fact that our devices could not be used as weapons, it was a "no-brainer."

Naturally, during the following months, I was compelled to continue to navigate the regulatory obstacle course, which I did

---

[5] See Claire Priest, "Cuba's History and Transformation through the Lens of the Sugar Industry," Yale Library, May 23, 2016, 2, https://law.yale.edu/sites/default/files/area/center/kamel/sela16_priest_cv_eng_20160523.pdf.

in earnest. Even so, I received various threats and warnings about our project and doing business with the Cuban government.

There are no more fervent anti-communists on the planet than people who have escaped such a tyrannical system. In 1959, the guerrilla campaign against the government of Fulgencio Batista evolved into a full-blown revolution, culminating in Batista's removal and the ascendance of Fidel Castro. Castro crushed all opposition, resulting in wave after wave of dissidents fleeing the island, with most receiving sanctuary in and around Miami, Florida. Cuban exiles dreamed of retaking their homeland and formed many resistance groups, such as "Alpha 66,"[6] which is still active today. I had no idea that my project would be perceived as a threat to their mission to destroy Fidel and his government at all costs. Until my project, I really hadn't taken that resistance activity too seriously as the people making the threats were conservative, patriotic, family- and God-loving—my kind of people, or so I thought. End of history lesson. Let's get back to Miami ATC's question:

"Roger Eight-Five, One-Two Yankee, standby...uh...uh... do you have an authorization or some kind of permission to go there?"

I replied, "Affirm—yes, I actually put the OFAC [Office of Foreign Assets Control] license number in the notes of my flight plan."

By that time, I was nearing Cuban airspace and the hair on the back of my neck stood to attention. I anxiously pondered my

---

[6] María Cristina García, "Hardliners v. 'Dialogueros': Cuban Exile Political Groups and United States-Cuba Policy," *Journal of American Ethnic History* 17, no. 4 (1998): 3–28.

journey into the unknown as I droned along in the clouds toward my final destination. I was approaching Havana for the first time, and was without navigational aids, specifically, recent aeronautical maps or updated approach plates.[7] Because of the Cuban embargo, information about the country was nearly impossible for the public to attain—including those critical tools. Even though the Bahamas, where I stopped to refuel, is ruled by the United Kingdom, not the United States, it respects US Export Administration laws, including those pertaining to high-tech equipment. Thus, trade with Cuba was limited, and Bahamians could be sanctioned for doing business with the Cuban government if deemed in violation of the same laws that required me to obtain that temporary export license just to fly my airplane into Cuban airspace.

Getting the licenses and US Food and Drug Administration's buy-in for our medical device's application support (in other words, the clinical trials) was the product of a year's worth of specialized lawyering alone. If not for a recent piece of legislation tabled in Congress that eased the restrictions for medical, religious, and educational pursuits, I would not be in Nassau breathing easier and buying Avgas to complete my mission in pursuit of the first licensed export of the device.

That Vietnam-era Creedence Clearwater Revival song played in my head, a warning to anyone facing danger who needed to flee the jaws of death. The lyrics echoed through my brain, reminding me that I needed to keep running through the jungle, just keep running through the jungle because the Devil was definitely on

---

[7] *Aeronautical Chart User's Guide, Terminal Procedure Publications* (PDF), FAA Aeronautical Information Services, 2018, 9.

the loose. This reminder was especially pertinent, as it brought to my mind the 1996 shootdown of two aircraft flown by the Cuban exile organization, Brothers to the Rescue.[8] The Cuban American pilots of the Cessna 337 Skymasters (twin-engine civilian light aircraft) flew into Cuban airspace to drop leaflets over Havana without permission or approved flight plans. The 24th of February 1996 was not the first time Brothers to the Rescue flew such a mission, but for these dedicated freedom fighters, it was to be their last. Their airplanes were quickly and easily detected and shot down for violating Cuban airspace.

The humanitarian mission on which I had embarked was somewhat reminiscent of those conducted by Brothers to the Rescue. That Florida-based band of expatriate Cubans diligently struck back at the tyrannical Cuban government in a variety of peaceful ways. For example, they patrolled the international airspace between Cuba and the US, on the lookout for Cuban refugees adrift on the perilous open seas in their hastily fabricated creative vessels (sometimes only a tractor tire inner tube). Upon sighting those in distress, they dropped food and water or signaled friendly boats to pick them up. The hope of navigating the Straits of Florida for freedom outweighed the obvious danger. If they were to avoid interception and set foot on American soil, they automatically became US permanent residents.

The 1996 shootdown was condemned by other nations. But the Cubans had reason to become increasingly reactive to

---

[8]   See *Report on the Investigation Regarding the Shooting Down of Two U.S.-Registered Private Civil Aircraft by Cuban Military Aircraft on 24 February 1996*, C-WP/10441, United Nations Security Council, June 20, 1996, https://documents.un.org/doc/undoc/gen/n96/164/16/img/n9616416.pdf?OpenElement.

incursions from the north in particular, as our CIA and other divisions of the US intelligence community continued to anger Cuba by encouraging, and even directly supporting, the Cuban exile group's occasional provocative acts, such as those flyovers to drop resistance materials. Those missions kept the dissident dreams of retaking the island alive, yet poked the tiger. How was Cuba to differentiate between humanitarianism and invasion?

The US embargo against Cuba began in part in 1958,[9] and by 1962, after the Cuban Missile Crisis,[10] it was extended to include almost all exports. Since the island nation is located just ninety miles from Florida, it would take only a few short minutes to destroy many parts of the US if Cuba were to obtain nuclear weapons. The fear of such an event became the US's pretext to completely isolate the newly poor formally tropical paradise. As soon as Castro took control of Cuba and increasingly relied upon the Soviet Union for support, the CIA began training and arming Cuban exiles to invade and retake their homeland. The CIA enabled the exiles to form "Brigade 2506," and a plan to overthrow Castro was prepared and approved by President Dwight D. Eisenhower in March of 1960. Later that year, newly elected President John F. Kennedy was briefed on the plan, which moved forward in April 1961. The new president was not sold on the plan to begin with, and when it went terribly wrong from the start, he refused to allow further air support for the CIA-funded

---

[9]   Isabella Oliver and Mariakarla Nodarse Venancio, "Understanding the Failure of the U.S. Embargo on Cuba," WOLA, February 4, 2022. https://www.wola.org/analysis/understanding-failure-of-us-cuba-embargo/.

[10] See "The Cuban Missile Crisis, October 1962," US Department of State, Office of the Historian, https://history.state.gov/milestones/1961-1968/cuban-missile-crisis.

and Mafia-recruited counter-revolutionaries. The effort quickly devolved into a bloodbath for the brigade and an international relations nightmare for Kennedy. Castro had his guard up and moved quickly to create protective assets.

The Cuban intelligence services quickly became an invaluable—although little known—asset. Cuba's intelligence community and apparatus have been compared to Israel's Mossad, infiltrating their intelligence machine into every corner of the world. The Soviets trained the Cubans well, and they caught on to the spy game quickly. Cuba's abundance of beautiful and exotic females enabled the development of an effective cadre of intel honeypots.[11] Back to the skies, approaching Havana on that day in March, I was to fly over the general area of the Brothers to the Rescue shootdown. I was thinking of those Brothers to the Rescue pilots who died for their cause. Would I reach Havana or soon be with them at their final destination? I was piloting the first privately owned aircraft licensed and authorized by both sides of the conflict to fly into Cuban airspace. I was trusting both parties to respect the mission and behave accordingly since my license required special dispensation from the Trading with the Enemy Act (TWEA).

The TWEA came into being during World War I as a means to manage the property of US enemies, such as patents filed in the US by German nationals.[12] The TWEA took on new inter-

---

[11] John Irvine, "The Ideological Spy: Ana Montes and the Havana Starbucks," National Office for Intelligence Reconciliation, January 6, 2015, https://noir4usa.org/the-ideological-spy-ana-montes-and-the-havana-starbucks/.

[12] Michael P. Malloy, "Trading with the Enemy Act (1917)," in *Major Acts of Congress, Volume 3: N–Z*, ed. Brian K. Landsberg (Macmillan Reference USA, 2004), 239-241.

est in 1940, while Germany was at war with European nations such as Norway and Denmark. Even though the US was yet to enter World War II, President Franklin D. Roosevelt expanded the application of TWEA to times of national emergency and imposed broad prohibitions upon the transfer of property to or from America involving persons and organizations, including the Ford Motor Company, unless licensed under regulation of the Department of Treasury.[13] Whatever the case, my flight to Havana transporting donated medical equipment and US manufactured and licensed vaccines was especially important regarding international relations, as it afforded the White House and Castro regime a means to deescalate tensions and appease citizens in both the US and Cuba. What I was doing enabled the two sides to outwardly project cooperation through a needle-free injection of large doses of "Hopium" (unfounded hope), resulting in a welcome period of peace and calm following the world-ending apocalypse potential of the previous decade. However, even as the '90s were drawing to a close, the deaths of those two expatriate Cuban pilots fueled thinly veiled animosity among the Cuban exiles, which continued to manifest pure hatred of Fidel Castro and his communist regime.

I was not born into a Cuban family or even a Latino one. I had no frame of reference for this hatred—I am the quintessential gringo with no dog in this fight. I suspect my disconnect from the fray provided a layer of insulation to the US government and a defensible rationale to allow a twenty-seven-year-old and newly licensed lawyer to become the first person to test the "good" intentions of the two enemy nations.

---

[13]   Malloy, "Trading with the Enemy Act (1917)."

In some ways I found the hatred irrational, but I also didn't know much about the people of Cuba and their conditions, so I was in no place to form a firm opinion. Only later did I understand where the true hatred lay—it turns out Fidel and Cuba had much more serious and vehement concerns with a Swiss entity than they did with the US government—which I later came to find out runs the US government and most governments of this world.

The fact that Fidel played both sides against the middle in his march to remove the firmly entrenched Mafia-backed Batista regime in Havana was another wild card. Some of the sticky issues plaguing Cuba today result from Fidel's mutual financial and military support from the CIA,[14] the KGB,[15] and the drug trade. It is unclear who knew what, and how espionage, drugs, sex, and the other pieces on the international chessboard fit together. The open interconnections and overlaps indicate all parties knew or should have expected that they were often mere pawns of the cigar-smoking revolutionary. Fidel's persona, a mix of brilliance, charisma, and betrayal, manifested relationships based alternatively upon courting, supporting, undermining, and destroying.

Fidel, along with his very worldly, famous, educated, and ruthless cohort Dr. Che Guevara,[16] understood that all wars are economic. It is by *no* coincidence that the International Monetary

---

[14] Thomas Coffey, "Castro's Secrets: The CIA and Cuba's Intelligence Machine," *Studies in Intelligence* 56, no. 3 (2012): 79–81, https://www.cia.gov/resources/csi/static/Castros-Secrets.pdf.

[15] 140 Cong. Rec. S7993 (daily ed. April 20, 1994) (statement by Sen. Helms).

[16] See History.com Editors, "Che Guevara," April 25, 2023, https://www.history.com/topics/latin-america/che-guevara. (Che Guevara, born Ernesto Guevara, was an Argentine Marxist revolutionary, guerrilla leader, and terrorist.)

Fund (IMF)[17] representatives were appearing everywhere in Latin America and the Caribbean at the same time as Fidel. The IMF was busy rallying poor Cubans to raise donated arms against the "criminal" Batista government. Not by coincidence, the CIA used Mafia hit men as part of the Bay of Pigs effort—they were reclaiming their turf as well.

Meanwhile, the IMF was busy making sweetheart deals for all the banana republics,[18] enabling them to enjoy giant budgets fueled by loans provided or guaranteed by the IMF and paid in US dollars. The IMF is, and always was, the preferred economic spear tip of the true Owners of this world—of those "people" that own the Swiss Bank for International Settlements. The IMF, being a subsidiary of the central bank to all central banks, was able to access cheap money (more or less free) in order to provide easy credit terms in hard currency (e.g. US dollars) to presidents and prime ministers who eagerly collateralized their national assets for those loans, including the taxable earnings of their citizens.

Why should a head of state care about the citizen taxpayers when given personal access to unlimited sums during their reign? It was the allure of a life of luxury—effectively a life estate in monetary terms, yet entirely beholden to the dictates of the

---

[17] See "The Case Against the International Monetary Fund," Hoover Institution, November 1, 1999, https://www.hoover.org/research/case-against-international-monetary-fund.

[18] See *Britannica*, "banana republic," last updated October 17, 2024, https://www.britannica.com/topic/banana-republic. (The term "banana republic" originated in the late twentieth century to describe Central American countries that were overthrown or otherwise heavily influenced by US CIA cutouts such as the United Fruit Company. The term has since been applied to other politically corrupt countries.)

provider. Golden chains for the ruler, shackles for the peasants/peons/slaves.

Fidel was different, and he understood the true cost of the IMF's promises of free money, particularly regarding the US dollar. Also, as a pragmatist, Fidel knew he had to enlist a thug/benefactor with the right combination of skills and resources to play the game in the Mafia-styled monetary protection racket. After all, the future of Cuba and its independence depended entirely on his choice between having a big brother or master. Of the three choices (CIA, KGB, or IMF) in this protection racket, Fidel chose the Soviets—because, among other things, Cuba would retain ownership of their central bank, have the ability to mint and print money, *and* the Soviets agreed to support an independent Cuban economy through highly inflated sugar purchases. Their communist brothers even promised to provide nuclear and other weapons as deterrents against US aggression.

For decades, the IMF, World Bank, European Bank for Reconstruction and Development, International Bank for Reconstruction and Development, et al (collectively just subsidiaries of the maker of money), all had a mutual mission to acquire and control every central bank in the world and thereby control the world's money supply. Fidel remained a stick in their craw and that is what fueled much of the private, public, and clandestine efforts to rid Cuba of Fidel Castro.[19] I became aware of all of this background information in the days and weeks after the incident that nearly cost me my life. In retrospect, the recent

---

[19] "Memorandum of Discussion at the 450th Meeting of the National Security Council, Washington, July 7, 1960," Office of the Historian, US Department of State, https://history.state.gov/historicaldocuments/frus1958-60v06/d545.

blossoming relations between the two feuding nations almost ignited a global nuclear holocaust in the 1960s. Had it not been for the calm heads of President Kennedy and Chairman Nikita Khrushchev,[20] our world would not likely exist. The same permanent bureaucrats who infect the levers of power in our "elected" government also exist in most all other nations, including the Soviet Union. The generals, professional advisers, cheerleaders, Satanists, and pawns surrounding the leadership of both nations during that period made impassioned pleas and speeches as to why a nuclear exchange was warranted and sought their level best to preclude the two leaders from talking directly. The Owners of the world's money supply, and therefore the world itself, could not rest, could not waiver, and could not wait to destroy Fidel due to his audacious attempt to withhold the Cuban money supply from them. Yet, the good guys behind the scenes, some might call "White Hats," existed in those days as well. The trusted back channels between nations have always existed and also do exist in international commerce.

It is true that the Soviet Union was also deemed an enemy nation by the US during practically all of Fidel's reign and life. Yet, the destruction of Fidel at all costs, even nuclear planetary annihilation, was deemed just punishment by the Owners who had achieved such great success with the debt slavery of other nations and whole continents.

We return again to the skies above the Straits of Florida.

---

[20] See "To the Brink: JFK and the Cuban Missile Crisis," Past Exhibits, John F. Kennedy Presidential Library and Museum, https://www. jfklibrary.org/visit-museum/exhibits/past-exhibits/to-the-brink-jfk-and-the-cuban-missile-crisis.

Miami ATC: "November Eight-Five, One-Two Yankee, you are leaving my airspace. Squawk new code four-one-five-six and contact Havana Center on one-three-two-point-seven-five."

The static on the radio crackled.

"Good luck." Miami's final words.

What the hell does that mean? I thought.

Controllers don't usually wish you safe travels or good luck. Rather, our aviation language is all matter of fact, clear, and concise to keep the radio channels clear of chatter and unnecessary commentary.

Undaunted, I responded, "Roger Miami Center, new squawk is four-one, five-six and going to Havana Center on one thirty-two, seventy-five. Thanks for the help."

Almost immediately after I crossed the southern coast of Andros, I was in the airborne equivalent of that Creedence Clearwater Revival jungle, about to encounter the forewarned tiger. The visual cue of the transponder's reddish-orange occasional blink, matching the song's audio cadence in the background, instantly changed to a red-hot poker, recalling to my mind the color of campfire embers.

Aircraft are typically painted with a unique tail number directly associated with its transponder. In those days, aircraft identification varied, with some numbers assigned in a seemingly random fashion. But all aircraft were assigned a number by ATC when no flight plan was opened and used. An airplane "squawking 1200" means it is flying under Visual Flight Rules. In such a case, controllers recognize that such an aircraft is flying without the assistance of a controller. In addition, the plane may not squawk at all, as in many cases the civilian radar simply won't recognize the aircraft as being airborne or existing at all.

Likewise, if an airplane is flying on a squawk code that does not correspond to an open flight plan, then the controller would see an unknown airplane, its altitude, and current heading but not know its origin, destination, or intentions. In such a case, the unidentified aircraft is called a "bogey." Identifying and/ or destroying bogies is the job of national military air defense authorities.

According to foundational international law, article 1 of the 1944 Chicago Convention concerns civil aviation: "The contracting States recognize that every State has complete and exclusive sovereignty over the airspace about its territory."[21] A nation has the right to repeal any unidentified invaders (bogies) with as much force as they deem necessary for the situation at hand. The difference between the start of an invasion and an incidental or other intrusion short of invasion is hard to determine when the decision window is short and history is involved. Naturally, nations vary in how they deal with potential border intrusions based upon their circumstances. Some nations consider any unknown aircraft or marine vessel entering their sovereign territory or airspace as hostile, others do not.

A cauldron of chaos formed in 1994 as a result of incendiary speeches by Castro. Riots erupted in Havana and Fidel "solved" the problem by telling disgruntled people to leave the island.

---

[21] *Convention on International Civil Aviation*, 9th ed. (International Civil Aviation Organization, 2006), https://www.icao.int/publications/ Documents/7300_9ed.pdf.

Over thirty-five thousand Cubans took to rafts[22] and entered the ocean in hopes of reaching America. The US Coast Guard detained many at sea and returned them to Cuba. Brothers to the Rescue dedicated itself to aiding the refugees find freedom in the US. Again, on January 9 and 13, 1996, the Brothers flew over Havana and dropped leaflets considered subversive propaganda by the Cuban regime that prompted locals to take action against the "Cuban constitutional order." Just over a month later, the Brothers paid the price as Cuban Air Force pilots were aching to take them down and leaped at the chance to unleash their fury.

Of course, the fury was not one sided, and little did I know or suspect that forces on both sides of the ocean were quickly in motion to take advantage of my presence. An expatriate air traffic controller in Miami hatched a scheme to create an incident to sour the newly warming relations between the US and Fidel. He made sure I would be bogie bate, flying straight toward Cuba's capital city without the correct frequency to talk to the controllers in Cuba.

Why not subvert and sacrifice a stupid gringo from Colorado, a buffalo in the china shop, who was ignorant of the horrors of communism and dictatorial regimes and unaware of what lengths the resistance would go in their fight?

Unbeknownst to any of the antagonists, I had already experienced the behavior of dictatorial regimes firsthand, having lived and worked in two communist countries over nearly three decades.

---

[22] *Cuban/Haitian Adjustment: Hearings on H.R. 4853, Before the Subcommittee on Immigration, Refugees, and International Law*, 98th Cong. 46 (1984), PDF, Library of Congress, May 9, 1984, 46.

I had lived and worked from 1993 to 1994 in Poland, as it was still a communist country with a declared communist party president (Lech Walesa) and a communist parliament. Cuba remains communist to this day, and I have represented clients throughout hot zones around the world, including the Democratic Republic of the Congo, Ecuador, and Venezuela.

My experience involves not just the vaccine business, and not just the creation of vaccines, but also vaccine delivery systems. In addition, I have actually done business with the very people described in this book, influential power players involved in global governance in this key healthcare area, including Peter Carrasco of the World Health Organization and top Pfizer executives, whom I introduced to the highest levels of the Cuban government.

But I digress—back once again to the unfriendly skies.

The music playing through my headset had moved on to "I Heard it Through the Grapevine," and as the song was winding down, the fire-hot red and glowing transponder light pierced my brain like an ice pick (figuratively). At that moment, I should have turned around immediately. Yet, I was heavy in the soup, handed off by Miami to no one. Although the Cuban government was well aware of my trip to deliver much needed medical supplies and equipment at no cost to the government or the people of Cuba, it was all in jeopardy.

As with all things involving airplanes in flight, pilots get themselves into trouble when they ignore little problems. Little problems have a tendency to cascade and multiply. Minimal problems become larger, and if ignored long enough, culminate into the biggest problem anyone will suffer in life—the end of it.

Still, I was falsely confident, receiving a fresh squawk code (which I should have realized was very unusual mid-flight). After all, Miami gave me the frequency and handed me off to Havana. Sure, the old maps I had acquired in Nassau were likely outdated (another mistake), but God was my copilot.

As I flew closer to Cuba, I repeatedly called the frequency Miami provided to no avail. Why no response? I even tried calling Miami Center back to confirm the code and frequency. Still no reply. Silence at both ends; no one was talking on the radios. The only sound I heard was that of the engines, usually a comforting thrum. Even that noise seemed to roar in my ears, amplifying the chilling silence on the other end. With each passing mile as I flew towards Cuba, a knot of dread tightened in my gut. I was starting to realize just how deep in the jungle I had ventured. Is that the sound of a tiger approaching?

The transponder light had stopped flickering. What was worse: yellow to orange to red or lights out? I had been in many hairy places and had experienced many a jungle-like encounter in my life, so I was not prone to panic. Yet, I do admit that I suffered cold sweats and felt a grade A pucker factor coming on when I realized death may be near. I sweated and puckered as I scrolled through all frequencies trying to raise someone, anyone. Communication was the key to my survival, with any ear capable of relaying a message or getting me to the right frequency.

I knew from that heavy, sick feeling in the pit of my stomach that my worst-case scenario was in play: some armed and potentially hostile force had a radar lock on my plane. At that point, I was flying under instrument meteorological conditions.[23] If missiles were incoming, I'd never even see their approach. With a new squawk code and seemingly inoperative radios or frequencies, I wasn't sure what I was about to encounter, but it all painted a grim picture.

The Cuban coastline loomed ahead. The peril of my situation was accentuated by that stark memory of the fate that befell the crew of the Cessna Skymasters. I was fighting an inner war, logic-battled fear. I prayed. Maybe, just maybe, I was flying too low, or too close for the Cuban's antique Soviet radios to pick up my signal. I formed a desperate evasive plan. I decided to fly five more nautical miles to the next waypoint on my flight plan. Surely someone would notice I was flying exactly at the filed altitude, speed, and heading as my flight plan indicated and pause the tiger.

If I had no luck on the comms, I'd turn around at the waypoint and fly back to Nassau. If I had enough fuel, the weather conditions in Nassau would still be good enough to land. I was sweating through my shirt and down my shorts with the sick realization that the Cubans were hunting me, and I was likely going to be shot down. Yes, run through the jungle Todd, run.

Would it be a surface-to-air missile or air-to-air missile?

I had heard one of the Skymasters was shot down old style, with lead from the 30 mm GSh-30 cannon by one of the bloodthirsty Cuban Air Force pilots who wanted to practice his dogfighting skills, OK Corral–style, against an unarmed target. Kinda cowardly, ain't it?

---

[23] See David Rowland, "Surviving VFR into IMC," AV Web, updated June 12, 2019, https://www.avweb.com/flight-safety/technique/surviving-vfr-into-imc/.

My nerves were high, but I tried to stay calm; I was in God's hands.

I kept praying and dialing, switching between different frequencies and transmitting the same message over and over: "This is Twin Comanche November Eight-Five, One-Two Yankee on south of Andros, en route to Havana and looking for a bridge."

Finally, my prayers were answered. All my fiddling around and switching frequencies bore fruit. I stumbled upon one of the old frequencies indicated on the ancient Bahamian aeronautical maps. I almost passed out with joy when a United Airlines captain heard me and replied. A voice that seemed from heaven broke the radio silence. My angel drowned out the almost-deafening engine noise. I had long stopped the music. Had I outrun the tiger?

Angel: "This is United Two-Two, Three-Zero. Was that a One-Two Yankee calling on one-two-four-point-six?"

I breathed deeply, thank God! I wasn't going to die alone in the middle of nowhere!

"AFFIRM!! United Two-Two, Three-Zero!!" I responded loudly.

Then calmly, I continued, "November Eight-Five, One-Two Yankee and I'm on an IFR [Instrument Flight Rules] flight plan from Nassau to Havana level ten thousand and one hundred miles west of IMELA intersection—India-Mike-Echo-Lima-Alfa.

Can you please let Havana Center know I'm on a new squawk four-one-five-six and looking for a good frequency. I've been trying to call them on one thirty-two, seventy-five and couldn't reach them."

I was starting to breathe a bit more regularly.

The apple I previously felt stuck in my throat eased down to my already pitted stomach as United 2230 relayed the message and responded back to me, "Comanche Eight-Five, One-Two Yankee, Havana now sees you and invites you to speak with them on one-twenty-three-point five; that's twenty-three, fifty-five."

What a strange way to convey that break in comms. I was being "invited" to speak with the Cuban controllers. Perhaps the Cubans were just happy that I was bringing free medical stuff, or I really messed up, and they were going to throw me in a Cuban Gulag for the rest of my life. Adding insult to injury, they'd most likely add my airplane for their Cuban Air Force!

"Good afternoon, Havana Center, this is Twin Comanche November Eight-Five, One-Two Yankee," I said slowly, pronouncing every syllable clearly, not knowing the full extent of their English.

I knew they would speak at least some English, the universal language of aviation. All pilots and controllers must speak and communicate in English.

"Havana, I'm squawking four-one, five-six and one hundred ten miles west of IMELA," I said. "I've been trying to raise you for the last forty-five minutes." I realized how pitiful it was to admit that I had flown along the entire route before making contact with the United captain. Just another cascading mistake that pilots make and die from as a result. Obviously, my cascade came close to ending with my death.

By the grace of God, each cascading mistake that day was evened out with what some would say is luck, but I looked upward for explanation. As I spoke to the Cuban controllers, they seemed extremely happy to be speaking with me. Weird, but I came to understand their relief when I broke out of the soup at eight hundred feet above the ground (jungle?). The menacing MiG-29s, my tigers that day, still had a radar lock on me the whole time, which clarified why the transponder was incessantly glowing like a demonic ember.

Our company representative and official liaison with the Cuban government was an extremely well-respected and established older gentleman by the name of Aristides Ruiz. I was not expecting hugs and kisses, or even his presence on the ramp, after I shut the engines down and exited the airplane.

Aristides was the former president of CIMEX, which is one of Cuba's largest government enterprises. Although he was officially retired, people greeted him like an important president but more endearing, like a folk hero. Aristides was known and loved like a movie star everywhere we went together, and he was with me almost everywhere I went. He was clearly assigned to me as a handler, and although he was my friend and facilitator in this project, Aristides was also an agent of the government. I'm sure his reports up the chain of command reassured the authorities that I wasn't a spy or there with malicious intentions. If I were a threat in any way, the Cuban intel/police apparatus was prepared to deal with me accordingly. Gulp.

After landing without any holes in my airplane or body, that near miracle seemed to draw us together, almost like family. Aristides had been a Cuban soldier earlier in his life. He spent time in Africa during the Angolan Civil War. He avoided talking about his involvement, if any, in the Cuban Revolution. I was wet with sweat, as was he, having been in the control tower talking to the Air Force commanders and other people seeking my destruction and the subversion of our joint medical mission—a mission that would ultimately warm relations and end the embargo.

Aristides, unlike regular Cubans, was allowed to do pretty much whatever he wanted due to his age and position in the communist public-private partnership (government enterprise),[24] together with his endearing personal qualities that made him a national treasure.

So, after sparing me and saving the mission through intercession with the controllers and air force, Aristides walked right out onto the ramp reserved for dignitaries (private aircraft in Cuba was unheard of). He stood patiently with a smile on his face at my wingtip while I shut down the airplane's engines and systems. He was gleeful in a very strange way because he didn't know what I had seen: He had the look of a father seeing a son leave the hospital after a lifesaving surgery.

I'll never forget the way he hugged me and shook my hand over and over in the most animated way I've ever experienced. I have never seen a septuagenarian behave with such youthful vigor. He literally had to catch himself for a moment in order to begin speaking. About that same time, I heard the two MiG-29s roar by overhead, everyone peering skyward into the soup just one thousand feet above us—or, should I say, the large bowl of chili into which my small spoon had almost disappeared.

Aristides teared up when he finally spoke. "Those same MiGs were ordered to shoot you down. Thankfully, you beat the clock by bridging with the United captain by a mere thirty seconds."

As this experience wound down, I realized that my worst suspicions were true. The MiGs had a radar lock on me for many

---

[24] See Darién García Linsuaín, "On the Emergence of Domestic Public-Private Partnerships in Cuba," Cuba Study Group, December 9, 2021, https://cubastudygroup.org/blog_posts/on-the-emergence-of-domestic-public-private-partnerships-in-cuba/.

miles and it was by the grace of God that I was sent the United captain (angel one) and Aristides (angel two) to rescue me. By their intervention and Aristides's steady measured response, I survived the day. It took a long while for me to truly appreciate the significance of the events of that day. After it was explained to me many times in many different ways by many different people in our government and the Cuban officials, I felt the full impact. Thank you, Lord!

Reflecting upon the events, it is obvious I was the very object of a planned international incident to destroy any hope of US/ Cuban peaceful relations. My demise would have been the pretext and excuse to further punish and sanction Cuba through pure shame and allegations of murder.

Most people don't know that after the US declared Cuba an enemy nation, Canada continued to trade with them and never stopped, even at the height of the Cuban Missile Crisis.[25] The expatriate Cuban community in the United States and abroad had planned to use my erroneous death to cut off even Canadian help to the island nation so that the Owners of the United States could finally obtain their goal—to acquire the Cuban central bank. Yet, there are many more layers to this story that intertwine with our current experiences in the act of fighting against the current democide in progress.

When you're in the middle of these odd situations between governments and their diplomats, who also do not understand the true paradigm, there are non sequiturs abound. It's confusing,

---

[25] See "Canada-Cuba Relations," Government of Canada, updated October 1, 2024, https://www.international.gc.ca/country-pays/cuba/relations.aspx?lang=eng.

and my three years in Cuba were full of non sequiturs—things that made no sense or were simply impossible yet visibly and verifiably true.

CHAPTER 2

THE JUNGLE STRIKES BACK

Cuba was a strange paradox with abject poverty according to housing conditions, yet a highly educated, highly employed populace. Everyone had access to food, clean water, and health care. The Cubans living on the island often seemed to look longingly for a different life as they went about their daily business. Yet, they flashed ready smiles, and the slightest sound of music sparked an instant and unexpectedly exuberant dance. The economic non sequitur was no different: somehow despite its restrictions, isolation, and limited resources, Cuba had developed the latest vaccine and drug manufacturing facilities of anywhere. Those facilities are run by extraordinarily educated staff and scientists, arriving at work every day on foot, by "camel" [26] (a strangely shaped trailer-like bus, described as the "poor man's subway"), jerry-rigged electric or motorized bicycle, or rare carpool.

---

[26] Anthony Boadle, "Over the hump? Cubans hope for end to 'camel' buses," Reuters, August 9, 2007, https://www.reuters.com/article/world/over-the-hump-cubans-hope-for-end-to-camel-buses-idUSN31189993/.

Todd S. Callender, J.D., Jerome R. Corsi, Ph.D., and Craig D. Campbell, Ph.D.

The whole economy ran in that way: brilliant, kind, wonderful people who possessed world-class knowledge, operating modern facilities while subsisting on a diet primarily of beans, rice, and pork.

The government employees I dealt with absolutely loved lunch meetings, rare opportunities for us to dine at a government-run restaurant. What a luxury—foods like beef, lobster, or shrimp were served and sold at US prices. Normal Cubans weren't allowed to go to these restaurants as they were reserved for precious tourists, with wallets full of what was even more precious, money. Meanwhile, the government had to procure dollars, euros, or other international currencies, which allowed the government to access hard currency for acquisitions, as they lacked the facilities to manufacture currency themselves.

The vaccine manufacturing facilities were good examples of this Cuban-specific business environment. Instituto Pedro Kouri[27] was one of the government enterprises with which we consulted and planned our field trials for scientific observation and recording. I feel certain that my multitudes of lunch and dinner meetings at most all of the government establishments paid for the sophisticated German equipment that comprised the large manufacturing campus. How did the Cuban scientists know how to operate this equipment? And more importantly, how did they design the first viable hepatitis B vaccine?[28] The field trials

---

[27] See Annmarie Christensen, "Cuba's Jewel of Tropical Medicine," *Perspectives in Health Magazine*, 2003, https://www3.paho.org/english/dd/pin/Number17_article4_4.htm.

[28] See Eduardo Pentón-Arias and Julio César Aguilar-Rubido, "Cuban Prophylactic and Therapeutic Vaccines for Controlling Hepatitis B," *MEDICC Review* 23, no. 1 (2021): 21–29, https://doi.org/10.37757/mr2021.v23.n1.6.

in Brazil for their hep B vaccine were going astoundingly well and catching lots of attention in the industry. Even the US Food and Drug Administration was aware and very upset about the advances that the Cubans had made.

Dr. Kouri, the namesake of the institution, and even today, a major figure in vaccinology, was very proud of this achievement and many others his team had made in preventing disease. They looked at their work as being patriotic because they were not just helping Cubans but demonstrating to the whole world that Cuba was a leader in that industry. They were literally curing disease while other nations and manufacturers continued to treat a disease while never curing it.

Realizing that lowly Cuba was able to succeed in ways that "advanced" counties could not was a non sequitur that stuck with me throughout the Cuban experience. It weighed heavily on my mind as I spoke to highly placed "economic" advisers at the US Interests Section in Havana. Because of the embargo, the US government did not have or maintain diplomatic relations with Cuba "officially." Yet, right on the Malecón, overlooking the bay of Havana Harbor and in the heart of Havana, was a gigantic, very imposing, stark but oddly elegant concrete building that flew a Swiss flag but boasted a huge inlaid US government symbol on the side of the building.

The building was *not* an embassy, but it had the usual security protocols for embassies with a fortified fence and was secured by US Marines on the inside and Cuban military on the outside. It was also the place where I had to check in regularly with "Gary," my official US government but non-existent (in Cuba) liaison.

Everyone knew Gary was a spook, a member of the American intelligence community.

Most embassies are replete with intelligence assets/agents no matter what county it belongs to or where it is located. It's a well-known feature of diplomacy that ambassadors appointed to political figurehead positions come and go, while the permanent diplomatic bureaucrats make all the important decisions and carry on the business of international relations.

Because the US had no official diplomatic relations with Cuba, no ambassador was assigned to the Interest Section. However, we did have Gary, and I was very pleased to have him as my contact in Havana. If anything went wrong and I needed to be bailed out or rescued from a Cuban prison, Gary was there to help. Being the first and only authorized US person in a hostile, enemy nation was initially a bit unnerving. Yet, the Cuban secret intelligence spooks were absolutely superb at their tradecraft. No wonder the Cubans were so effective as an intelligence power-house in the world of spies.

While traveling to and from meetings, dining at *paladars* (family-run restaurants in peoples' homes), or enjoying local music on a weekend near my *particular* (the Cuban version of an Airbnb), the Cuban intel agents carefully observed and cataloged all of my tastes and habits. Whether I lingered at a certain shop, glanced at a landmark, or second-glanced at a pretty lady walking by, it was noted. I eventually figured out that pieces of the chess board were moved around to increase the odds of me dining in a particular *paladar*, staying in one *particular* more than others, or encountering pretty women that looked similar and familiar.

Spiders spin webs; spy masters weave more elaborate traps. It is up to the target to avoid becoming a fly.

It could have been just the rhythms of life, but the longer I spent in Cuba, the more these personal preferences would "incidentally" appear in my path. Likewise, the more I got to engage with the Cuban scientists, doctors, and government representatives that eventually formed our local team, the more I felt at ease. Cuba very quickly became my new part-time home. I say "part-time" because my license from the US government only allowed me to be there temporarily; it expressly forbid becoming a resident in Cuba.

As time passed, my travels to and from Cuba became more routine and mundane. When I wasn't moving cargo (field trial supplies) with me, I would catch a Cubana flight to or from Nassau. I decided to keep a condo in the sunny Bahamas, avoiding the long journey to and from Denver, sometimes through snow and ice storms.

After two long years of preparations for the later stages of the field trials,[29] the animal studies[30] were successfully completed. I prepared for the human portion of the clinical field trials.[31] We

---

[29] "Exploring Medical Device Clinical Trials and Their Development Pipeline," Vial.com, https://vial.com/blog/articles/medical-device-clinical-trials/?https://vial.com/blog/articles/medical-device-clinical-trials/?utm_source=organic.

[30] US Food and Drug Administration, Guidance Document, "General Considerations for Animal Studies Intended to Evaluate Medical Devices," March 2023, https://www.fda.gov/regulatory-information/search-fda-guidance-documents/general-considerations-animal-studies-intended-ed-evaluate-medical-devices.

[31] "What is Human Subjects Research?" University of Texas at Austin, https://web.archive.org/web/20120207032034/http://www.utexas.edu/research/rsc/humansubjects/whatis.html.

were setting up for the kickoff of a small pilot study, with film crews from BBC, CNN, and local news agencies arriving. The crews seemed to descend on the area from nowhere and every-where all at the same time. It was as if they simply appeared out of thin air, along with various Cuban and foreign officials that I had never seen before. The only "official" I recognized was Vice Minister (of Health) Regla Arango, with whom I spent two years working in preparation for this day, who I thought was the only "official" in my mind.

I did not realize that much negotiation and discussion was happening in Washington and Havana between various govern-ment entities, including a sponsored congressional bill to ease the embargo.

This particular trial was just a pilot trial with a few "volunteers" from the nearby village and organized by the local Committees for the Defense of the Revolution commander,[32] who acted much like a colonial governor with the authority to efficiently organize people and places. I was surprised by the attendance of the news crews at that particular event because the main trial was still sev-eral months away. The Hollywood-esque feel came through the remarkably fast setup. The "volunteers" magically appeared and rolled up their sleeves for a shot of tetanus toxoid, with the hopes of making international news. Did they think an escapee would recognize them? It would not matter, as regular Cubans weren't allowed access to international sources of information.[33]

---

[32] John Pike, "Committee for the Defense of the Revolution," Global Security, October 20, 2018.

[33] "Six Facts about Censorship in Cuba," Amnesty International, March 11, 2016, https://www.amnesty.org/en/latest/campaigns/2016/03/six-facts-about-censorship-in-cuba/.

But as you may have already gathered, Cubans are a crafty and creative bunch. Aristides had a TV set for local broadcasts. He configured the cooking grate from a barbeque grill, which hung carefully and precariously outside of his tenth-story balcony, to serve as an antenna. He was then able to pick up a fuzzy and intermittent newscast from channel 9 in Tampa. The only places with cable TV were the government hotels, forbidden to ordinary Cubans. While on the island, it was nearly impossible to find an internet connection for my laptop. I succeeded two years into the process. Regardless, this was a *big* deal because the Cuban government said it was a "Big Deal." I had not noticed with all the fuss that none of the participants in the trial were in a control group, meaning that every one of our test subjects had received tetanus toxoid vaccines at some point earlier in their life. If their vaccine status was as I suspected, it would be a *disaster*, as the entire pilot trial would be invalid.

The reception that followed the pilot test the next day back in downtown Havana was quite a surprise. After giving a few interviews to the reporters, including a BBC film crew, I was told that I was too bland and unanimated. The BBC actually reshot the entire interview. I obliged by gesticulating like a baby eagle trying to fly for the first time. I really didn't get it.

Immediately after my media debut, I was sped through the traffic and hordes of Cuban people getting on and off the typical traffic circus act of camels, homemade motorcycles, bicycles, and pedestrians. It was Havana's version of rush hour: the end of their day or shift and the struggle homeward. After a remarkably fast ride through these busy streets of downtown Havana to a well-appointed government building that could have been a skyscraper in Chicago, I found myself ill-prepared for what came next.

Aristides never mentioned there was a meeting after the sweaty day in the country and that I would meet the magically appearing film crews again. I found myself feeling way outdressed, ill-prepared, and surprised to see a spread of hors d'oeuvres among the many neatly suited gentlemen and even a few formally dressed women. Cuba had learned how to put on a show.

The "meeting" attendees were all chatting rapidly and animatedly in Spanish while devouring the cheese and ham nuggets, wine, and local beer. I felt completely out of place and alone in a room full of strangers. Those strangers kept glancing at me while they talked in rapid and hushed tones. I felt like a science experiment until a kind and familiar face eventually appeared, who I knew as Señor Machado.

Sr. José Ramón Machado Ventura was the former minister of health. He came over quite calmly and in a commanding way that I find difficult to describe. It was as though the man in front of me was sizing me up for a boxing match, not malevolent in any way, just analytically and calmly, with the hint of a smile. He, of course, spoke perfect English, which I always welcomed to offset my deficient Spanish and difficulty understanding Cuban colloquialisms that made little or no sense to me. For example, whenever the name "Maldonado" was referenced, people would burst out laughing. It appears calling someone "Maldonado" was a Cuban inside joke meaning someone short on thinking skills, a dolt.

Sr. Machado was anything but a Maldonado, and I felt myself the lesser man, being new to the country and overseeing what turned out to be a complete disaster.

But the trials were not a disaster in the eyes of the minister. Unbeknownst to me, I was in the middle of a grand celebration among the power brokers of the Cuban government. The room was full of them, including old and dear friends of Fidel who had helped him fight through the mountains to take Havana from the Batista regime. The retired generals who supported Fidel all wore long pants and Che Guevara shirts that kept them cool in the heat and well-appointed in Cuban fashion, as well as marking their seniority in the society as Fidel's former chosen leaders.

The now retired revolutionaries, like Aristides, were all his contemporaries, comfortable enough in each other's presence to laugh and throw out loud accusations of faux pas. Such joking would not have been accepted lightly in other company and without the free-flowing beer and wine that was otherwise absolutely forbidden from government meetings.

I was wearing a dark green suit that was durable like a Class "A" Army service uniform. It was the appropriate choice as I got dressed that morning, expecting to be in the field all day. At end of day, I would also be required to buy dinner for all the Committees for the Defense of the Revolution commanders in the area at the nearest government restaurant so they could tank up on meat, shrimp, and lobster. But it was not exactly party fare.

The minister examined my attire for a few seconds, and with a wry but authentic smile, he simply said, "You look like a soldier for the second time I've seen you recently."

I couldn't reason why he had recently seen me elsewhere looking like a soldier. I hadn't worn this same suit earlier in the trip? Did he review my Cuban secret intelligence file before that gathering?

The minister called the meeting to order. "Today is a grand celebration for the champions of our Republic who have brought us this exciting technology that we are pursuing with our norteamericano partners, which we demonstrated today in the first of many field trials in our glorious Republic."

All of this was stated in perfect English, and the room full of career Cuban leaders seemingly understood perfectly too.

Aristides then continued, "Let me remind you of the great words of our revolutionary leader whose wisdom and foresight bring us this treasured opportunity."

After a pause, he resumed, "The health of the population constitutes, from the programmatic platform of the revolutionary triumph expressed in the saying, 'History will absolve me,' a matter of special interest for our government, one of the most precious conquests..."

There it was. To my surprise, my mission to successfully complete a single test was taking on a life of its own. *The* minister just announced that our needle-free testing project in Cuba had become a state-appointed enterprise and joint venture.

I felt shocked and slightly sick because I had not negotiated *any* kind of long-term business relationship with the Cubans, and despite asking for the costs to organize and run the trial that day, Aristides kept putting me off by telling me the process would take a long time.

My mind raced. *What am I going to tell the embassy [the Interests Section] people? I don't know if my license to be in Cuba and do the trials is sufficient for a joint venture.*

I sensed the possibility of serious trouble. Was I back in the jungle? A tiger was sure to pick up my scent.

The minister had just announced that I was officially "trading with the enemy"; and for all I knew, he had just helped himself and his government to all the intellectual property we had worked so diligently to protect with the extraordinarily expensive Patent Cooperation Treaty and patent applications.[34] I continued to ask myself questions: *What do I tell my parents (after all, I was merely representing the company they founded, Genesis Medical Technologies) and the other shareholders about this? I've lost the company and its sole product to the communist government of Cuba?!*

How does one exactly get their product back from a communist, dictatorial regime with nuclear weapons and an air force with MiG-29s that just demonstrated their long-range, air-to-air capabilities by locking their targeting radar on me when I was at least fifty miles away the other day?

I was in some serious personal and professional peril.

Some things are universal. For me it was a learning process. Either the US intelligence apparatus in Cuba was working very well, or the grapevine (the "coconut telegraph") worked equally well in Cuba as in other parts of the Caribbean. I soon found out Gary knew all about that meeting. You know, the meeting during which

---

[34] "PCT – The International Patent System," World Intellectual Property Organization (WIPO), https://www.wipo.int/pct/en/.

I discovered I had mistakenly and inadvertently veered our company into a forbidden joint venture without me telling him first.

I was the sole director for the company in Cuba, and I was sure no one else signed any papers because I would have been the lawyer drafting them. No one else would risk agreeing to something without getting my buy-in beforehand.

To my surprise, Gary smiled as he greeted me on the fourth floor of the gigantic Interests Section building overlooking the Malecón. I was even more surprised and most happy at the gregarious meeting in Gary's office. It was a large room full of various piles of his work papers. Being a chief economist undoubtedly required him to be aware of all the business happenings in Cuba. My project was clearly a big deal, but I did not understand that it was also a big deal in Washington, Geneva, and even Basel, Switzerland.

It seemed odd to me that Gary knew a great deal about the recent meeting with Aristides and the other ministers, senior bureaucrats, and loyal communist party friends of Fidel. However, it appeared that Gary did not realize that the entire clinical trial protocol was invalid. There was no way to measure the seroconversion[35] of the test subjects. We injected them with tetanus, and there was *no* control group. Little did I know that the Cuban scientists had conducted the study differently, in a way that may have preserved its validity, without informing us. They had lined up two groups of people and gave a set of tetanus shots using a traditional needle to one group. Another group received the same

---

[35] See Sara Ryding, "What is Seroconversion?" News-Medical.net, updated March 3, 2021, https://www.news-medical.net/health/What-is-Seroconversion.aspx.

vaccine using the needle-free injector. The scientists and health officials were instantly excited about the new technology. I even saw a couple "volunteers" try to switch lines into the needle-free line, which was most encouraging.

Still, it bothered me that we would not be able to tell from this test whether the injector had delivered a dose of vaccine into the right area of the body and if it was in an amount sufficient to produce the seroconversion. Without such knowledge, I would not know if the preventive medicine was working.

I asked Dr. Angela, our top government scientist and doctor responsible for running this trial, to verify the results. I did not realize at the time that she had already been chosen by the room full of ministers and Fidelistas to be the project head for the Cuban government. They chose her wisely. Dr. Angela was trained as a medical doctor and PhD scientist in Russia, Germany, and various other countries.

After the trial, we'd occasionally enjoy her company for informal dinners at a *paladar*, and she would sing magnificent Russian folk songs and American country and Western tunes like a pro. Her English was superb but a bit dusty from her short scientific training in Canada. I appreciated her linguistic skills, ensuring my sixth grade "Merican" Spanish didn't confuse members of the team. Yet, there was that one time when she openly referred to me in her accented English as a "gay boy," bringing his Colorado ranching and rodeo skills to Havana. Did that description open speculation that I had enjoyed a *Brokeback Mountain* experience? My concern was soon dispelled, as during a subsequent dinner, people at our table made it clear that they understood that Dr.

Angela was merely calling me a high spirited "cowboy." I eagerly accepted the new moniker of "cowboy."

On these dining occasions, the large groups of Cuban junior partners to our venture opened up a bit about their lives and entrapment on the communist island. Many of the stories were both fascinating and heartbreaking. They shared dreams of a future in which they could leave the island. One way or another, pretty much everyone worked for the government. In those days, there were nine different classifications of private enterprise jobs. Such a job would be in addition to one to which a person had been formally appointed.

The amount of organization, command, and control of such a massive population of workers to make the entire island machine run was nothing short of miraculous, although largely unapparent.

After the pilot trial and big reveal of the joint enterprise, I noticed that our on-island staff, at that point a dedicated team of Cubans assigned solely to that project, were more open and inclined to share what clearly should have been kept as secrets.

As our project progressed, the team members realized the inconsistencies of their behavior and the non sequiturs of their protocols. For instance, I asked them, "Who made the decision to unblind the pilot study [injecting all of the test subjects with tetanus instead of half tetanus and the rest saline]? Are double-blind studies required for your clinical trials to be valid?"

None of the team knew who made the unblind decision, but they all agreed it would have had to come from the minister, or at the least made with his knowledge and consent. They all knew the required features of clinical trials, but they did as instructed and found that the needle-free injector had a 2,300 percent better seroconversion than the regular needles.

"Does that mean we could use a smaller dose, perhaps one-fourth of the usual dose to obtain the same seroconversion?" I asked. This was especially interesting to the Cubans because budgets for vaccines acquired abroad were very thin. The Cubans did not want to rely upon foreign vaccines anyway and developed their own in accordance with the international standards of the Food and Drug Administration. The FDA played no role at all in our efforts, never commenting on the informational updates we provided.

In order to drive vaccine development, Cuba had developed public-private partnerships. Our project was becoming one. Therefore, the accounting aspects of the project (costs and budget) required special expertise. An accountant, Antonio, was assigned to our team. Antonio was a true gentleman, reappointed from a different industry in the CIMEX empire. At that time, CIMEX was one of three large government enterprises that provided everything to the citizens and tourists, from Crystal beer to rooms in $400,000,000 hotels on the beach at Varadero.

Antonio was an engineer by training but handled the money coming in and out of the CIMEX enterprises, which eventually comprised the Cuban national budget.

At the time, I did not understand that Cuba was completely cut off from the International Monetary Fund (IMF)/World Bank "free money" spigot, and Fidel (along with the whole nation) was being punished for refusing to play along with the Bank for International Settlements' Ponzi scheme. Of course, absolutely *nothing* is free, and the charismatic, athletic, and foxlike revolutionary fully understood this fact.

From the start, Fidel knew he needed to control Cuba's national finances. He recognized the US government and the CIA for what it was—an arm, tool, or weapon of the IMF. Loansharking Che Guevara, a medical doctor, created the Ministry of Health before moving on to start or expand revolutions in other countries. The Mafia owned the Batista government,[36] and Fidel didn't want any part of it. Fidel understood that the long arms of the IMF/World Bank and Bank for International Settlements would infect every aspect of Cuba's economy if he allowed foreign nongovernmental organizations. To avoid entrapment, he only did business with specific companies and specific countries that were free from the Owners. The Spanish, the Canadians, and the Italians were good and loyal trading partners after the Soviet Union went bankrupt. It was impossible for the Soviets to keep up spending when their economy required the production of goods and services to fund their defense and other government services, such as healthcare. When the Soviets withdrew their heavily subsidized sugar purchases from Cuba, the Cubans had to be creative to avoid the IMF debt trap. They changed their strategy from agronomy and industry production to tourism. That change ushered in the nine lawful private sector jobs. Those jobs were essential after the Russians pulled out.

Cuba also invested heavily in the vaccine industry, buying brand-new equipment from Germany to compete on the world

---

[36] Simon Worrall, "When the Mob Owned Cuba," *Smithsonian Magazine*, October 28, 2016, https://www.smithsonianmag.com/travel/mob-havana-cuba-culture-music-book-tj-english-cultural-travel-180960610/.

stage. It was remarkable how fast they geared up. They saw the money Bill Gates was investing, along with the US government, and they were distrustful of the US-manufactured vaccines.

At the time, I did not know why our vaccines were pure poison. The Cubans knew it and tried to test other vaccines throughout the trials, but we weren't allowed to do so for reasons they did not disclose.

The tetanus toxoid vaccine was developed by Pfizer. The Cubans were interested in exploring opportunities with Pfizer after free samples of Viagra were handed out at Cuba's Pabexpo Exhibition Complex.

As Cuba opened up to international tourism and business with countries other than their Soviet partners, there was a huge expansion of efforts to "Westernize" the country.

Westernization meant building country clubs, golf courses, and other tourist draws. Such development perked the interest of Spanish real estate conglomerate Inmobiliaria, the banking lenders for our enterprise.

Russian-built Illyusin IL-62s were used to fly US dollars to Taiwan to open banking operations, enabling access to the world's money supply. The project team acquired computers from Acer, and the team created the documentation required to present the findings of the field trial. Once the documentation was finished, it was time for the field trial results to be revealed to the world.

Soon thereafter, I was introduced to the World Health Organization (WHO), as WHO representatives attended our Pfizer grand field trial introduction at Hotel Nacional. In the press release for the event, I purposely included the fact that the device was dual-use technology.[37] The US Department of Commerce wanted State Department acquiescence in order to open the US door to trade with Cuba.[38] Cuba was hoping to establish a mutual legal assistance treaty (MLAT) with the US. That pursuit was the other reason I was allowed to be the first American to go down this path. The Cuban Ministry of Health sought to develop relationships with both the US FDA and Centers for Disease Control and Prevention. The US government was not so inclined; however, the WHO followed up with Cuba directly. As a result, I was not included nor updated regarding changes in protocols. My exclusion led to the subversion of the injector, as new requirements for shock resistance were imposed. Engineers were then running the project, not doctors or scientists. Enter Dulce Maria Martinez, the Cuban regulator of medical devices, who would later become the head of the Center for the State Control of Medicines, Equipment, and Medical Devices, the Cuban equivalent of the FDA. She was hard and siloed—definitely on a mission. US Commerce knew that our own State Department was not acting in best interest of our country. The State Department was, and is today, merely a branch of the CIA.

By the end of 1999, I was called to the ninth floor of the State Department building in Washington DC. They did not appreciate my commentary to the Cubans about further cooperation with

---

[37] *United States Government Policy for Oversight of Dual Use Research of Concern and Pathogens with Enhanced Pandemic Potential*, National Science and Technology Council, May 2024, https://www.whitehouse.gov/wp-content/uploads/2024/05/USG-Policy-for-Oversight-of-DURC-and-PEPP.pdf.

[38] See "U.S. Relations With Cuba: Bilateral Relations Fact Sheet," US Department of State, November 22, 2019, https://www.state.gov/u-s-relations-with-cuba/.

other branches of our government because the State Department *owns* foreign policy to the exclusion of all other agencies. About that time, our project had been subverted in Cuba due to evolving engineering standards and new health standards that were based on that engineering. I was not privy to nor able to adapt to the changes that doomed the project.

My license from the Treasury Department to be in Cuba was not renewed; however, I did receive FDA approval for the injector and the work we had performed while I was in Cuba.

My Cuban adventure had met a tragic end considering that it had exceeded expectations for its purpose, and it was the basis for both sides to check their guns at the door, which they eventually did in the following years. Today, there are numerous direct flights to various parts of Cuba, and travel is allowed on a general license as long as one receives an exemption to the Office of Foreign Assets Control regulations.

That end did include a small bit of fanfare. The *Financial Times* in the United Kingdom published a short article that announced to the world what we had done. I am sure bird cages throughout the UK were lined with that paper as the story came and went quickly.

> A small U.S. medical company has been given permission by U.S. and Cuban authorities to test a new product in Cuba in what appears to be a groundbreaking step under the existing U.S. trade embargo against Cuba.
>
> Cuban health officials will test a needle-free vaccine injector which has been developed

by Genesis Medical Technologies, a company based in Denver. The three-month trial involving 6,000 volunteer Cuban patients and using a Cuban anti-tetanus vaccine will start on Monday.

It's believed to be the first case of its kind involving a U.S. commercial company operating in Cuba since Washington imposed an embargo barring U.S. trade and financial transactions with the communist-ruled island 36 years ago.

Nine injector devices and 2,000 vaccine vials produced by Genesis for the trial have been delivered to Cuba with a temporary export license from the U.S. Commerce Department.

The device uses a spring to drive a piston through a vial of vaccine, injecting a fine high-speed jet of medicine into the patient. Existing U.S. embargo regulations permit the licensed sale and donation of medicines to Cuba.[39]

---

[39] Pascal Batcher, "Go-ahead for Cuba test of US product," *Financial Times* (UK), December 18, 1998, archived November 29, 2016, https://archive. org/stream/FinancialTimes1998UKEnglish/Dec%2018%201998%2C%20 Financial%20Times%2C%20%2318%2C%20UK%20%28en%29_djvu.txt

CHAPTER 3

TODD'S COMMUNIST FLASHBACK

I have practiced international law for nearly thirty years, including time living and working in two communist countries. I arrived in Poland in 1993, just after the Soviets left. It was still a communist country with a declared Communist Party president (Lech Walesa) and a communist parliament. Cuba remains communist to this day, and I have represented clients throughout hot zones around the world, including the Democratic Republic of the Congo, Ecuador, and Venezuela.

While in Poland, I worked for the largest law firm in Poland at that time, Soltyzinski, Kawecki & Zshykowski (now Soltysinski Kawecki & Szlezak). I was assigned to the international tax and acquisition team, responsible for the sale of newly privatized government enterprises, global companies, and groups that acquired entire enterprises, from factories to farms. Frequently, an insurance component or an insurance company (such as American International Group, better known as AIG) would make the acquisitions or insure the "guarantee" of the acquisitions.

When the Soviet Union collapsed and the Russians left Poland, as a parting gift, they left their 94 percent tax rate as well. Under the communist regime, the state kept all but a tiny fraction of its citizen's earnings. Upon gaining their freedom, one of the first priorities of the Poles was to take back their rightful share of earnings and prosper. Prosperity depended upon Poland's ability to operate as a free nation in all sectors, especially the economy.

In order to rejoin the financial community of free nations, Poland then had to restore its conformance to the US Code of Federal Regulations about commercial zones.[40] The restoration was no easy process as Poland had been disconnected from the enterprise system of law (e.g. private property rights) for decades.

Another critical change in governance involved the establishment of normal relations with foreign nations, including, and especially, the United States. The majority of US embassy personnel were working for the United States Agency for International Development (USAID), which is replete with spooks as it is a major cutout for the CIA.

USAID employees all enjoyed diplomatic immunity and supplies, including fresh food, flown in routinely using US military aircraft. As US military aircraft were allowed free travel to and from Poland, building an alliance with the US military was easy, and American troops immediately started training with and training the Polish military. The Poles needed to ensure that their separation from the newly forming Russian Federation would be permanent.

By July 1994, senior leadership of the US Navy traveled to Warsaw to jointly announce, with their Polish counterparts, the

---

[40] See Commercial Zones, 49 C. F. R. §170 (1938).

creation and development of a US Naval Support Facility in Redzikowo. The base is located two hours west of Gdansk on the Baltic Sea coast. The base is crucial to Polish efforts to guard against Russian aggression.

Many *Spetsnaz* troops (Russian special forces) remained in Poland after the Russians pulled out. I used to skydive and fly with them in Wroclaw, in southwestern Poland. The *Spetznaz* loved to sing patriotic Soviet songs about their government-guaranteed freedom. Yes, "freedom" is in the eyes and throat of the beholder, and every country, regardless of how tyrannical, proclaims freedom at the core. In some cases, citizens are actually free, in other cases somewhat free, and the case of Cuba, freedom is but an elusive goal. In the case of these young members of a Jeans Revolution,[41] wearing Western denim had become a symbol of democratic opposition in communist states. The young warriors were technically expatriates, yet without allegiance to Poland. Betwixt and between, they were apart from US operations there and what their fellow specops (special operations) brethren were doing back in Mother Russia. The *Spetznaz* had checked out, but they were used as a menace to justify the existence of the Naval Support Facility, among other things.

Afterward, the International Monetary Fund (IMF) moved in to work along with USAID, the European Bank for Reconstruction and Development, and International Bank for Reconstruction and Development. The Polish stock market was launched soon after, euphemistically exiting Earth's orbit to the tune of an 1,800

---

[41] Iryna Halip, "Choosing the Colour and Symbol of Future Revolution Is One of the Year's Events," Belarus News, December 16, 2005, https://web.archive.org/web/20110516092614/http://www.charter97.org/eng/news/2005/12/16/halip

percent increase in the first year. That success lopped two or three zeros off the national currency, the zloty.

In short order, inflation was back under control as the Poles mysteriously produced unknown wealth. Actually, they had hidden stashes under their mattresses, buried it in the back yard, and/or secreted it away in closet and attics. Of the crumbs the communist rats were unable to sniff out, the Poles had become masters of saving for rainy days. Yet the clouds of tyranny had parted, the sun was shining, and the skies were bright.

The Poles quickly realized that their stock market was the way to make up for financial lost time. They turned their pocket watches, rubles, and deutschmarks into zlotys that could be exchanged into dollars. These instant capitalists displayed exceptional market acumen and financial finesse. The turnaround during the first few months was very impressive.

From the start of the transition, the US State Department (DOS) was nation-building a capitalist ally and did a really good job. The DOS empowered the Poles and firmly backed the new democratic leader of Poland, Lech Walesa, and his Solidarity movement.[42] When sworn in, Walesa and his entire cabinet and parliament were registered Communist Party members. They all quickly burned their membership cards after the stock market launched and claimed credit for the turn around.

---

[42] See Maciej Bartkowski, "Poland's Solidarity Movement (1980-1989)," International Center on Nonviolent Conflict, December 2009, https://www.nonviolent-conflict.org/polands-solidarity-movement-1980-1989/. (The Solidarity movement, also known as Solidarność, was a Polish trade union founded on August 14, 1980, at the Lenin Shipyards (now Gdańsk Shipyards) by Lech Wałęsa and others. It became the first independent labor union in a Soviet bloc country.)

It is clear to me that Walesa was IMF-created and owned, and it just took that long for the IMF/US to insert a willing proxy capitalist into the government as an "outsider." Think Ukraine's color revolution in reverse.

At this point, the US did a good thing by bringing Poland into capitalism, drastically improving the life of the Poles. The capitalist revolution away from the Soviet model was a complete success.

In 2014, US President Barack Obama achieved his definition of "hope" by changing Ukraine from an elected democratic state to a US/NATO proxy. All he had to do was green-light Victoria Nuland, ruthless neo-con extraordinaire. They initiated a bloody color revolution transforming historically corrupt Ukraine into a puppet regime to counter the capitalist/free market Russians. Does Nuland's dart board have a likeness of Putin? The Owners hate peace because war is their bottomless well of money, power, and control. Peaceful and free people with free markets prevent them from accomplishing their end game. Avoiding war is not their dream, it is their nightmare. War is their Valhalla.

In 2014, Ukraine was increasingly forming a peaceful relationship with Russia. The Owners passed down orders to their puppet Obama and others to come to their rescue. All it took was a color revolution (the Maidan "protest").[43] Nuland passed out cookies while the country declined into death and madness. The result is a destroyed Ukraine, the loss of a generation of young men, and a future defined by a non-Ukrainian speaking gay actor with a drug problem. How is this possible?

Think Klaus Schwab, the Bank for International Settlements, and others who are busily changing the world into a Soviet-model economy under the guise of the elite acclaimed "public-private partnership." An essential cog in that wheel is the government bureaucrat. Anthony "Fraudci" Fauci, Francis Collins, and other bureaucrats of the National Institutes of Health, Centers for Disease Control and Prevention, and the myriad of other government agencies were deployed.

Private property rights and personal ownership is in direct conflict with the government power grab. The trajectory *is* toward the Soviet model. Groomed and owned oligarchs (Jeff Bezos, Mark Zuckerberg, and others) now run fully integrated industries. They are but two examples. There are also the puppets running Target, Walmart, United, and American Airlines…the list is

---

[43] See *Britannica*, "The Maidan protest movement," accessed October 6, 2024, https://www.britannica.com/place/Ukraine/The-Maidan-protest-movement. (The Obama Administration State Department staged the 2014 uprisings in Ukraine to overthrow duly elected Ukrainian leader Viktor Yanukovych, who promoted a peaceful relationship with Russia, so an anti-Russian puppet of the CIA, Petro Poroshenko, could be installed to destabilize the region and pave the way for Ukraine to join NATO. In 1990, as the Soviet Union dissolved and the Russian Federation was created, US Secretary of State James Baker promised Russia's new leader, Mikhail S. Gorbachev, that the US would not violate the one clear red line that would threaten the new peace, enabling Ukraine to join NATO. Since 2014, bad actors in the CIA/DOS have taken action to ensure escalation of its cold war against Russia and Vladimir Putin.

endless. The captives to a no longer free US market dance to the tunes of the Owners. The political class is owned, bribed, and extorted. They are but political underlings receiving occasional extra rations in reward for their enslavement and abuse of the miserable communist slave class.

Again, I experienced the communist nightmare from within, rubbed shoulders with the survivors, and worked with them to resurrect broken systems and lives from the ashes of totalitarianism.

PART II
THE "OWNERS" TAKE CONTROL

CHAPTER 4

THE WORLD HEALTH ORGANIZATION'S GLOBAL POWER GRAB

As mentioned, I have practiced international law for nearly thirty years, and my experience involves not just the vaccine business or the creation of vaccines, but also vaccine delivery systems. In addition, I have actually done business with the very people described in this book, influential power players involved in global governance in this key healthcare area. One of those people is Peter Carrasco of the WHO. I've also worked with others, including top Pfizer executives whom I introduced to the highest levels of the Cuban government as previously explained.

In 1974, Henry Kissinger, President Richard Nixon's secretary of state, wrote *National Security Study Memorandum 200*, "Implications of Worldwide Population Growth for US Security and Overseas Interests," also known as *The Kissinger Report*.[44]

---

[44] See *National Security Study Memorandum, NSSM 200*, National Security Council, December 10, 1974, https://pdf.usaid.gov/pdf_docs/pcaab500.pdf.

TODD S. CALLENDER, J.D., JEROME R. CORSI, PH.D.,
AND CRAIG D. CAMPBELL, PH.D.

The report presented concern for US national security due to projected population growth. A presumption was made therein that civil unrest and political instability would occur if the population in countries with a high potential for economic development were to continue increasing. That report set the stage for more draconian population controls that would be proposed twenty years later. In 1994, the United Nations (UN), and its 194 member countries, held the International Conference on Population and Development,[45] which became known as the Cairo Population Accords. That nine-day event effectively began the formal process of bringing all nations of the world to the most critical decision point in history through their UN representatives. The representatives at that gathering decided and agreed to reduce the population of this planet by seven billion people. Although the UN is the visible entity driving global governance, there is actually a hierarchy of people that are truly in charge, albeit behind a black curtain of secrecy as this graphic details.

---

[45] See "Report of the International Conference on Population and Development, Cairo, 5-13 September 1994," United Nations Digital Library, October 18, 1994, https://digitallibrary.un.org/record/172777?v=pdf.

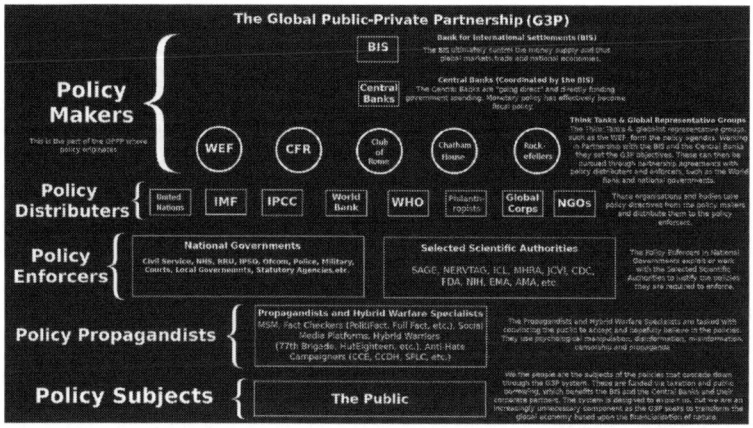

UN member states and their various legislative bodies are really just lowly level field administrators carrying out the plans devised by the select few Owners. The main drivers of the 1994 Cairo Population Accords were US Secretary of State Henry Kissinger and the Bank for International Settlements (BIS), as indicated at the top of the graphic. The BIS is, in essence, the financial *capo dei capi* of central banks, above all other central banks in this top-down, Owner-controlled financial network.

In practical terms, the BIS "owns" every private central bank on this planet, with three exceptions. As such, the head of the BIS, currently Agustin Carstens, has ultimate authority over the underlings, effectively owning everything. No matter if it's controlling the world's money supply—whether that be in yen, dollars, pounds, or euros—printing any currency out of thin air, and facilitating loans to governments in order the fund their operating budgets, Carstens has become the global puppet master. With such power and influence, what can't you own? But cheer up, we've been promised that we will own nothing, but we'll be happy.[46]

That is the point; they literally own everything. Power and control cascades downward through think tanks, special interest groups, and nongovernmental organizations. These entities are the tools of the overlords, the hammers and chisels that pound us down and chip away at all aspects of our lives. Over the decades, they have taken charge of the destiny of this planet. By and through their different organizations, including government bodies themselves, they control what happens to the world and its inhabitants—or more precisely, slaves.

By virtue of the 1994 Cairo Population Accords, the decision to reduce the population by seven billion people was set in motion. Like-minded lower-level commanders were groomed and put in place. They, in turn, recruited and trained loyal foot soldiers, and the "Army of Darkness" was mobilized. It has taken fifty years for this beast to reach the point today, by which it feels unstoppable, even as the mask has been peeled back. This giant unidirectional mass marginalizes or crushes all resistance.

In legislative hearings around the world, the slightest perceived pushback against the Owners, even innocuous questions, is met with the equivalent of nuclear retaliation. The totalitarianism displayed during the 2000 "plandemic" was just a pretext for global governance. It was a manifestation, or perhaps test run, for the subsequent more-serious launch of the Owners' mass depopulation plan—the plan being a global fear-based attack

---

[46] See Hannah, Felicity, "Why you'll own nothing by 2030," *The Independent*, March 1, 2017, https://www.independent.co.uk/money/why-you-ll-own-nothing-by-2030-a7582111.html.

using freedom-ending tactics through international relationships, including governments.

Governments became the blunt instruments that carried out the scheme. Let me guide you through that very process and how it happened. Over the last fifty years or so, countries' laws were all changed to bring us to this very point in time. The result is a confluence of events causing people to panic and thereby surrender their rights for independent choice regarding their own safety.

The Owners based their rollout plan on the assumption that all people would surrender to the fear they were ready to unleash. All notions of due process, people-centric governance, rational decision-making, and rule of law would be sacrificed in furtherance of supposed safety for all. We now know that the actions of the Owners had nothing to do with our well-being and were maliciously calculated to strip us of freedom, wealth, and even life to consolidate the wealth, control, and power of the Owners themselves.[47] The onerous ambitions of the Owners were exposed by an event that was scheduled for 2019 as explained henceforth.

As the Owners' lab-grown bioweapon was nearing release in the fall of 2019, the demonic pieces were coming together. Event 201was organized by the World Economic Forum.[48] Hosted by the Bill & Melinda Gates Foundation, a who's who of like-minded elites gathered in New York and conducted a "high-level simu-

---

[47] See James Kwak, "The End of Small Business," *The Washington Post*, July 9, 2020, https://www.washingtonpost.com/outlook/2020/07/09/after-covid-19-giant-corporations-chains-may-be-only-ones-left/.

[48] See Kirsten Salyer, "Live Simulation Exercise to Prepare Public and Private Leaders for Pandemic Response," news release, World Economic Forum, October 15, 2019, https://www.weforum.org/press/2019/10/live-simulation-exercise-to-prepare-public-and-private-leaders-for-pandemic-response/.

lation exercise." Did they just dust off the 1980s Japanese just-in-time[49] model, or was it just "lucky timing"? That symposium was either an incredible coincidence or the last preparation step for what was to follow. Was the release of the virus just another lab accident in Wuhan[50] (one of many)? Or, realistically, was it a planned event to bring the world to its knees using a weapon called COVID-19, (a coronavirus)?[51] In this new "improved" form, it was labeled "SARS-CoV-2." A patent application for Coronavirus 1 was initially filed by the Centers for Disease Control and Prevention (CDC) in 2004, and the application was granted in 2007.[52] In July of 2007, the patent was assigned to the US Department of Health and Human Services (HHS). So America effectively owns the pathogen, or a variation of it, that was released by a mortal enemy of the US, Communist China.[53] This fact endorses my point that global governance is above governments; it is done supra of governments. Otherwise, this event would have been considered an act of war against the US. Yet, since the US is considered by the Owners as just one other their many assets, it was business as usual.

---

[49] See Caroline Banton, "Just-in-Time (JIT): Definition, Example, and Pros & Cons," Investopedia, updated June 29, 2024, https://www.investopedia.com/terms/j/jit.asp.

[50] See, "Fact Sheet: Activity at the Wuhan Institute of Virology," Office of the Spokesman, US Department of State, January 15, 2021, https://2017-2021.state.gov/fact-sheet-activity-at-the-wuhan-institute-of-virology/.

[51] See Linda Rath, "What Is the History of Coronavirus?" WebMD, November 21, 2023, https://www.webmd.com/covid/coronavirus-history.

[52] Paul A. Rota et al. Coronavirus isolated from humans. US Patent 7220852B1, filed April 12, 2004, and issued May 22, 2007, https://patents.google.com/patent/US7220852B1/en.

[53] "The Chinese Communist Party's Coronavirus Cover-up," House Foreign Affairs Committee Republicans, updated June 22, 2020, https://foreignaffairs.house.gov/chinas-coronavirus-cover-up/.

Every country has had their laws changed in the last four years all for the very same purpose—the weaponization of public health. The master plan is to eliminate people at the end of the day, without any due process rights whatsoever, and without any hope of recourse in the courts. We are in the middle of a military-style plan being implemented with military precision. Regardless of one's position on the plan and tactics, the populace, the people who are, in fact, being depopulated, are to have no means of escape.

Inquiring minds might ask, "How did this actually happen?" Let me share my conclusions based upon my unique knowledge.

On April 4, 2003, then–US President George W. Bush signed Executive Order 13295.[54] The EO created a task force as a public health and national priority to prevent disruption to military operations. For that reason, a military response was in order. The Department of Defense (DOD) effectively took control of the public health response in the United States by virtue of this EO. The mission to establish the Owners' legal foundation was complete. Also in 2003, the US Congress passed the Turning Point Model State Public Health Act. This "historic" piece of legislation created a template to be used by state and local authorities on which to base their new healthcare laws. Key components of the act are to delegate authority, encourage collaboration, and provide ethical and constitutional public health services. The premise was to create a more robust public health infrastructure based upon legally sound powers, duties, and practices. But as history teaches

---

[54] "Executive Order 13295—Revised List of Quarantinable Communicable Diseases," in *Public Papers of the Presidents of the United States: George W. Bush, Book 1: January 1 to June 30, 2003* (United States Government Printing Office, 2006), 408, https://www.govinfo.gov/content/pkg/WCPD-2003-04-07/pdf/WCPD-2003-04-07-Pg408.pdf.

us, the best laid plans of mice and men often lead to horrendous dumpster fires. We should have started to smell smoke.

Then, in 2004, the United States passed the Project BioShield Act.[55] This act set the major pretext for mass depopulation, using public health as the primary weapon in coordination with the WHO. The smoke was becoming thicker and darker. Both acts were pieces of federal law that the bureaucracy, by its very nature, used as authority to crank out voluminous regulations and further laws through the course of events and time.[56] Refer back to the graphic and review the interplay between the Cairo Population Accords, the Turning Point Act, and the BioShield Act. Take particular note of Johns Hopkins University. Johns Hopkins was paid $26 million in taxpayer funds to further this model public health legislation. The overt goal of the enterprise was to ensure that state and federal governments would operate as one, should there be a public health emergency declaration. The covert goal was to ensure that all human rights and all constitutional rights would be suspended. Upon the mere declaration alone of those magic words "public health emergency," all human, constitutional, and charter rights would be suspended.

So, just how did the Owners make this dark magic happen? In the case of COVID-19, President Trump declared a national emergency on March 13, 2020. That act had the effect of suspending our constitution. In so much, the Article III courts were

---

[55] US Congress, "S.15 - Project BioShield Act of 2004," https://www.congress.gov/bill/108th-congress/senate-bill/15/text.

[56] See James G. Hodge, Jr., "The Evolution of Law in Biopreparedness," *Biosecurity and Bioterrorism: Biodefense Strategy, Practice, and Science,* 2012, https://www.nga.org/wp-content/uploads/2019/06/Evolution-of-Law-in-Biopreparedness.pdf.

no longer available. The FDA process was accelerated and began to follow a military process. Elements of martial law were implemented in that the executive branch of our government gained the function of the legislature as well. In some cases, aspects of judiciary discretion were also layered on top.

So, the three branches of government were grafted onto a newly planted tree of state, a dangerous hybrid made possible by the national emergency declaration.

The Turning Point Act started the legislative ball rolling, with each and every state adopting their own legislation. Upon the declaration of a public health emergency, people lost their right to free travel and were subject to immediate and indefinite quarantine (based upon mere suspicion of contamination and transmissibility). Upon quarantine, anyone could be forced to accept a medical device. As defined by the WHO, "a medical device can be any instrument, apparatus, implement, machine, appliance, implant, reagent for in vitro use, software, material or other similar or related article, intended by the manufacturer to be used, alone or in combination for a medical purpose."[57] Quarantining is, in essence, a form of detention, the application of which is for anyone identified as "unclean" by any medical personnel or medical treatments/procedures, shots, and drugs. People could even be jailed if resisting.

As the laws and regulations were being structured, there was no recourse for dissidents. Johns Hopkins University was responsible for getting these draconian measures passed in the US Congress and for the measures to flow downward for passage

---

[57] "Medical devices," World Health Organization, https://www.who.int/health-topics/medical-devices#tab=tab_1.

in each and every state. That is how the Turning Point Act came into effect.

When EO 13295 revised the list of quarantinable communicable diseases, it added severe acute respiratory syndrome (SARS)[58] to the list. In 2005, Bush signed the amendment to EO 132895, adding "Influenza caused by novel or reemergent influenza viruses that are causing, or have the potential to cause, a pandemic."[59] The stage was being set for the great unfolding (reset?).

The 140 member nations and two territories of the WHO all agreed to abide by extraordinary health regulations upon declaration of a "public health emergency of international concern." Those six words, if stated by the head of the WHO, would set in motion the tyranny these acts and EOs were designed to create. The Turning Point Act and related instruments enacted in the United States were being elevated to worldwide status—so, downward to the states and localities and upward to the other nations.

In the international context, should a public health declaration of international concern be declared by the WHO, all of its signatory nations would operate in the exact same way. Indeed, that is what happened in 2020.

The language from the 2003 Turning Point Act was all that was needed, and it propagated in a more deadly fashion than any virus it was intended to mitigate. It became the model state act,

---

[58] "Executive Order 13295."

[59] "Executive Order: Amendment to E.O. 13295 Relating to Certain Influenza Viruses and Quarantinable Communicable Diseases," The White House (archived), April 1, 2005, https://georgewbush-whitehouse.archives.gov/news/releases/2005/04/20050401-6.html.

and International Health Regulations (IHR)[60] became the model for all aspects of government action and intergovernmental agreement. In 2005, the WHO's IHR and movement toward an international pandemic treaty were put into effect. Emergency powers were enumerated under Section 361(b) of the Public Health Services Act (which goes back to 1944). Upon the invocation of a public health emergency, the entire government would operate under martial law. The list of diseases included cholera; diphtheria; infectious tuberculosis; plague; smallpox; yellow fever; viral hemorrhagic fevers, including Lassa, Marburg, Ebola, and Crimean-Congo; SARS; and SARS-like diseases.

So the model health act, the international model health regulations, and the pandemic treaty, as you can see, were all harmonized with the laws of the United States, happening at the exact same time. Certain specific diseases were identified, knowing full well that any scientist—or government for that matter—declaring that any one of those diseases was on the loose was enough for the specified reactions to take place. Such a declaration set the legal basis for the world powers, and for those controlling those governments, to invoke the IHR. Each and every one of those countries would be required to take the exact same actions in unison.

Comes now the year 2020, a year which will live in infamy for a variety of reasons. Right after the declaration of a national emergency by President Trump, Tedros Adhanom Ghebreyesus, the director general of the World Health Organization, made a

---

[60] See "International Health Regulations," World Health Organization, https://www.who.int/health-topics/international-health-regulations #tab=tab_1.

proclamation of his own. He announced a "public health emergency of international concern."

Yes, he said the six magic words, and the words on paper took full flight. Immediately thereafter, the IHR were adopted and put into force. The Organisation for Economic Co-operation and Development (OECD) appointed "competent authorities" to take charge in all of the countries.

Upon the invocation of this "treaty," the one-world government seized power over all sovereigns, signatories, and member nations of the WHO. Their power was fully relinquished through their various competent authorities. In agreements executed with the OECD, they gave their power to Ghebreyesus, enabling him to choose his "experts" and impose their opinions as edicts upon the worldwide slave population.

In America, in the case of COVID-19, those experts became the FDA, the CDC, and its National Institutes of Health (NIH), among others. The NIH instantly rose to the top of the pecking order, with Dr. Anthony Fauci taking center stage. Command and control was delegated to the very people involved in the creation of SARS-CoV-1, having genetically modified that disease to be contagious and to spread like wildfire through gain-of-function research and development.

Those same people became the primary advisers to Ghebreyesus. Ghebreyesus was born in Ethiopia and is not a PhD in medical science but "community health." As a Marxist and member of the Tigray People's Liberation Front,[61] which was classified by the Ethiopian government as a terrorist organization,

---

[61] Tefera Negash Gebregziabher, "Ideology and power in TPLF's Ethiopia: A historic reversal in the making?" African Affairs, 2019.

Ghebreyesus is by extension, a terrorist. He had a running relationship with a terrorist warlord, according to sources around him. While Ghebreyesus was the health minister for Ethiopia, there were three significant cholera outbreaks (2006, 2009, and 2011). Allegations continue to this day that Ghebreyesus covered up the outbreaks to avoid international embarrassment.[62] One would think the WHO would only appoint someone with superior medical science credentials, a dynamic career, and a spotless reputation to its highest position. However, considering how Ghebreyesus handled the COVID-19 response and ran cover for the Chinese Communist Party,[63] is it possible that Ghebreyesus was handpicked for the position by Xi Jinping for just such a time as this?

Or is it possible that the man in charge of the entire planet upon the invocation of a public health emergency, the Wuhan lab involvement, and the Ethiopian leadership failure are just coincidence times three? He's just the wrong person in the wrong time at the wrong place. Unless your intention is to truly depopulate the planet. That's a real poser.

Yet, Ghebreyesus remains in his position to this day, ready and anxious to declare the next "public health emergency of international concern." Can we rest assured that he learned from his mistakes and will do a much better job next time? Oh, wait, according to Ghebreyesus, he made no mistakes. Never mind.

---

[62] Avijit Goel, "Dr Cover-up: Tedros Adhanom's controversial journey to the WHO," Observer Research Foundation, May 1, 2020, https://www.orfonline.org/expert-speak/dr-cover-up-tedros-adhanoms-controversial-journey-to-the-who-65493.

[63] Michael Collins, "The WHO and China: Dereliction of Duty," Council on Foreign Relations, February 27, 2020, https://www.cfr.org/blog/who-and-china-dereliction-duty.

Based on the opinion of Ghebreyesus alone, the mere suspicion of a communicable disease requires all of the member nations to submit all of their jurisdictional power, their sovereignty, and all decision-making to this Marxist/Terrorist/Chinese Communist Party agent. Ghebreyesus is, in my view, the most powerful and potentially dangerous person on the planet. With his connections and self-professed infallibility, what could possibly go wrong?

In the US, upon Ghebreyesus making a declaration of a "public health emergency of international concern," the Department of Homeland Security takes charge of everything. In 2020, this department opened quarantine centers in each and every state, and in some cases, there were multiple centers.

Later, the US Federal Emergency Management Agency was also put in charge of "medical sheltering" (quarantine camps) and other key aspects of health protection during outbreaks. With the way the law is written, the Federal Emergency Management Agency has the authority to designate any location as a quarantine center.

So, if the public health authorities were to designate your house as a quarantine center, you're under house arrest. So be it. The feds can afford the same designation to a pig pen. If they declare that pig pen to be the place you will be confined, then that's where you're confined. Oink. There is no recourse to you as a person; effectively, you're just the accused. You're accused of being sick or having a communicable disease. Mere accusation equals presumed guilt, and you have no recourse. There is no judicial appeal. You are simply stuck there indefinitely until the public health services say otherwise.

In the CDC's quarantine map, they also put in place various governors in charge of those regions. After that, we see the creation of the Defense Health Agency (DHA), along with seventy-plus COVID-19 patents that were put into effect based on the original SARS-CoV-1 patent in 2007. The DHA is where the rubber hits the road under the DOD.

The DHA was created in 2013. Later, it formed the uniformed officer component of the DOD, which falls under the purview of the president. At the same time, in 2016, the federal laws that formed the basis of pandemic response finally made it into existence. Remember the model health act (Turning Point Model State Public Health Act)—that is the primary reference. It can be found in the Code of Federal Regulations, parts 70 and 71.[64]

In these model health regulations, if there's a public health emergency, the CDC is in control. The quarantine provisions go into place. Mandatory testing is enabled. Vaccine passports may be required. The federal statutes for all of these laws are now contained within the Code of Federal Regulations. Immediately thereafter, they create an enforcement network (see image below).

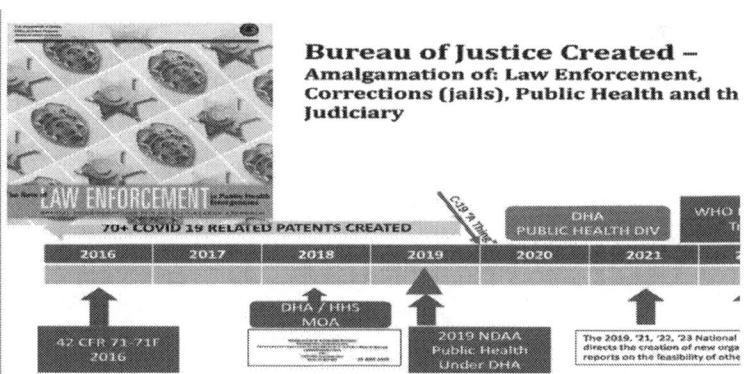

---

[64] *Interstate Quarantine*, 42 C. F. R. § 70 (2000); *Foreign Quarantine*, 42 C. F. R. § 71 (1985).

Todd S. Callender, J.D., Jerome R. Corsi, Ph.D.,
and Craig D. Campbell, Ph.D.

The Bureau of Justice Assistance (BJA)[65] was created with the authority to issue its own regulations. Again, the BJA contains an amalgamation of functions created to be the enforcement mechanism, not just a service organization to "achieve safer communities" as the BJA website implies.[66] I have since concluded that the Department of Justice's (DOJ) canned responsive pleadings, which all read alike in ten different federal suits following mine, came from years of preparation by the BJA. Upon the declaration of a public health emergency, the law enforcement arm is activated. The Constitution and human rights are suspended, and a substitute law goes into effect (parts 70 and 71 of the Code of Federal Regulations).[67] As such, incarceration by the public health authorities is both enabled and unquestioned and enforced by law enforcement. County hospitals and administrators, along with the judiciary, are in control of all things health related. Corrections departments, law enforcement arms, public health agencies, and the judiciary merge into one functionary. All wheels begin spinning in the same direction, driving us over the cliff. How can that possibly be? What happened to separation of powers? The courts are supposed to be separate from the other government branches. But contrary to very basis of our different governing branches, these public health regulations create a martial law situation in which citizens have no rights.

---

[65] "About the Bureau of Justice Assistance," US Bureau of Justice Assistance (BJA), September 5, 2019, https://bja.ojp.gov/about.

[66] "Leadership and Service to Achieve Safer Communities," US Bureau of Justice Assistance, https://bja.ojp.gov/.

[67] *Interstate Quarantine*, 42 C. F. R. § 70 (2000); *Foreign Quarantine*, 42 C. F. R. § 71 (1985).

Suspension of human rights includes the possibility of imposed medical experimentation on people. These actions are in violation of two UN conventions: the UN Universal Declaration of Human Rights[68] and the UN International Covenant on Civil and Political Rights.[69] It is also in violation of the Nuremberg Code[70] established by the international military tribunal in 1947, insisting that human experimentation had to be humane and respectful of human rights.

These international criminal laws were created to protect citizens anywhere on the earth; yet this set of laws have been twisted to enable forced medical experimentation. An entire planet of lab rats, Fauci's dream come true. Once again, the Owners have turned things 180 degrees to achieve their evil goals.

Medical experimentation is precisely what took place by the development and introduction of four different sets of COVID shots. AstraZeneca, Johnson & Johnson, Moderna, and Pfizer developed their own versions of the "vaccines"[71] during the race

---

68 See "Universal Declaration of Human Rights," December 10, 1948, United Nations, https://www.un.org/en/about-us/universal-declaration-of-human-rights.

69 See "International Covenant on Civil and Political Rights," United Nations Human Rights, Office of the High Commissioner, December 16, 1966, https://www.ohchr.org/en/instruments-mechanisms/instruments/international-covenant-civil-and-political-rights.

70 "The Nuremberg Code (1947)," *British Medical Journal* 313, no. 7070 (1996): 1448, https://media.tghn.org/medialibrary/2011/04/BMJ_No_7070_Volume_313_The_Nuremberg_Code.pdf.

71 "COVID-19 Vaccine Basics," US Centers for Disease Control and Prevention, https://www.cdc.gov/covid/vaccines/how-they-work.html?s_cid=SEM.MS:PAI:RG_AO_MS_TM_A18_C-CVD-VaccineTypes-Brd:best%20covid%20vaccine:SEM00071&utm_id=SEM.MS:PAI:RG_AO_MS_TM_A18_C-CVD-VaccineTypes-Brd:best%20covid%20vaccine:SEM00071.

to take advantage of Operation Warp Speed, a partnership to produce and deliver 300 million doses of COVID-19 vaccines.[72] All of these concoctions were "pre-clinical" or in various stages of clinical trials,[73] meaning clinical trials were incomplete at the time that the shots were issued and released to the public in 2020.

Looking back, it is difficult to believe that any government, let alone almost all governments, would be able to waive laws and enforce panic measures that have been proven to cause more harm than good. From the beginning, some citizens and medical professionals were sounding alarms and forming resistance movements. But the Owners were prepared for such a reaction, and that's when the law enforcement entities (now even part of the hospital apparatus), court system, and correctional institutions flexed their newly grown muscles. The mandates were to be followed without question or pushback. Dissidents were fined, censured, and even jailed indefinitely. Dissenters were given no due process and were indiscriminately treated as criminals.

The WHO's 2005 IHR had become the primary weapon used to pervert laws in every country. All of the signatory countries to the WHO passed their own compliant legislation—laws that could be unleashed merely upon the whimsical declaration by Ghebreyesus of those six magic words: "public health emergency of international concern." That Sword of Damocles is now

---

[72] "Fact Sheet: Explaining Operation Warp Speed," US Department of Health and Human Services, last modified January 21, 2021 (archived), https://public3.pagefreezer.com/content/HHS.gov/26-01-2021T05:48/https://www.hhs.gov/coronavirus/explaining-operation-warp-speed/index.html.

[73] Sagheer Ahmed et al., "Vaccine Development against COVID-19: Study from Pre-Clinical Phases to Clinical Trials and Global Use," *Vaccines* 9, no. 8 (July 2021): 836, https://www.ncbi.nlm.nih.gov/pmc/articles/PMC8402459/.

hanging over all of our heads. The revocation of all human and constitutional charter rights can be suspended at any time.

In 2017, Donald J. Trump took office, posing an existential threat to the Owners and disruption of the sixteen-year plan to follow the disastrous Obama/Biden regime, with the coup de grâce to be delivered by Hillary Clinton. The Owners quickly retaliated, and a new pandemic release operation was mobilized and bioweapon designed. In 2019, the bioweapon was released and emergency declared. In 2020, Operation Warp Speed, under the leadership of then-Vice President Mike Pence, a key asset of the Owners, expedited the creation of what were supposed to be vaccines.

Based upon the advice Trump received from Pence, the CDC, NIH, and others, he called forth a national public health emergency,[74] a declaration that soon echoed across the globe. By virtue of that declaration, the US government bypassed much of the institutional and public reluctance, and the full power of the Owners' plan, decades in the making, was launched. The governmental power base was increased again through EO 13887.[75] Critical elements of the public health apparatus were moved under the DOD's DHA. By virtue of this EO, knowingly or not, the final

---

[74] "Proclamation on Declaring a National Emergency Concerning the Novel Coronavirus Disease (COVID-19) Outbreak," The White House (archived), March 13, 2020, https://trumpwhitehouse.archives.gov/presidential-actions/proclamation-declaring-national-emergency-concerning-novel-coronavirus-disease-covid-19-outbreak/.

[75] "Executive Order 13887—Modernizing Influenza Vaccines in the United States To Promote National Security and Public Health," The American Presidency Project, UC Santa Barbara, September 19, 2019, https://www.presidency.ucsb.edu/documents/executive-order-13887-modernizing-influenza-vaccines-the-united-states-promote-national.

preparation for the militarization of the public health apparatus was complete. The government body in the United States became homogeneous. All powers now rested effectively in the executive branch, starting with the president, who by these acts was also subservient in power to the secretary of the HHS. The secretary was then in charge of all government responses, all the military responses, and use of the military to effectuate this public health response.

It was the US military that hired Pfizer, Moderna, and Johnson & Johnson to make the shots. Thus, the military was part of the development. The military moved the shots around the globe using military equipment.

I describe this reality as "militarized public health." It is, in essence, medical martial law. That is a precise description of what has been put in place by virtue of these legal wranglings. It took decades, but the Owners think long-term, and their plan has been put into full effect. The road from health protection to health tyranny was long and bumpy, but the final phases have been accomplished at warp speed.

Each year, the US Congress passes an updated National Defense Authorization Act (NDAA).[76] Executive Order 13887 in 2019 was incorporated into the NDAA to permit the development of certain cell-based or recombinant vaccines that affected cell structure by modifying RNA and/or DNA. Yet, a team of expert witnesses and military leaders advising our legal team pleaded, "We, dissent," based on a concern that genetically modi-

---

[76] See "History of the NDAA," House Armed Services Committee, archived December 22, 2018, at https://web.archive.org/web/20181222000607/ https://armedservices.house.gov/ndaa/history-ndaa.

fied vaccines would be required to be taken by all military personnel regardless of objections. We failed to win our case as subsequent NDAAs continued to allow the development of genetically modified vaccines.

As a result, the military is now in charge of all public health responses, and everyone is responsible for adhering to the military's public health mandates. The public health of all Americans falls under the control of the US military through medical martial law under the jurisdiction of the secretary of HHS. Until January 2025, when President Trump withdrew the United States from the World Health Organization, the head of the WHO had the authority to declare a "public health emergency of international concern" under which all natural sovereign health rights over the entire world would become subservient to United Nations authority, making the WHO the defacto health ruler over the entire world. The result would be that all health rights would be lost, leaving no one with a moral or ethical basis to object to whatever medical treatment the WHO would demand. The public health division of the DHA is responsible for vaccine creation and decides what are communicable diseases and their locations of origin. Again, the entire apparatus for these functions was moved to the DHA, not just the response mechanisms.

The DHA has created "global health engagement"[77] partners and a "whole-of-government" approach."[78] "Whole of government" means that all government agencies and employees work

---

[77] "Global Health Engagement," Military Health System, https://www.health.mil/Military-Health-Topics/Health-Readiness/Global-Health-Engagement.

[78] Adegboyega Ojo, "The Whole of Government Approach: Models and Tools for EGOV Strategy & Alignment," SlidePlayer, https://slideplayer.com/slide/6133559/.

together during a public health emergency. We experienced the whole-of-government approach starting in 2020, as all of the state public health entities, county health officials, all the way up to the federal government, and everywhere in between acted as one… from the DHA to the Department of Agriculture to the United States Agency for International Development (provider of support to foreign nations). So, the DHA is responsible for both domestic and foreign affairs, gaining extraterritorial reach.

Beyond just territorial issues, the separation between public and private enterprise has been co-opted. The private sector is being drawn into control by the Owners through public-private partnerships.

The US government has been investing in a multitude of businesses and their enterprises. In effect, at any moment in time, if there is a public health emergency, all sectors of the economy are controlled. If an international public health emergency is declared, it has the same effect, only globally. Everything has been militarized, and Ghebreyesus has been given the power to be the global dictator. Heil Tedros.

The official public health emergency expired on May 11, 2023. The US Congress declared that public health emergency in 2020 as a Marburg[79] pandemic. Marburg is a viral hemorrhagic fever, and Congress included it in that declaration. Funds from the Centers for Medicare and Medicaid Services were diverted to fund operations under the declaration. The funds were used to build quarantine centers and a variety of items on the Owners'

---

[79] Anna Rovid Spickler, "Ebolavirus and Marburgvirus Infections," The Center for Food Security and Public Health, July 2021, https://www.cfsph.iastate.edu/Factsheets/pdfs/viral_hemorrhagic_fever_filovirus.pdf.

wish list. To reiterate, the US government has been, remains to be, and will continue be under medical martial law until at least the first of August 2025. At this very moment in time, the government has the right to indefinitely quarantine anybody. Government agents can forcibly treat us with any medication they want, and there is nothing that we can do about it because the Article III courts[80] will not hear our cases.

In May of 2021, the DOD started saber-rattling about using the newly updated public health policy relating to mRNA technology—the use of synthetic ribonucleic acid as a means of instructing the victims' bodies to produce pathogens similar or identical to the pathogens du jour (meaning man-made by our DOD, Department of Energy, NIH, and others) as a replacement to long-established vaccine manufacturing protocols, which theretofore used disabled or dead "viruses." There is a vigorous debate among very learned scientists and medical practitioners as to whether viruses, introduced in vivo, actually exist to challenge a person's immune system to a rigged fight. EO 13887 made "upgrading" vaccine technology a national priority—a national security priority. This action struck me as odd at the time because I had never thought of the flu as a national security priority. It was an alarming first clue as to what was coming and hinted to: the one-hundred-year plan to eradicate or transmute humanity that was unfolding before us. By that time, large public-private-partnership oligopolies were beginning to mandate that this new mRNA technology be used among its workforce.

Many doctors and scientists were already coalescing, along with a handful of lawyers, out of concern that this brand-new gene

---

[80]   U.S. Const. art. III, § 1.8.1.

modification technology had not gone through rigorous testing. It was *not* an approved medicine by the FDA, despite the commercial media's best attempts to convince people that mRNA was a "safe and effective" technology. How could it be "safe and effective" if it was so new?! Classifying a medicine as safe and effective would require years of reaction studies of patients, not just words spoken by supposed experts to achieve compliance.

I knew better because of my family's needle-free company. My mother and sister ran the company after our successful device testing done through the FDA's investigational device exemption process. Over a period of twenty years, our company had tested almost every new vaccine and injectable through "collaborations" with manufacturers worldwide.

I received regular updates and reports, produced as a result of those collaborations. I knew that for the previous twenty years, mRNA technology *always* ended with dead humanized laboratory animals upon a "challenge test." A challenge test is a process during which the vaccinated animal is later exposed to the same pathogen that it was synthetically programmed to produce, using synthetic DNA and RNA genetic coding—something anti-human historian and philosopher Yuval Noah Harari calls "hacking life."

In every instance, the humanized test animals (genetically modified chimeric rats, mice, rabbits, ferrets, and guinea pigs) were mixed with human DNA/RNA to better mimic the immuno-reaction of their experimental genetic therapy. The animals that were given the challenge test developed an "antibody-dependent enhancement"[81] in response to which its body would overproduce the pathogens, causing shedding (transmission of the manufactured/synthetic pathogens programmed into the animal's body) and overwhelm all of the animal's bodily systems and functions, resulting in death.[82]

These results represented twenty years of science and data. I *knew* that mRNA and/or synthetic DNA vaccines were deadly; yet the government and commercial media hailed them as "safe and effective" when nothing could be further from the truth. The commercial media and almost every government in the world hid that information and that these shots were merely experimental, with components never before tested in acceptably large human clinical trials.

There had been two human clinical trials involving military personnel, starting in 2019. These were trials for which the results were fabricated and used to support an "emergency use authorization" by the FDA. That emergency use authorization was used to sell the unwitting public the lie that the shots were "licensed" products and were actually used to kill or genetically transform their target: seven billion people around the planet.

When I learned of all the evil actions being taken by various government agencies, I sued Lloyd Austin (secretary of defense), Xavier Becerra (secretary of HHS), and Janet Woodcock (then-commissioner of the FDA). I had them *personally served*

---

[81] Sol M. Cancel Tirado and Kyoung-Jin Yoon, "Antibody-Dependent Enhancement of Virus Infection and Disease," *Viral Immunology* 16, no.1 (2004): 69–86, https://doi.org/10.1089/088282403763635465.

[82] Lele Xu et al., "Chapter Three - Antibody dependent enhancement: Unavoidable problems in vaccine development," in *Advances in Immunology*, ed. Frederick W. Alt and Kenneth M. Murphy, vol. 151, (Elsevier, 2021), 99–133, https://doi.org/10.1016/bs.ai.2021.08.003.

with *all* of that data as evidence, along with expert testimony from highly qualified professionals—roughly one thousand pages of evidence between the temporary restraining order and preliminary injunction.

In an effort to tell the world what I knew, and prior to filing the suit, I linked-up with America's Frontline Doctors (AFLDS). Per the AFLDS website:

> America's Frontline Doctors (AFLDS) stands up for every American looking for the best quality healthcare by empowering doctors working on the front lines of our nation's most pressing healthcare challenges. We help to amplify the voices of concerned physicians and patients nationwide to combat those who push political and economic agendas at the expense of science and quality healthcare solutions.[83]

My collaboration with AFLDS and other organizations and experts enabled us to all uncover the evil and spread the truth. Our network grew as more and more people became active and were concerned about the same issues. I met all the leading doctors and scientists involved in the fight. I also formed relationships with a very, very small handful of lawyers, paralegals, and volunteers who had the same mission as mine. We became fiercely dedicated to alert the world to the deadly "vaccines" being pushed, mandated, and sold like snake oil to the public.

---

[83] "Who We Are," America's Frontline Doctors, https://americasfrontline doctors.org/about-us.

I am forever grateful to have had the experience of collaborating with the group of people at AFLDS who all very quickly became colleagues, friends, and trench-sharing "battle buddies" (US Army lingo). We remain resistance partners to this day.

Yet, unfortunately, money does weird things to people, and there was a great deal of money flowing into AFLDS at that time. The primary mission of the charity seemed to change from saving lives to attracting charitable contributions. As a result, most of us abandoned the organization.

Yet, all was not lost, as during that time I met some of the finest lawyers and people I've ever known. Two of them, Dawn Uballe and David (Dave) Wilson, joined me in forming a pro bono law firm called Disabled Rights Advocates, PLLC.[84] Dave is a retired judge advocate general ("JAG") Army officer. He was hearing similar concerns regarding the shots among active-duty military service members.

The knowledge I gained from Dave led to us to putting together a late-night video conference in May of 2021. The various concerned military members included Dr./Lt. Col. Theresa Long. Dr. Long is a highly regarded Army flight surgeon and formally trained expert in chemical, biological, radiological, and nuclear weapons at Fort Detrick, which is the Army's chemical, biological, radiological, and nuclear weapons educator and allegedly the former manufacturer of these weapons technologies.

We have since come to find that Ft. Detrick had a long, active, and intricate involvement with the bioweapons unleashed on humanity. Dr. Long later became the soldier who caused an entire standing army to reevaluate its thinking regarding the shots. Lt.

---

[84] Disabled Rights Advocates, https://dradvocates.com/.

Col. Long testified that polyethylene glycol comprised of between third and half of the contents of the Moderna and Pfizer shots. Polyethylene glycol had never before been used intravenously in humans. Her affidavit made headlines around the world, and I recall getting calls from New Guinea seeking to validate the contents of her sworn affidavit.

Also present in this meeting were highly respected servicemen Air Force Lt. Gen. Thomas McInerney and Army Drill Sgt. Dan Robert, and various other concerned service members. These dedicated warriors all knew the shots presented a real and significant danger to service members. They were seeking ways for duly concerned service members to seek exemptions from the shots. They risked their reputations, and for those still on active duty, their careers, to stop what was surely coming—a mandate by the military that all active-duty personnel would be forced to take the shot, or else.[85] That "or else" meant expulsion from service, loss of pay, and other punitive action. During that meeting, I shared my experiences in Cuba and the twenty years of knowledge regarding the testing of this deadly mRNA technology. Testing that always ended in the same result—dead test animals.

I recall vividly that General McInerney was deeply bothered by my explanation, and after hearing it, he excused himself from the meeting to alert other people he characterized as being too important for the military to lose.

Also during that meeting, Dan Robert volunteered to be the plaintiff in a lawsuit to be filed to stop the shots. Dan reasoned

---

[85] Jessica Schneider, Ellie Kaufman, and Veronica Stracqualursi, "Pentagon mandates US military service members receive Covid vaccine immediately," CNN, August 25, 2021, https://www.cnn.com/2021/08/25/politics/us-military-covid-vaccine-mandate/index.html.

that since he had already contracted and defeated COVID that indicated his body had already developed the antibodies, thus making him resistant to the virus. Therefore, he did not need to take the shots. In fact, he was the ideal plaintiff for our action, because there was operative law exactly on point in the Army Regulations.[86] That regulation provided service members with an exemption from the shots for various reasons, including religious, disability, medical reactions, and previous exposure. The combination of previous exposure and his deep-seated spiritual faith gave Dan two solid reasons that should have prevented the administration of these shots against his will, and in violation of Army Regulations. As such action violated his religious rights, this gave us additional causation to sue the government to stop the mandate and force the DOD to honor its own regulations.

Denial of a legitimate faith exemption would open the military up to a discrimination violation on top of the failure to accept the previous exposure exemption. Almost within the same breath, Dr. Long volunteered to be our expert witness in the legal proceedings, and Dave agreed to help get our legal house in order.

The project would require more legal horsepower than just Dave and I could present, given the size, scope, and deep pockets of the opposing legal counsel—the DOJ.

As always, whether the government had been engaged in proper action or not, it would fight to the death with almost unlimited resources to defend itself. We had some associates from

---

[86] *Immunizations and Chemoprophylaxis for the Prevention of Infectious Diseases*, Departments of the Army, the Navy, the Air Force, and the Coast Guard, October 7, 2013, https://health.mil/Reference-Center/Policies/2013/10/07/Immunizations-and-Chemoprophylaxis-for-the-Prevention-of-Infectious-Diseases.

America's Frontline Doctors who agreed to chip in as well, so in the end, the more the merrier.

However, this was clearly to be a federal lawsuit, and I was the only lawyer on the team with the appropriate federal legal license to file the complaint. Having drawn the short straw, which I suppose is a reflection of God's wonderful sense of humor, I gathered my senses to begin the uphill battle to prevail against such a mighty foe. It would be a David-versus-Goliath contest, and the mighty Goliath does not take kindly to being challenged. It would take more than five smooth stones and a slingshot for us to prevail. I had not tried a lawsuit in more than two decades, and the prospect of squaring off against the secretary of defense and others was daunting at a minimum.

As such, I filed the first lawsuit against the US DOD, being the only lawyer of standing in our Lilliputian cohort. The Federal District Court of Colorado recognized my standing, thus enabling the initial filing. Several other lawyers on our team quickly applied to the federal courts for admittance. The temporary restraining order complaint, although supported by five-hundred-plus pages of evidence, was rejected by the court out of hand. Concurrently, my co-counsels were all admitted by the court and already working hard on the preliminary injunction we had immediately filed following the dismissal. That filing was supported by yet another five hundred pages of evidence damning to the government's position.

Our legal position was expanding like a hydrogel in the ocean as we welcomed Dr./Lt. Col. Theresa Long to the team. Dr. Long became world-famous for her "antifreeze affidavit."[87] Dr. Long truthfully claimed that both COVID shots and antifreeze contain hydrogels. She warned that although hydrogels in antifreeze are an enhancement, their presence in the shots, and ultimately the human body, pose significant health risks. Even to the lay person, her argument should have warranted additional investigation. Why are hydrogels present in the COVID shots? What benefit do they provide? What risk do they pose? Sounds reasonable. But to the media, obviously prompted by their intelligence community masters, it was just another conspiracy theory dog whistle. The hounds came running.

The DOD entered their appearance on behalf of the defendants and immediately started a paper barrage of responsive pleadings. I felt so horribly naïve upon receiving those non-answers to our complaints, along with a DOD-wide order from the secretary of defense.

The shots were to be compulsory on all service members and non-uniformed DOD personnel—with the Use of Force authorized. Any service member refusing to take the shot could be literally restrained, or otherwise physically compelled, to comply— shot with an experimental liquid, or shot with well-tested lead.

In other words, the secretary of defense was personally served with one thousand pages of evidence clearly proving that the shots are deadly. Not just deadly, but untested and unlicensed. We

---

[87] See Leada Gore, "Alabama-based Army surgeon says she warned of COVID 'vaccine injuries,' was ignored," November 4, 2021, https://www.al.com/news/2021/11/alabama-based-army-surgeon-says-she-warned-of-covid-vaccine-injuries-was-ignored.html.

proved that new, never used before ingredients, like SM-102[88] and ALC 3015,[89] both "hydrogels," were listed as components of the "gene therapy" shots. As described in the textbook *Introductory Biomaterials*: "Hydrogels are polymeric materials that are hydrated and highly cross-linked at a three-dimensional (3D) level and have high elasticity and the ability to swell and collapse depending on the hydration level of their structure."[90] I actually thought that the lawyers at the DOJ and DOD would review our evidence and put a halt to the plan to forcibly hold service members down and, in essence, rape their bodies with a known toxic material that would genetically transform and potentially kill the troops. I would be proven wrong, dead wrong.

I kept waiting for a call from the DOJ to enable me to set up an opportunity for DOJ representatives to speak with our expert witnesses. It was essential for the evidence to be put into the official court record. Once entered into the official record, the evidence would remain enshrined forever. But perhaps that is the very reason our expert witnesses were denied the ability to tell the truth and expose the evil afoot. Plausible deniability only exists in the darkness and is vanquished under the heat of bright light.

John 1:5 (ESV)

The light shines in the darkness, and the darkness has not overcome it

---

[88] See "SM-102," Cayman Chemical, https://www.caymanchem.com/product/33474/sm-102#reference61317.

[89] See "ALC-0315," BroadPharm, https://broadpharm.com/product/bp-25498.

[90] Lia Stanciu and Susana Diaz-Amaya, "Chapter 7 – Composite biomaterials," in *Introductory Biomaterials*, (Elsevier, 2022), 149–169, https://www.sciencedirect.com/topics/materials-science/hydrogel.

At that point in time, I could not believe, let alone even remotely conceive, that our government would allow our troops to be forcibly injected with the equivalent of antifreeze. It just could not be true!! But, I have come to reluctantly realize that truth is now to our government actors as Kryptonite is to Superman—a radioactive element that drains them of their evil power and ability to control the US, their slave class.

Previously, when America existed as a nation of laws, such legal action would have followed the centuries-old standard protocol. A grievant would file a lawsuit and the party being sued would then be compelled to answer the complaint in a very formal manner. Such a response would follow the traditional lines of "With regard to Plaintiffs allegations in paragraphs one to ten, the Defendant admits, and in reference to all others, the Defendants deny the allegations."

That approach to begin a legal contest was the norm under the United States Constitution and Bill of Rights. Such a method enables the parties involved to boil down points of contention to the core truths. In that way, a judge and/or jury is able to impartially consider the matters in dispute in a way that promotes fairness.

Once that essential framework for justice is in place, the discovery process can begin. Both sides are allowed to freely disclose their facts and evidence in a manner that enables the truth to be known. That is *not* what the DOJ lawyers did. The DOJ filed immediate and vehement "motions to dismiss" without ever answering the complaint and its allegations. They dodged the issues and questions presented by the plaintiffs. The government refused to address the one thousand pages of evidence in their entirety. A darkness descended upon our once-proud nation.

Realizing the darkness was threatening to cover the land, other "lawyers of light" from all over the US started filing their own lawsuits to stop the mandates. We collaborated by sharing information, evidence, experts, and pleadings. It was the truly remarkable part of that episode in the fight for humanity's survival.

In every one of the eleven different federal lawsuits filed to try to stop the shots or exempt plaintiffs from them, *not a single* plaintiff received an answer to their complaint. All of the responsive pleadings from the DOJ from all over the United States were basically the same. It sounds like an actual conspiracy at the least, or the Borg mind at work at the worst. Is it possible that evil minds act in unison without collusion?

Ephesians 6:12 (ESV)

For we do not wrestle against flesh and blood, but against principalities, against powers, against the rulers of the darkness of this age, against spiritual hosts of wickedness in the heavenly places.

In other words, the DOJ had prepared canned pleadings and a strategy to *not answer* any of the allegations. Every single case filed was met with "motions to dismiss" for the exact same reasons. The obvious conclusion is that these were long prepared in advance just in case a legal resistance was initiated.

We all wondered if the DOJ itself was even responding to our lawsuits, but a higher entity was in control, as the fact patterns did not even match. If the same response is provided to pleadings of disparate natures, that is more than a clue that these responsive pleadings had been worked on long in advance, perhaps years.

Operation Overlord,[91] the Allied plan to retake the European mainland from the Axis powers, took two years to develop. It makes sense that one of the key initiatives to destroy the United States would be equally long in development. In other words, the evil powers were ready and waiting for the complaints and were going to do their damnedest (literally) to ensure that no plaintiff would receive their day in court. In essence, that turned out to be the case but only as a somewhat successful strategy.

We knew we were not just involved in a mere difference of opinion that required adjudication. We were not facing a spat between intransigent foes. We were literally involved in a life-and-death struggle between good and evil. The very well-being and lives of the men and women who voluntarily enlisted to serve and protect their nation and families were at stake.

Ergo, we were not deterred when we discovered a piece of evidence proving that the entire Operation Warp Speed program was a preplanned, intentional attack on our troops. Vast elements of our own government had developed a multi-pronged attack so nefarious, the culprits so devious in preparing the attack, that they even pre-wrote the pleadings we were facing countrywide.

There is, and was, no other conclusion to draw—*Lloyd Austin III, the secretary of defense was in the process of fragging*[92] *his own troops.* No one at the time, me included, could allow their minds to accept the reality that this ultimate evil was fact. The responsive pleadings were not well received by any of us. Our presumptive

---

[91] Dwight D. Eisenhower Presidential Library, "World War II: D-Day, The Invasion of Normandy," https://www.eisenhowerlibrary.gov/research/online-documents/world-war-ii-d-day-invasion-normandy.

[92] Encyclopedia.com, "Fragging," https://www.encyclopedia.com/history/encyclopedias-almanacs-transcripts-and-maps/fragging.

class of 210,000 service members, the other lawyers, their clients who were also stonewalled by the government, and our little law firm's pro bono practice became overwhelmed.

The troops were calling, faxing, texting, emailing, and exploring any means possible to become exempt from accepting the shots. We were concurrently writing legal opinions and developing other documents that the troops could use to receive an exemption to the shots.

We knew that we were on fertile ground, on a mission to fight back against the darkness. The obvious intentionality of the attack on humanity opened a legal Pandora's box. Criminal, administrative, quasi-criminal, civil, and international law claims were filed. The worldwide push back should have ended the mandated shots for everyone, not just our troops.

By day five of the legal fight to save the troops—and by extension, all of humanity—we paused to gather our resources and wits. Dave, Dawn, and I each had our individual needs and cases, but it was obvious a unified strategy was essential.

We held an impromptu meeting to establish a common legal means and protocol. We agreed that our number one priority must be to help as many service members as we could. Everything and everyone else would have to wait in line.

Dave suggested that we make a set of legal templates from the work we had already done. The templates were to include lengthy criminal complaints supported by exhibits, refined, and filed by thirty thousand "momma bears" across the US and six other countries. We drafted a master template many months prior and, with the updates, were clear on the intentionality of our attack.

Looking back, it feels like a battle plan in need of a name…perhaps "Operation Sink Warp Speed."

Other templates included Nuremberg notices, the Uniform Code of Military Justice Article 138[93] complaints, religious and medical exemptions, and my personal favorite, complaints against complicit senior military officers for treason and sedition.[94] Over the course of several weeks, we continued to litigate our case in what became a "motions practice of law." We sought hearings for any reason possible just to get in front of the judge in a court room. We had trained many clients in the completion, use, and service of the seven templates we had developed.

The clients we trained held seminars and symposia demonstrating to others exactly what they were doing and had filed. The activities of our clients quickly morphed into extended working groups.

Colleges throughout the military, across every branch, developed collaborative, fully integrated, asymmetrical "lawfare" models the world had never before encountered.

In the end, four hundred thousand service members stood up in defiance of Sith Lord Lloyd Austin and his rogue government regime. Hundreds of thousands of legal documents were filed and served upon almost every complicit member of the senior officer corps, Pentagon, and civilian leadership in the DOD.

---

[93] "ARTICLE 138, UCMJ, COMPLAINT," Opinion of the Judge Advocate General of the Air Force, November 9, 2016, https://www.afjag.af.mil/LinkClick.aspx?fileticket=nEQo2bvpqOI%3D&portalid=77#:~:text=Article%20138%2C%20UCMJ%2C%20provides%2C,the%20officer%20exercising%20general%20court%2D.

[94] Treason, Sedition, and Subversive Activities, 18 U. S. C. § 115 (1940).

In addition to the paper avalanche that befell the DOD, a huge life raft of military and civilian DOD whistleblowers parted the sinking SS *Austin*. Brave truth tellers from all ranks, positions, military operations specialties, and bureaucracies within the DOD put God and country over loyalty to out-of-control superiors.

The whistleblowers brought forward enormous amounts of previously hidden evidence. For example, an Army officer, remaining anonymous due to threats of arrest, court-martial, and other forms of persecution, was interviewed by Elizabeth Lee Vliet, MD. In an article about that interview, Vliet described her shock "to learn of the massive command-level violations of military regulations regarding the Department of Defense mandate for all service members to receive the COVID shots, a clear departure from safeguarding the general welfare of those under their command."[95]

The volume of information we received, filed, shared, and investigated was staggering. A treasure trove of new evidence, templates, and schools took shape.

To share all of this valuable information with the public free of charge, we created a website: www.vaxxchoice.com. Upon its inception, the sole focus of the website was to wage a legal war against these illegally mandated shots. The website has become a giant how-to library for the enlightened ones who saw the truth and felt the need to share their information with fellow light seekers.

---

[95] Elizabeth Lee Vliet, "Army whistleblower exposes command violations on vax mandates," WorldNetDaily, December 19, 2024, https://www.wnd.com/2022/03/army-whistleblower-exposes-command-violations-vax-mandates/.

One such prophetic piece of information on the site included evidence of a secret legal memorandum (a legal opinion), drafted by John Ashcroft's DOJ in 2005. The memo was addressed to then-secretary of defense Donald Rumsfeld. This memorandum discussed the use of genetic modification ("gene therapy"), which the military called "military genomics." Military genomics is the use of genetic information to improve the health and readiness of military personnel. It includes research, screening, and treatment based on genetics.

Years later, the DOD was spanked by the federal district court in Washington, DC, by Judge Emmet Sullivan in *Doe v. Rumsfeld*.[96] The proceedings brought to light the fact that the DOD had tested another deadly "vaccine" on its troops serving in the Middle East. In that case, the government failed to follow the proper FDA approval process for an investigative new drug, and my co-counsel, Dale Saran and Lou Michels, prevailed in their case to stop an experimental anthrax shot mandated for their noble plaintiff, Captain Thomas Rempfer.

The federal district court upheld an injunction and the anthrax shots were stopped after the DOD had already poisoned hundreds of thousands of service members, many of whom died horrible deaths or continue to suffer the ill effects to this day.

The DOJ lawyers figured out that an entirely new type of permission ("license") could be granted by the FDA to bypass the regulatory protections put in place to prevent unnecessary death and injury. But they could be avoided if the decision-makers just

---

[96] *Doe v. Rumsfeld*, No. CIV.A.03-707 (EGS), Casetext (D.D.C. October 27, 2024), https://casetext.com/case/doe-v-rumsfeld.

classified their experimental bioweapons as "emergency use authorization" vaccines.

Congress dutifully accommodated the DOD, as did the FDA. In fact, they conspired to make sure that they were fully armed and ready for the next event, which was the COVID-19 "plandemic." The DOD was permitted to widely require, mandate, coerce, and convince the whole planet, let alone the military service members, to take these "safe and effective" shots. Unfortunately for humans, the shots were not safe but rather highly effective in injuring, harming, and killing masses of people—which, of course, was the plan all along.

We learned a great deal from this litigation and were ready by the time we appealed to the Tenth Circuit Court of Appeals. We received a hearing date of November 18, 2022. We fully understood that the shots were designed to genetically modify the troops or kill them in the process. At the same time, the noncompliant would be identified and removed from service.

Because of our filing of the temporary restraining order and preliminary injunction, along with papering the hell out of the DOD, we were able to shelve the Use of Force authorization. That little win gave countless people, both troops and civilians working in the DOD, the clout they needed to abstain from the shots and stand their ground.

Throughout this period, the war cry *"Hold the line"* was echoed in every corner of the world. Members of all ranks, from E-1 enlisted privates through O-6 "full bird" colonels, were leading and educating others regarding the dangerous attack in progress. Not a single flag officer (general officers) sided with the troops, and *they all* followed, forced, and enforced illegal orders to frag their own troops.

Only now do we hear a few soft moans of regret by the sick and dying commanders who refused to believe that their own government would attack the whole of its standing military. All service branches—Army, Air Force, Marines, Navy, Coast Guard, and Space Force—and all of the civilian personnel supporting the DOD mission were targeted. I still scratch my head and wonder how the lawyers representing the DOD and others read the evidence we presented and still vigorously defended and protected their democidal client—our compromised government.

It can be argued that the continued feigned ignorance and compliance in lieu of proper action is worse than the original reaction to the pleadings. By the time we presented oral arguments before the Tenth Circuit that November, the truth was widely known. We proved the shots were genetically modifying the victims.

The undeniable truth was revealed through the results of the Pfizer six-month post-marketing study.[97] It was a study mandated, buried, and hidden from the greater public by the FDA. The results demonstrated in the appendix that the forty-four thousand service members *and their families* that took part in the COVID-19 kill shot clinical trials (study C4591000/1010) went home with 1,291 new diseases they did not go to the trials with. They went home carrying some of the most horrible diseases known

[97] Hannah G. Rosenblum et al., "Safety of mRNA vaccines administered during the initial 6 months of the US COVID-19 vaccination programme: an observational study of reports to the Vaccine Adverse Event Reporting System and v-safe," *The Lancet* 22, no. 6 (2022): 802–812, https://www.thelancet.com/journals/laninf/article/PIIS1473-3099(22)00054-8/fulltext.

to science, a third of which were genetic diseases that people are rarely born with (meaning not congenital diseases) showing up as side effects after the participation in the clinical trial—it's what the FDA and Pfizer innocuously referred to as "serious adverse events of special concern."

The very first such serious adverse event of special concern was the 1p36 gene deletion disorder, which only affects a handful of people born with it; yet it was the number one serious adverse event from the study, which means that lots of test victims went home without the genetic coding (ability) to regulate the health of their frontal cortex—the thinking part of the brain. Today, we wonder why people can't seem to process information as quickly or are showing up with dementia symptoms at very early ages, now including infants.[98]

Dr. Long was the first to note that pilots at Fort Rucker (now Fort Novosel) and other military training facilities were struggling to get through the courses and even failing out of their flight programs from being too sick; three pilots on her base self-grounded, meaning they went to the base flight surgeon (Dr. Long) and surrendered their wings—no small decision for a pilot.

Of course, masses of cases of pilots falling ill or dead at the controls is now commonplace and even recorded with the Federal Aviation Administration's chief flight surgeon and secretary of transportation by another brave whistleblower who is a senior flight safety officer by the name of Bruce McGray. For three years, McGray, Dr. Long, and various other aviation safety experts have

---

[98] Aparajita Chatterjee and Ambar Chakravarty, "Neurological Complications Following COVID-19 Vaccination," *Current Neurology Neuroscience Reports* 23, no. 1 (2022): 1–14, https://doi.org/10.1007/s11910-022-01247-x.

tried to stop the shots and pilots from taking them while the FAA, fully briefed on the dangers, continues to allow them being mandated by the owners and boards of airlines.

That piece of litigation opposing the shot mandates, *Robert v. Austin*, No. 22-1032 (10th Cir. 2023), interrupted the "use of force." But our case was eventually thrown out of the courts, first by the federal district courts,[99] then by the appellate courts (Tenth Circuit).[100] We presented oral arguments in 2022, an important part of the process, and we filed a petition in the US Supreme Court in December 2023.[101]

The threshold question from the Supreme Court relates to not just military and medical martial law, but also the characterization of anyone having received the shots, as the DOD was delivering these agents not just for the military, but the civilian population as well. The "vaccines" were gene modification shots.[102] In 2023, the US Supreme Court issued an opinion that applies to all federal employees including military service members.[103] People receiving those gene modification shots are, in all likeli-

---

[99] *Robert et al v. Austin et al*, No. 1:2021cv02228-RM-STV, JUSTIA (D. Colo. 2022), https://law.justia.com/cases/federal/district-courts/colorado/codce/1:2021cv02228/209086/48/.

[100] *Robert et al*, JUSTIA.

[101] *Dan Robert, et al., Petitioners v. Lloyd J. Austin, III, Secretary of Defense, et al.*, No. 23-600 (US Ct. App. 10th Cir., July 6, 2023), https://www.supremecourt.gov/docket/docketfiles/html/public/23-600.html.

[102] Joanne Cono et al., "mRNA COVID-19 Vaccines: An Incredible Feat of Genomic Technology," Genomics and Precision Health Blog, US Centers for Disease Control and Prevention, March 5, 2021, https://blogs.cdc.gov/genomics/2021/03/05/mrna-covid-19-vaccines/.

[103] *Vivek H. Murthy, Surgeon General, et al., Petitioners, v. Missouri, et al.*, No. 23-411 (US Ct. App. 5th Circuit, 2024), https://www.supremecourt.gov/DocketPDF/23/23-411/300032/20240207151527024_AAPS%20amicus%20brief%20Murthy%20v%20Missouri%2023-411.pdf.

hood, becoming a new species and are thereby owned by the patent holders, if you can imagine something that evil.

The Thirteenth Amendment to the US Constitution outlaws slavery, the ownership of people by other people. So, theoretically, this law cannot exist; people of any vaccination status cannot be considered slaves, at least in principle. However, since the principles of government have been so drastically changed, why not the principles of humanity itself?

People having gone through genetic modification due to the shots are believed by some as belonging to a new species, "Homoborgenesis," nicknamed "Borg"[104] DNA. Although a feckless new breed of humanoid, "fact checkers" (*Factoid refuto*), object to the term,[105] either as a result of binge-watching reruns of *Star Trek: The Next Generation* while on breaks or actually making scientific discoveries, both the NIH and University of Berkeley College of Chemistry have found and are studying "Borg" DNA.[106]

Again, when the ultimate public health emergency is declared, both constitutional and all other human rights are suspended. At that point, if the Owners have already succeeded in forcing everyone to take the shots that change their DNA, what did they

---

[104] Amber Dance, "Massive DNA 'Borg' structures perplex scientists," *Nature*, July 16, 2021, https://www.nature.com/articles/d41586-021-01947-3.

[105] Bruce Y. Lee, 'Homoborgenesis': Here Are Unfounded Claims Covid-19 Vaccinated Are No Longer Human," *Forbes*, November 2, 2022, https://www.forbes.com/sites/brucelee/2022/11/02/homoborgenesis-here-are-unfounded-claims-covid-19-vaccinated-are-no-longer-human/.

[106] William A. Wells, "Beware the Borg," *Journal of Cell Biology* 155, no. 1 (2001): 13, https://rupress.org/jcb/article-abstract/155/1/13/32316/Beware-the-Borg?redirectedFrom=fulltext.

become? If that change results in them crossing the threshold into becoming an entirely new species? If deemed no longer human, do the hybrid beings become "chattel property" of the Owners? After all, the Owners engineered the changes establishing their ownership rights, right?

As of this writing, the question is pending before the US Supreme Court. All lower-level leftist courts either refused to even hear or quickly dismissed this hot potato. I am praying that God willing, the Supreme Court will not have to finally address and answer that question, as the readers of this book will have banded together to fight and defeat the darkness. In this way, the only way, the mandates will be defeated. It will take a worldwide resistance—no, more than a resistance: a resolute and unstoppable uprising of humanity to save themselves. A movement of the "Army of Light" against the "Forces of Darkness."

If we do not prevail in *Robert v. Austin*, and people do not rise to defeat this madness, does our legal persistence constitute an offense of the Constitution? When totalitarian rule is pervasive, no dissent will be allowed, even retroactively. In that case, January 6 will be seen as just the warm-up. The DC Gulag will overflow, and the Federal Emergency Management Agency, or "FEMA," camps and other government-run detention centers will be open for business.

The *Robert v. Austin* case gives rise to the same concerns presented in *Association for Molecular Pathology v. Myriad Genetics*, 2013.[107] Public health laws made these issues a military function.

---

[107] *Assoc. for Molecular Pathology v. Myriad Genetics, Inc.*, 569 U.S. 576 (2013), https://supreme.justia.com/cases/federal/us/569/576/.

Whether those concerns pertain to the US government, or any other government, the application is all the same.

Again, the goal of the entire evil enterprise is depopulation. We don't have to wonder, because the forces of darkness have converted good intentions into nefarious actions that have been unfolding for decades—in particular, the 1994[108] Cairo population conference and the revisiting of the program in a report ten years later.[109] These actions bring together diverse factions with seemingly common altruistic goals that, over time, are subverted to serve the overriding dark plans of the Owners.

Lori Ashford, technical director for policy information at the Population Reference Bureau, reported on the focus and progress between the two events, separated by a decade. First, her comments on the 1994 conference:

A turning point in international discussions on population was the 1994 International Conference on Population and Development (ICPD), held in Cairo. Whereas earlier world conferences on population had focused on controlling population growth in developing countries, mainly through family planning, the Cairo conference enlarged the scope of policy discussions....

[108] "Cairo Declaration on Population & Development," United Nations Population Fund, https://www.unfpa.org/resources/cairo-declaration-population-development.

[109] "State of World Population 2004: the Cairo Consensus at ten: population, reproductive health and the global effort to end poverty," Health and Education Resource Centre, UNESCO, https://healtheducationresources.unesco.org/library/documents/state-world-population-2004-cairo-consensus-ten-population-reproductive-health.

[That conference] brought together 11,000 representatives from governments, nongovernmental organizations (NGOs), international agencies, and citizen activists. The diversity of views contributed to the unprecedented international consensus achieved in 1994.[110]

New "focus"..."enlarged scope"..."citizen activism"—clearly, Ashford was setting the stage for a new strategy. As indicated by the midpoint status as addressed in the 1999 progress review:

[T]he five-year review of the ICPD documented a great deal of commitment and progress, perhaps in part because of the widespread appeal of the concepts in the Cairo agreement and the activism of NGOs.[111]

By using the code of "activism of NGOs," Ashford, either covertly or overtly, knowingly or unknowingly, signaled that a significant shift had taken place. Abortion was becoming a "human right" driven by the UN,[112] to be cloaked in "prevent[ing] maternal deaths." Mothers were to be protected by murdering their

---

[110] Lori S. Ashford, "What Was Cairo? The Promise and Reality of ICPD," Population Reference Bureau, September 2004, https://www.prb.org/resources/what-was-cairo-the-promise-and-reality-of-icpd/.

[111] Ashford, "What Was Cairo?"

[112] "UN Human Rights Committee Asserts that Access to Abortion and Prevention of Maternal Mortality are Human Rights," press release, Center for Reproductive Rights, October 31, 2018, https://reproductiverights.org/un-human-rights-committee-asserts-that-access-to-abortion-and-prevention-of-maternal-mortality-are-human-rights/.

babies in the womb. To unbelievers it makes perfect sense, but to a Christ follower, the devil is in the details. Creating legal justification for females to abort their babies began in 1992 with Bill Clinton's "inspiring" credo of, "safe, legal, and rare."[113] Such platitudes have purposely led to pro-abortion zealots demanding that abortions be performed anyway, for any reason, and without limitation. "My body, my choice" on steroids.

> *Changing laws and policies.* Continuing the momentum that began during the Cairo process, governments around the world have drafted an impressive array of new legislation and strategy documents. The UN reported in 1999 that, since the Cairo conference, more than 40 countries had taken concrete policy actions toward the goal of providing universal access to reproductive health care.[114]

The emphasis of these "covenants" evolved from independent action by individual governments to promote family planning (in other words, contraception) to UN-guided policy change that would take on a darker tone and give unfettered access to abortion: abortion as a virtue.

The 2004 review revealed the motive to be used for the UN to exert even greater control: Money, with a capital *M*.

---

[113] Caitlin Flanagan, "Losing the Rare in 'Safe, Legal, and Rare,'" *The Atlantic*, December 6, 2019, https://www.theatlantic.com/ideas/archive/2019/12/the-brilliance-of-safe-legal-and-rare/603151/.

[114] Ashford, "What Was Cairo?"

Many countries have attempted to implement the recommendations of the Cairo conference, although progress has been uneven. In many low-income countries, addressing such a wide range of health and social concerns requires greater resources and organizational capacity than are currently available.

Also, funding from donor agencies to support these changes has fallen below expectations. Under the Cairo guidelines, the donor/developing country breakdown would have translated to $5.7 billion and $11.3 billion, respectively, in 2000. In fact, the UN estimates that donor funding levels in 2000 were less than half the required amount.[115]

By 2018, the UN was clearly in the driver's seat of this initiative to form an international death covenant. The Center for Reproductive Rights welcomed and firmly supported the United Nations Human Rights Committee's General Comment on the Right to Life. "Reproductive rights" versus "right to life." A battle of evil versus good.

"Reproductive rights" is code for unrestricted warfare against humanity using Satan's preferred weapon of choice, child sacrifice. The language of the UN affirms that abortion is a basic and undeniable human right, that "preventable" maternal deaths are a violation of the right to life, even though the baby is denied that same right.

---

[115] Ashford, "What Was Cairo?"

TODD S. CALLENDER, J.D., JEROME R. CORSI, PH.D.,
AND CRAIG D. CAMPBELL, PH.D.

The world has been moving from passing out condoms in order to prevent pregnancy to Planned Parenthood cutting up preborn human beings, the pieces of which could be sold in a meat market. The door to the operating room of death was flung wide open by the growing movement of the "depopulationists."

Harping on "reproductive health care" is particularly significant in this regard as the "my body, my choice" movement gains steam and intensity. In recent years, in the US in particular, a variety of forces have united behind the classification of abortion as a key component of "health care." So the initial Cairo conference regarding slowing population growth, protecting female health, and preventing pregnancies in overpopulated and under-resourced areas has morphed into an aggressive move to depopulate the planet through killing babies in the womb. The road to hell is paved with good intentions.

Another component of the plan to eliminate us, the non-elite, is the use of genetic modification shots.

These "vaccines" are completely hazardous, dangerous and deadly. But beyond those facts, the Owners may actually be stealing people's humanity, one injection at a time. We must literally outlaw the use of this technology. The vaccines contain altered messenger RNA, or more accurately, synthetic DNA and synthetic RNA.

Calling these molecules RNA ignores the facts and science; the process is actually gene modification using the CRISPR/Cas9[116] system. The creation of these shots is just the first

---

[116] See Melody Redman et al., "What is CRISPR/Cas9?" *Archives of Disease in Childhood: Education and Practice Edition* 101, no. 4 (2016): 213–215, https://doi.org/10.1136/archdischild-2016-310459.

step. The next step is to ensure that every human being on the planet takes the shots. The reaction of the evil "vaxhive" by a single dissenter is reminiscent to the attack waged against Neo in *The Matrix*, invoking a similar "all-points bulletin" systemic response. The virus detects the antivirus and deploys overwhelming countermeasures. Dissent is a threat so dangerous to the plan that all assets of the evil ones are engaged to end that threat before it spreads. Ergo, if some dissident says, "No shot for me, thank you," all hell is unleashed. Dissidents are considered the real virus by the ultimate shot callers, our Owners.

Although the Owners took draconian steps to ensure compliance by everyone, as already detailed in this book, the planners have that eventuality covered as well. A primary goal of their evil plan was to make resistance futile, and they almost succeeded.

But a resistance movement came together from the outset of the launch of the bioweapons, and has been growing ever since. The Owners greatly underestimated the will of free people to avoid slavery.

That resistance has forced the evil ones to go to their "Plan B." When faced with noncompliance, unlimited force has been authorized. Again, according to US law, the government can line dissidents up against the wall and shoot them right now, without any due process whatsoever, with liquid or lead. The enforcers are determined to shoot you up or shoot you down. Government agents can illegally detain those who do not comply, and there is nothing to stop them. Obey or else!

The Seventy-Seventh World Health Assembly[117] was held in Geneva, Switzerland, from May 27 to June 1, 2024. The theme of the assembly was: "All for Health, Health for All." Playing off the famous motto chanted by the heroes in Alexandre Dumas's *The Three Musketeers*, it is meant to frighten people into compliance with their agenda. The health of everyone is at risk unless all rally to the UN/WHO cause. Anyone who does not respond to the call is a feckless traitor and danger to the "UN-ibody." As the world is awakening to the coming darkness, independent physicians, medical researchers, and even ordinary humans are speaking out ever more loudly and forming resistance groups. The Owners are no longer able to keep the false narratives alive. Even with the complicit "Mockingbird Media,"[118] the light is shining on this darkness. However, the Owners feel that they are so close to their end goal, have come so far and labored for so long, and are determined to press forward regardless of the strength of the opposition. The fact is that the truth will always come out.

Luke 8:17 (ESV)

For nothing is hidden that will not be made manifest, nor is anything secret that will not be known and come to light.

For the evil ones, it is all or none, now or never.

---

[117] "Seventy-seventh World Health Assembly," World Health Organization, https://www.who.int/about/governance/world-health-assembly/seventy-seventh.

[118] Kaleena Fraga, "What Is Operation Mockingbird, The CIA's Alleged Program That Infiltrated America's Top News Organizations?," All That's Interesting, updated December 2, 2024, https://allthatsinteresting.com/operation-mockingbird.

Our sum of all health fears may now be coming together. The six black magic words have been spoken. On August 14, 2024, per the headline of the WHO news release: "WHO Director-General declares mpox outbreak a public health emergency of international concern":

> WHO Director-General Dr Tedros Adhanom Ghebreyesus has determined that the upsurge of mpox in the Democratic Republic of the Congo (DRC) and a growing number of countries in Africa constitutes a public health emergency of international concern (PHEIC) under the International Health Regulations (2005) (IHR).[119]

The containment of the outbreak of a virus as serious as mpox is naturally a primary concern of the WHO, but it may be a chicken or egg consideration. How so? Consider that the nature of spike proteins,[120] which enable viruses to breach cells and cause infection, are potentially deadly. Medical researchers in Australia have concluded, based upon extensive research, that spike proteins may be the product of a virus but also of the vaccine

---

[119] "WHO Director-General declares mpox outbreak a public health emergency of international concern," World Health Organization, August 14, 2024, https://www.who.int/news/item/14-08-2024-who-director-general-declares-mpox-outbreak-a-public-health-emergency-of-international-concern.

[120] See Benedette Cuffari, "What are Spike Proteins?" News-Medical.net, updated February 24, 2021, https://www.news-medical.net/health/What-are-Spike-Proteins.aspx.

mRNA.[121]According to the abstract: "The COVID-19 pandemic caused much illness, many deaths, and profound disruption to society. The production of 'safe and effective' vaccines was a key public health target. Sadly, unprecedented high rates of adverse events have overshadowed the benefits."

If VAERS, the Vaccine Adverse Event Reporting System, were to contain all of the data, not just a fraction, that statement would be considered a vast understatement. Continuing from the abstract, the "review presents evidence for the widespread harms of novel product COVID-19 mRNA and adenovectorDNA vaccines and is novel in attempting to provide a thorough overview of harms arising from the new technology in vaccines that relied on human cells producing a foreign antigen that has evidence of pathogenicity." This proves again the statement "the cure may be worse than the disease."

Surely, other research teams must be working overtime to prove that the shots are all safe and effective. Or, are these intrepid investigators bucking "VAX Inc." at their own peril? The word from these researchers from "the land down under" is enlightening. "This first paper explores peer-reviewed data counter to the 'safe and effective' narrative attached to these new technologies."

"First paper"? I guess that answers my question. One might wonder why the truth does not break through the shroud of darkness more often. Perhaps the answer is found in the death of the transparency of free and open dialogue in the legacy media. There

---

[121] Peter I. Parry et al., "'Spikeopathy': COVID-19 Spike Protein Is Pathogenic, from Both Virus and Vaccine mRNA," *Biomedicines* 11, no. 8 (2023): 2287, https://doi.org/10.3390/biomedicines11082287.

are, however, glimmers of hope as the tide may be shifting as the alternative media is on the rise.

Unlike in 2020, today, with free speech platforms like X, and the movement of the public away from mainstream sources to such alternatives, the truth is getting out. The resistance is alive and loud, and the examples of change are growing.

On June 21, 2024, the article, "A systematic review of autopsy findings in deaths after COVID-19 vaccination" appeared in the *Forensic Science International* journal. Some highlights of their findings are truly alarming:

- We found that 73.9 percent of deaths were directly due to or significantly contributed to by COVID-19 vaccination.
- Our data suggest a high likelihood of a causal link between COVID-19 vaccination and death.
- These findings indicate the urgent need to elucidate the pathophysiologic mechanisms of death with the goal of risk stratification and avoidance of death for the large numbers of individuals who have taken or will receive one or more COVID-19 vaccines in the future.[122]

The conclusions of the researchers do not bode well for humanity:

The consistency seen among cases in this review with known COVID-19 vaccine mechanisms of injury and death, coupled with autopsy

---

[122] Nicolas Hulscher et al., "Withdrawn: A systematic review of autopsy findings in deaths after COVID-19 vaccination," *Forensic Science International,* June 21, 2024, https://doi.org/10.1016/j.forsciint.2024.112115.

> confirmation by physician adjudication, suggests
> there is a high likelihood of a causal link between
> COVID-19 vaccines and death. Further urgent
> investigation is required for the purpose of clari-
> fying our findings.[123]

So much for safe and effective. Perhaps, although the shots are definitely *not* safe, they may truly be effective if the definition of effective is depopulation. In that case, they are highly effective and an indispensable component of the plans of the Owners. Dark side kudos to Fauci.

But rest assured, I am sure now that the entire world is aware of such findings, the "further urgent investigation" is surely underway. Unless of course, these findings are not reported, and the only urgency is to launch the next round of death shots.

On August 23, 2024, award-winning international journalist Alex Newman interviewed Dr. David Martin as part of Newman's series *Conversations That Matter* for the *New American* magazine. The title of the show was "Monkeypox a Cover for Covid Injection Side Effects, Warns Dr. David Martin." Dr. Martin began with the following:

> And the reason why this is a cause from concern,
> Alex, is not because the theater of monkeypox.
> Let's set that aside for a moment. There is no
> monkeypox outbreak of any concern whatsoever.

---

[123] Hulscher et al., "Withdrawn: A systematic review."

But what there is, is a pox-like side effect of people's response to their immune failures around receiving the injections of spike protein. And when you have surface skin lesions, which are increasing in their frequency, when you have side effects that are associated with autoimmune diseases that are upcoming, which look like pox-like skin disorders, Alex, it's important to build a cover story that says that when somebody has a thing that looks like a rash that advances to quite a serious disease, and sometimes actually fatal outcomes, what is being done is they're selling the side effect of the COVID injection as a new outbreak. So the numbers are going to match up.

Dr. Martin reflected back to 2022:

That's the interesting thing. And that's why I said that back in 2022. They forecast that we were going to have as many as 200 million deaths.

They were looking at 187 million to 200 million deaths in their scenario. They said that there was going to be as much as half the world's population allegedly suffering these side effects. They called it from the infection.

But the point is, yes, we should be concerned, but we shouldn't be concerned about monkeypox. We should be concerned about the fact that the institutional lie is being sold to cover up a genuine consequence of the mRNA injection. And they knew that was coming.

Dr. Martin finished with the following:

There was no question that this was going to be coming, so much so that it was published. And if anybody wants to go back, just go into any browser, type "nuclear threat initiative," type "monkeypox."[124] And lo and behold, you're going to find out that they told us what was coming, lo and behold, three years ago.[125]

But undaunted, the Evil Empire struck back. On September 1, 2024, WHO director general Dr. Tedros said the following:

On Friday, we received the information we needed from one of the manufacturers to evaluate its [mpox] vaccine. We expect to issue an emergency use listing within [the] next three weeks. In the meantime, I have given the green

---

[124] See Margaret A. Hamburg and Ernest J. Moniz, "Monkeypox Response Shortcomings Highlight Urgent Need to Invest in Pandemic Preparedness Across the Globe," Nuclear Threat Initiative, August 11, 2002, https://www. nti.org/news/statement-by-dr-margaret-a-hamburg-and-ernest-j-moniz-monkeypox-response-shortcomings-highlight-urgent-need-to-invest-in-pandemic-preparedness-across-the-globe/.

[125] Alex Newman, "Monkeypox a Cover for Covid Injection Side Effects, Warns Dr. David Martin," video, Rumble, August 23, 2024, 3:31–5:22, https:// thenewamerican.com/video/monkeypox-a-cover-for-covid-injection-side-effects-warns-dr-david-martin/.

light to the Gavi and UNICEF to proceed with procurement of vaccines pending EUL [emergency use listing] decision.[126]

Gavi is "the Vaccine Alliance," a consortium of the usual players (culprits): WHO, UNICEF, the Bill and Melinda Gates Foundation, and the World Bank. Their stated mission is to mobilize the world with a "wake up call for all global health leaders" to react to the "public health emergency of international concern" regarding mpox.

The Gavi website states that this is a way to "protect our future" through this "investment opportunity" for 2026–2030. The alliance "needs… US$9 billion from…donors to fund [their] most ambitious strategy ever: protecting 500 million children and saving at least 8 million lives." Naturally, Gavi states that this is another reason "we need a strong pandemic agreement."[127] UNICEF's slogan is "for every child." Living down to their stated mission, UNICEF has been involved in several "scandals" including, according to Google's artificial intelligence engine:

---

[126] "Sudden and Unexpected" (@toobaffled), "WHO Director General Dr. Tedros: 'On Friday we received the information we needed from one of the manufacturers to evaluate its (mpox) vaccine. We expect to issue an emergency use listing within the next 3 weeks. In the meantime I have given the green light to the Gavi and UNICEF to proceed with procurement of vaccines pending EUL decision,'" video, X, September 1, 2024, https://x.com/toobaffled/status/1830159749809418556.

[127] Pascal Barollier, "Mpox outbreak: one more reason we need a strong pandemic agreement," VaccinesWork, Gavi, the Vaccine Alliance, September 4, 2024, https://www.gavi.org/vaccineswork/mpox-outbreak-one-more-reason-we-need-strong-pandemic-agreement.

Contrary to its slogan, UNICEF has been accused of child sexual abuse in the Central African Republic. In 2015, UNICEF was heavily criticized for failing to adequately respond to reports of widespread child sexual abuse by UN peacekeepers in the Central African Republic (CAR), with accusations that they did not properly investigate or protect victims of abuse by French, Chadian, and Equatorial Guinean troops stationed there; this resulted in a major controversy regarding the UN's handling of the situation and a "gross institutional failure" according to an independent panel.[128]

The allegations regarding the sex crimes are not isolated to the Central African Republic, as similar credible accusations have been made regarding sexual exploitation and abuse in the Democratic Republic of the Congo.

UNICEF statement on allegations of sexual exploitation and abuse in the Democratic Republic of the Congo. NEW YORK, 30 September 2020—"UNICEF is appalled that people who identify as UNICEF workers have reportedly committed abuse against

---

[128] Text generated by Google AI, https://www.google.com/search?q=Child+sexual+abuse+in+the+Central+African+Republic+(CAR)+In+2015%2C+UNICEF+was+criticized&rlz=1C1_____en-USUS1090US1090&oq=Child+sexual+abuse+in+the+Central+African+Republic+(CAR)+In+2015%2C+UNICEF+was+criticized&gs_lcrp=EgZjaHJvbWUyBggAE EUYOdIBBzMxNGowajSoAgCwAgE&sourceid=chrome&ie=UTF-8.

vulnerable women in the Democratic Republic of the Congo."[129]

The abuses by UN-funded UNICEF are not confined to Africa, as cases have been found in Europe as well. Whistleblower Kathryn Bolkovac made shocking revelations that were later exposed in a Hollywood movie. She shared her thoughts on the UN in an interview with a newspaper:

> The thing that stood out about these cases in Bosnia, and cases that have been reported in other [UN] mission areas, is...that police and humanitarian workers were frequently involved in not only the facilitation of forced sexual abuse, and the use of children and young women in brothels, but in many instances became involved in the trade by racketeering, bribery and outright falsifying of documents as part of a broader criminal syndicate.[130]

---

[129] Text generated by Google AI, https://www.google.com/search?q=Sexual+exploitation+and+abuse+in+the+Democratic+Republic+of+the+Congo+In+2020%2C+UNICEF+released+a+statement&rlz=1C1____en-USUS1090US1090&oq=Sexual+exploitation+and+abuse+in+the+Democratic+Republic+of+the+Congo+In+2020%2C+UNICEF+released+a+statement&gs_lcrp=EgZjaHJvbWUyBggAEEUYOdIBBzM5OGowajGoAgCwAgA&sourceid=chrome&ie=UTF-8.

[130] Ed Vulliamy, "Has the UN learned lessons of Bosnian sex slavery revealed in Rachel Weisz film?" *The Guardian*, January 14, 2012, https://www.theguardian.com/world/2012/jan/15/bosnia-sex-trafficking-whistleblower.

Just how rampant is the issue regarding sexual crimes by the UN in general, and UNICEF in particular? A 2018 article in *The Jerusalem Post* describes the extent:

> UN staff have carried out thousands of rapes and other sexual violations against women and children over the last decade, according to a former senior United Nations official.
>
> "There are tens of thousands of aid workers around the world with pedophile tendencies, but if you wear a UNICEF T-shirt, nobody will ask what you're up to," Andrew MacLeod, the former chief of operations at the UN's Emergency Co-ordination Center, said in an interview with british tabloid *The Sun* on Monday, adding that an estimated 60,000 cases of sexual exploitation had been committed over the last decade by 3,300 pedophiles working in the organization.[131]

These are but four examples of the dozens of incidents. Most of these events are not reported due to the lack of survivors, or fear on the part of the victims that retribution by the perpetrators would be worse than the original abuse.

So, with partners like UNICEF, the UN emphatically states that we can place full confidence and support behind Gavi as it

---

[131] Juliane Helmhold, "UN staff allegedly responsible for over 60,000 cases of sexual exploitation" *The Jerusalem Post*, February 16, 2018, https://www.jpost.com/international/un-staff-allegedly-responsbile-for-over-60000-cases-of-sexual-exploitation-542817.

plows forward, advancing its children-centric agenda. Is it possible that the stated agenda differs from its real intent? Inquiring minds might wonder.

CHAPTER 5

DISEASE X: THE WEAPONIZATION OF MEDICINE TO DEPOPULATE THE GLOBE

Disease X, the Official Story

In February 2018, the World Health Organization (WHO) began using the term "Disease X" to prioritize diseases for research and development in order to prepare for emergency outbreaks, as indicated in WHO's updated blueprint list.[132] Disease X represents a hypothetical, unknown pathogen with the potential to cause a future epidemic. The WHO adopted Disease X as a placeholder name to ensure that its planning and investment strategy was flexible in order to adapt to an unknown pathogen.

Anthony Fauci, former director of the US National Institute of Allergy and Infectious Diseases promoted the concept of Disease

---

[132] "Prioritizing diseases for research and development in emergency contexts," World Health Organization, https://www.who.int/activities/prioritizing-diseases-for-research-and-development-in-emergency-contexts.

X as a method for the WHO to focus research efforts on entire classes of viruses, instead of just individual strains. Fauci asserted that the WHO's capability to respond to unforeseen strains would be greatly improved.[133] In 2020, the WHO's science advisers posited that COVID-19, caused by the SARS-CoV-2 virus, was the first such Disease X.[134] How ironic is it that as of the date we are writing this book, Fauci has admitted to having come down with COVID for the third time? So much for "take the shot and you will not contract the disease," the primary purpose and selling point of the shots. The marketing campaign was wildly successful, but unfortunately for humanity, the snake oil caused more harm than good while not providing its advertised benefits. In the real world, a company this deceitful, providing a product having failed so completely, with numerous adverse effects, would be sued into nonexistence. But government bureaucrats are rarely fired, and pharmaceutical giants are untouchable. Vaccine manufacturers are immune from prosecution even if, as in the proximate case, they knowingly distributed deadly liquids with hidden toxins to the entire world.

Although trusted by the public in 2020, the case can be made that Fauci is both a malevolent fraud and chronic liar. When left-leading online publication Slate is lowered to admitting Fauci's lies and reduced to explaining them away as "noble," there is fire beneath that smoke.

---

[133] Susan Scutti, "World Health Organization gets ready for 'Disease X,'" CNN Health, March 12, 2018, https://edition.cnn.com/2018/03/12/health/disease-x-blueprint-who/index.html.

[134] Shibo Jiang and Zheng-Li Shi, "The First Disease X is Caused by a Highly Transmissible Acute Respiratory Syndrome Coronavirus," *Virologica Sinica* 35 (February 2020): 263–265, https://link.springer.com/article/10.1007/s12250-020-00206-5.

Although some have claimed that the evidence changed substantively in the early weeks of March, our assessment of the literature does not concur. We believe the evidence at the time of Fauci's *60 Minutes* interview was largely similar to that in April 2020. Thus, there are two ways to consider Fauci's statement. One possibility is, as he says, that his initial statement was dishonest but motivated to avoid a run on masks needed by health care workers. The other is that he believed his initial statements were accurate, and he subsequently decided to advocate for cloth masks to divert attention from surgical or N95 masks, or to provide a sense of hope and control to a fearful and anxious public.[135]

So, the need for "hope and control" is to be understood with the same unquestioned benevolence as "hope and change"? The lofty pontifications of the "vaxxer in chief" are elevated to the same level as still vaunted "divider in chief"?

The management of the so-called pandemic has shown, thanks in part to leaks and insider testimony, that its ultimate purpose was to impose forms of control and limitations on the basic freedoms of citizens. This was while simultaneously eliminating some of them through the spread of a virus and the concomitant banning of existing treatments. It would then impose an experimental gene serum—fraudulently passed off as a "vaccine"—that

---

[135] Kerrington Powell and Vinay Prasad, "The Noble Lies of COVID-19," *Slate*, July 28, 2021, https://slate.com/technology/2021/07/noble-lies-covid-fauci-cdc-masks.html.

would, dose after dose, severely weaken the population's immune defenses, genetically modify them, and insert relentless self-synthesizing factors (mRNAs) that would lead to death, with timelines as unrelated to the inoculation as possible.

The number of sudden deaths, miscarriages, seemingly unexplained deaths (but all concomitant with the distribution of the gene serum), and adverse reactions (including the frightening explosion of neoplasms; autoimmune diseases; neurodegenerative diseases; and prion-like, cardiac, circulatory, fertility, and gestation diseases) confirm the danger posed to society by the architects of this criminal plan and their intention to carry it out without any respect for human life.

Imagine after all of the intentionally inflicted global carnage and insistence that he was just following the science, he has had to admit that there was no science at all involved.[136] Worse yet, he did so with an unrepentant smirk and bulging bank account.

Disease X, the Rest of the Story

As noted before, the Johns Hopkins Center for Health Security, that once-prestigious medical institution, in partnership with the World Economic Forum and the Bill and Melinda Gates Foundation, hosted Event 201. It sponsored a high-level pandemic exercise on October 18, 2019, in New York city. As stated on the event's website, "The exercise illustrated areas where public/private partnerships will be necessary during the response to a severe pandemic in order to diminish large-scale economic and

---

[136] Nicole Russell, "COVID guidelines caused millions to suffer. Now Fauci admits 'there was no science behind it.'" *USA Today*, June 5, 2024,

societal consequences."[137] How prophetic. On December 12, 2019, less than two months later, people in the city of Wuhan in Communist China were found to be suffering from an "atypical pneumonia-like illness that does not respond well to standard treatments."[138] Do you believe in coincidences? The tooth fairy? Hope and change? On December 31, 2019, Communist China notified the WHO through its country office in China of the spreading disease.

2020: A year which will live in infamy

The Chinese zodiac consists of a twelve-year cycle, with each year symbolized by an animal. The year 2020 was the year of the "metal rat," the first animal in the cycle, which is believed by the Chinese to bring new beginnings. The new beginning for this cycle could be labeled "the greatest reset, and maybe the last."

Communist China invented the story that the Huanan Seafood Wholesale Market[139] was the location where patient

---

[137] "Tabletop Exercise: Event 201," Center for Health Security, https://centerforhealthsecurity.org/our-work/tabletop-exercises/event-201-pandemic-tabletop-exercise.

[138] Cate Martel, "The Hill's 12:30 Report — Scientific breakthrough in energy; Best 'White Lotus' reactions," *The Hill*, December 13, 2022, https://thehill.com/homenews/1230-report/3773469-the-hills-1230-report-scientific-breakthrough-in-energy-best-white-lotus-reactions-who-is-sbf-why-was-he-charged-in-ftx-what-the-nuclear-fusion-development-means-for-powering-houses-best-white/.

[139] Michael Worobey et al., "The Huanan Seafood Wholesale Market in Wuhan was the early epicenter of the COVID-19 pandemic," Science Online, July 26, 2022, https://www.science.org/doi/10.1126/science.abp8715.

zero[140] contracted the illness. On January 2, 2020, the WHO activated its incident management support team. A day later, Communist China announced that the patient list had increased to forty. On January 5, 2020, the Centers for Disease Control and Prevention (CDC)'s National Center for Immunization and Respiratory Diseases activated a "center-level response" to investigate the disease.[141] Two days later, public health officials in Communist China stated that a novel coronavirus was causing the outbreak. On January 10, 2020, the WHO labeled the disease "2019 Novel Coronavirus" with a specific reference to Wuhan as "2019-nCoV."[142] I am sure alarm bells went off in Emperor Xi's personal residence, as the mere naming of the bioweapon would point directly, and correctly, to the Chinese Communist Party (CCP)'s leaky lab of secrets. It was all media hands on deck for "The Great Deception." Everyone repeat after Xi, "Those dirty wet markets are to blame; the lab connection is a conspiracy theory!"

At the same time, medical scientists in India were studying the genome of COVID-19, and on January 31, 2020, and

---

[140] Michaeleen Doucleff, "Newly published evidence points to Wuhan seafood market as pandemic origin point," *Goats and Soda*, NPR, July 27, 2022, https://www.npr.org/sections/goatsandsoda/2022/03/03/1083751272/striking-new-evidence-points-to-seafood-market-in-wuhan-as-pandemic-origin-point.

[141] "COVID-19 Timeline," David J. Sencer CDC Museum, US Department of Health and Human Services, last reviewed March 15, 2023, https://www.cdc.gov/museum/timeline/covid19.html.

[142] "COVID-19 Timeline."

published their alarming findings.[143] During their swift and collaborative research, the scientists discovered a spike glycoprotein that was unique to COVID-19. Yet, the glycoprotein was similar to residues of amino acids present in HIV-1. Other pathogenic and transformative glycoproteins were also introduced, including the Opsin, mCherry, which has the ability to stop a person's heart from beating when exposed to a certain terahertz frequency. Although not ready to present their initial findings for peer review and publication, the group realized that the virus was not usually found in nature and could be engineered in a laboratory. Was this virus the result of gain-of-function research done in order to create a bioweapon? Their initial inclinations would prove to be correct as time passed.

In his book, *The Anti-Globalist Manifesto*, Jerome Corsi, PhD, pursued the logical questions regarding the nature and purpose of what had led mankind to this turning point in history.

> We must ask: Why does Fauci's name appear on four US patents for a key glycoprotein that appears related to the HIV genome elements inserted in the SARS virus chassis to create the current COVID-19 epidemic?[144]

---

[143] Raju Das, "FLASHBACK: In January 2020 Indian scientists found unique HIV-like 'insertions' in Covid-19 virus genome," Two Plus Two Equals Four, June 21, 2021, https://twoplustwoequalsfournews.wordpress.com/2022/02/04/flashback-in-january-2020-indian-scientists-found-unique-hiv-like-insertions-in-covid-19-virus-genome/.

[144] Jerome Corsi, *The Anti-Globalist Manifesto* (Skyhorse Publishing, 2024), 94.

TODD S. CALLENDER, J.D., JEROME R. CORSI, PH.D., AND CRAIG D. CAMPBELL, PH.D.

Dr. Corsi found the answer in the book by Robert F. Kennedy, Jr.: *The Real Anthony Fauci: Bill Gates, Big Pharma, and the Global War on Democracy and Public Health.* The answer was money, lots and lots of money.

I was astonished to realize that the pervasive web of deep financial entanglements between Pharma and the government health agencies had put regulatory capture on steroids. The CDC, for example, owns 57 vaccine patents and spends $4.9 of its $12.0 billion-dollar annual budget (as of 2019) buying and distributing vaccines. NIH [National Institutes of Health] owns hundreds of vaccine patents and often profits from the sale of products it supposedly regulates. High level officials, including Dr. Fauci, receive yearly emoluments of up to $150,000 in royalty payments on products that they help develop and then usher through the approval process. The FDA [Food and Drug Administration] receives 45 percent of its budget from the pharmaceutical industry, through what are euphemistically called "user fees." When I learned that extraordinary fact, the disastrous health of the American people was no longer a mystery; I wondered what the environment would look like if the EPA [Environmental

Protection Agency] received 45 percent of its budget from the coal industry![145]

The financial incentives provided to key players in this game of death for profit, such as Fauci, were and are enormous. The multibillion-dollar pharmaceutical industry knows its allies and rewards them well.

The Bible provides an explanation for just how strong an influence this incentive has been throughout history.

1 Timothy 6:10 (NLT)

For the love of money is the root of all kinds of evil. And some people, craving money, have wandered from the true faith and pierced themselves with many sorrows.

In this case, all of humanity would be pierced with innumerable sorrows.

The Huanan Seafood Wholesale Market red herring temporarily diverted attention away from the Wuhan lab and the culpability of Fauci and Communist China. The diversion worked for those of devious minds and/or evil intent, such as Bill Gates, who to this day insists that the virus was transferred from animal to human at the wet market.

Considering Gates's deep roots in the vaccine industry through his foundation and desperate need to preserve his thin veneer of a reputation, the backlash against truth seekers who would expose the lies would prove to be considerable.

---

[145] Robert F. Kennedy, Jr., *The Real Anthony Fauci: Bill Gates, Big Pharma, and the Global War on Democracy and Public Health* (Skyhorse Publishing, 2021), xv.

Shi Zhengli, a.k.a. "Bat Woman," a truly mad Communist Chinese scientist (is that redundant?), became obsessed with the study of viruses beginning in 2004 as she collected samples from bat colonies located in caves near the capital of Guangxi province of Communist China. Bat Woman described the experience as "spellbinding"[146] and has been under the spell of bats ever since. We can attribute much of what happened in 2020 to her nighttime ventures into caverns to collect bat blood and saliva. Put that on your resume. The development of Disease X, an enhanced (more deadly and contagious) hybrid of SARS, would not be possible without the gain-of-function (GoF) research. Although Fauci vehemently denied NIH participation in GoF,[147] it is indisputable that Fauci was up to his little rat lab ears in experimentation to make pathogens more contagious.

Why in the world would any medical scientist pursue GoF in the first place? Perhaps elements within the US government responsible for war fighting would think developing bioweapons was not only a necessary evil for defeating foreign enemies, but also crucial in achieving the long-sought depopulation goals both at home and abroad.

Regardless of the repercussions from exposing the truth that the virus was a bioweapon from the CCP's Wuhan lab, a few heroes would emerge. Dr. Corsi highlighted one such hero in his book.

---

[146] Jane Qiu, "How China's 'Bat Woman' Hunted Down Viruses from SARS to the New Coronavirus," *Scientific American*, June 1, 2020, https://www.scientificamerican.com/article/how-chinas-bat-woman-hunted-down-viruses-from-sars-to-the-new-coronavirus1/.

[147] Ed Browne, "Fauci Was 'Untruthful' to Congress About Wuhan Lab Research, New Documents Appear To Show," *Newsweek*, September 9, 2021, https://www.newsweek.com/fauci-untruthful-congress-wuhan-lab-research-documents-show-gain-function-1627351.

In April 2020, Li-Meng Yan, MD, PhD, an experienced Chinese virologist at the Hong Kong
School of Public Health, escaped to the United
States. While she remained in hiding, Li-Meng
Yan gave an interview to Tucker Carlson in
which she insisted COVID-19 was not a virus
that escaped from nature, transmitting from bats
to humans, but a bioweapon created in a lab.[148]

The reality of the nature and origin of the virus had to be suppressed at all costs. If the truth were to be known, decades of the
Owners' hard work would be severely hindered. Setbacks cannot
be tolerated when Satan knows his time is short, and his minions
are being outed.

But the powers that be knew they could rely on their not-so-
secret weapon, the mainstream media (MSM), to come to their
rescue. As dependable and compliant servants of the dark side,
the MSM leaped at the chance to display their unsavory talents. A
firestorm of intentional fear mongering, misdirection, and obfus-
cation, the MSM's stock in trade, was released. Hell hath no fury
like a scornful media.

Truth tellers were labeled crackpots and conspiracy theorists,
and the evildoers were hailed as saviors. An unrelenting torrent,
wave after wave of lies turned the public into a cowering herd
of confused and compliant lab rats. It was just what the doctor
ordered—a planet full of human guinea pigs begging for the shot
and the subsequent array of boosters.

---

[148] Corsi, *Anti-Globalist Manifesto*, 96.

Fauci was joined in what was the worst mass exploitation of humanity in history. Of course, Fauci basked in the false praise and growing bank account, while baring his fangs at anyone who had the audacity to kick against his goads. After all, the Bible states in Acts 26:14 that it is foolish to resist God's will, as the metaphor implies, and since Fauci has elevated himself to that stature, this application seems appropriate. The incentives were too high for the mere human purveyors of the lies to resist, and the punishments for speaking out were too brutal for the fainthearted to withstand.

The Bible foretold what we would encounter during this period in which we are now living:

2 Timothy 3:1-5 (KJV)

This know also, that in the last days perilous times shall come. For men shall be lovers of their own selves, covetous, boasters, proud, blasphemers, disobedient to parents, unthankful, unholy, Without natural affection, trucebreakers, false accusers, incontinent, fierce, despisers of those that are good, Traitors, heady, highminded, lovers of pleasures more than lovers of God; Having a form of godliness, but denying the power thereof: from such turn away.

Fauci and other "experts" stoked the fires of fear, chaos, and uncertainty by pretending they could tell the future. The CDC began projecting death forecasts, forcing people to feel subject to a roll of the dice based upon the supposed odds. Grouping people by age and health, the CDC painted a somewhat rosy picture for the young and a more dismal ending for the old and infirm. Using the CDC's numbers, Dr. Corsi explains:

According to the CDC, the COVID-19 surviv-
ability rate was 99.997 percent for those aged
0–19 years, 99.98 percent for 20–49 years,
99.5 percent for 50–69, and 94.6 percent for
70-plus years.[149]

With only a 5 percent, one in twenty, chance to die, that
sounds like long odds. But many oldsters, particularly those with
comorbidities, rushed to the shot-dispensing facilities. At the
same time, the voodoo science of paper masks and social distanc-
ing were added to the witches' brew. The streets filled with pan-
icked loners wearing useless face diapers. The exchanged looks
of horror with oncoming strangers, the fleeing from any possible
contact—such scenes from a zombie apocalypse played out across
the globe.

I am sure the panic was met with glee and satisfaction of the
Owners, benefactors of the madness as they achieved multiple
goals—depopulation, compliance, wealth, and power.

Again, a key factor to the upward trajectory of the human
die-off was the unrelenting and unsurpassed suppression of the
fact that the supposed cure was far more harmful than the disease
itself. Unbiased and unowned medical researchers did deep dives
into the data, and the results did not support the media or Fauci-
esque narrative.

J. Bart Classen, MD, is fortunately for team humanity and one
example of a true researcher. An extensive study he performed
and condensed to six pages was accepted by *Trends in Internal
Medicine* on August 25, 2021, under the title: "US COVID-19

---

[149] Corsi, *Anti-Globalist Manifesto*, 97.

Vaccines Proven to Cause More Harm than Good Based on Pivotal Clinical Trial Data Analyzed Using the Proper Scientific Endpoint, 'All Cause Severe Morbidity.'"[150] Dr. Classen studied the results of all three COVID-19 "vaccines" unleashed upon the public as a result of Big Pharma using the *Doe v. Rumsfeld*, United States District Court for the District of Columbia, 297 F. Supp. 2d 119 (2003) lessons (prior consent is required before administration of vaccinations) to fabricate and employ a new-ish feature of plandemic law called the "emergency use authorization" scheme.

Dr. Classen's introduction was illuminating, as the light always is when shining on the darkness.

> For decades, true scientists have warned that pivotal clinical trial designs for vaccines are dangerously flawed and outdated. Vaccines have been promoted and widely utilized under the false claim they have been shown to improve health. However, this claim is only a philosophical argument and not science based. In a true scientific fashion to show a health benefit one would need to show fewer overall deaths during an extended period in the vaccinated group compared to a control group. Less stringent indicators of a health benefit would include fewer severe events

---

[150] J. Bart Classen, "US COVID-19 Vaccines Proven to Cause More Harm than Good Based on Pivotal Clinical Trial Data Analyzed Using the Proper Scientific Endpoint, "All Cause Severe Morbidity," *Trends In Internal Medicine* 1, no. 1 (2021): 1–6, https://newsrescue.com/wp-content/uploads/2021/08/us-covid19-vaccines-proven-to-cause-more-harm-than-good-based-on-pivotal-clinical-trial-data-analyzed-using-the-proper-scientific-1811.pdf.

of all kinds, fewer days hospitalized for any reason, lower health care expenses of all types, fewer missed days from work for any health reason. No pivotal clinical trial for a vaccine preventing an infectious disease has ever demonstrated an improvement in health using these scientific measurements of health as a primary endpoint. Instead, vaccine clinical trials have relied on misleading surrogate endpoints of health such as infection rates with a specific infectious agent. Manufactures and government agents have made the scientifically disproved and dangerous philosophical argument that these surrogate endpoints equate to a health benefit.[151]

For decades "true scientists" warned that the methods being used by Fauci, Inc. (which we define as the "B team" of both government and Big Pharma) were flawed. Fauci, Inc.:

- offered a claim that was "only a philosophical argument and not science based";[152]
- has never improved health;
- mislead us with unscientific methods;
- forced disproved and dangerous substances on the public;
- inflicted pain, suffering, and death on a mass scale, perhaps the most massive effect in human history to date;
- profited enormously from all of the above; and

---

[151] Classen, "US COVID-19 Vaccines," 1.
[152] Classen, "US COVID-19 Vaccines," 1.

- completed the trial phase of the Owners' depopulation plan.

Dr. Classen concluded:

> In such a hostile government environment, the
> citizens need to individually evaluate the science
> of immunization with COVID-19 vaccines and
> not rely on philosophical arguments propagated
> by government officials. In this case there is no
> scientific evidence that the COVID-19 vaccines
> improve the health of the individual, much less
> of the population as a whole. Mass immunization
> with COVID-19 vaccines is certainly leading to
> a catastrophic public health event.[153]

Of course, Dr. Classen's impeccable research, anti-narrative conclusions, and dire warnings were not made known to the masses, and as ignorance is bliss, the Fauci death march continued on unabated. The lines of unknowing lab rats lined up for the shots and, in the false comfort of dutiful public servants merely following the science, proceeded toward the cliff.

How much different was today's chain of events from what had taken place in Germany eighty years prior? A government was faced with the need to solve a people problem, the problem being the existence of a group of people deemed to be unwanted. The problem is not easily solved if that group becomes aware of and thereby resistant to the end goal: their own demise.

---

[153] Classen, "US COVID-19 Vaccines," 5.

The solution, which proved to be the final solution for many members of the unwanted back then as today, was to gain their trust and compliance while the mission was accomplished. An expedient method was chosen to eliminate the pests using the calming balm of "it is just in their best interests." After all, the decision-makers and implementers are always acting in the best interests of people under their control.

Just read the assurances provided by Mao Zedong's campaign, "Great Leap Forward." It was the tried and true sales pitch of a leader just looking out for the best interests of the people: false promises of safety made to the target group, the march of smiling masses into wide trenches, the death shot delivered by lead or liquid. Liquid is so much cleaner.

So, with the truth suppressed, the initial depopulation scheme bore additional fruit, as culling out the useless eaters was but a first step. With fewer humans, a compliant remnant, and expanded personal wealth and power, the Owners would be hard-pressed to wish for more. The plan to eradicate the planet of but a few useful idiots they would control was proceeding nicely, and the fringe benefits were a welcomed bonus.

At the same time, the Owners were succeeding in their pursuit of larger game—economic destruction of the West. Nonessential operations such as gyms and churches were forced to close while liquor stores and funeral homes remained open. Of course, the making of the "remain open" and "must close" lists was left to the individual states, but there were many similarities between them. This episode brought back memories of my earlier life living in two Soviet-model economies in which only two public-private partnerships occupied and monopolized every domestic industry.

Soviet-sanctioned oligarchs paid enormous kickbacks to "party leaders" in return for their "semi-capitalist pig" enterprises.

Only a few brave governors, such as former Governor Pete Ricketts of Nebraska, endured the slanders of the doomsayers to allow all businesses to remain open. Of course, detractors were ready to rain hellfire upon Ricketts if his "gambling with the lives" of his constituents turned out to be a losing proposition.

Predictably, when Nebraskans fared much better than the people in states having taken draconian measures, such as New York, instead of being lauded, Ricketts's actions were still demeaned.

Governor Andrew Cuomo, on the other hand, was lifted up on high as the elderly in nursing homes died in vastly disproportionate numbers. Cuomo tried to hide the consequences of his failure by falsely understating the death numbers.[154] Even though he was able to weather the COVID storm, Cuomo was later forced to resign due to a sex scandal.[155] The COVID-19 plandemic is a case study of how Disease X will be weaponized to achieve global depopulation objectives. Research and development of bioweapons in America can be traced back to World War II. In the spring of 2020, Dr. Jerome Corsi wrote the now out-of-print e-book, *COVID-20: The Coming Killer Coronavirus.* In addition to

---

[154] Vaughn Golden et al., "Cuomo personally altered report that lowballed COVID nursing-home deaths, emails show – contradicting his claim to Congress," *New York Post*, September 19, 2024 https://nypost.com/2024/09/19/us-news/cuomo-personally-altered-covid-nursing-home-death-report-that-low-balled-fatalities-emails-show/.

[155] David Robinson, "How Cuomo's Sexual Harassment, Nursing Home Scandals Unraveled," *USA Today*, March 2, 2021, https://www.usatoday.com/story/news/politics/2021/03/02/how-cuomo-sexual-harassment-nursing-home-scandals-unfolded-timeline/6883274002/.

shedding light on the darkness covering the globe back then, Dr. Corsi prophetically saw what we are faced with today, he wrote:

> Writing this eBook in late-May 2020, the official narrative of governmental health authorities worldwide, parroted by lap-dog government-funded and government-controlled mainstream media worldwide, is that COVID-19 is not a bioweapon created in a laboratory with the intent to kill millions of people across the globe.
>
> Such a truth, if fully disclosed, would require the United States government to confess to the American public that we had in place a taxpayer-funded top-secret bioweapons program since 1943 under the auspices of the United States Army Biological Warfare Laboratories in Fort Detrick, Maryland.
>
> Despite public announcements these projects were discontinued in 1969, Fort Detrick continued as the U.S. "biological defense program" until July 2019, when the Centers for Disease Control and Prevention in Atlanta, Georgia, issued a "cease and desist" order to halt biological research at Fort Detrick because research into the Ebola virus was found "not to have sufficient

systems in place to decontaminate wastewater"
from its highest-security laboratories.[156]

Dr. Corsi put to rest Fauci's denials and warned the world
to be ready for the next wave of bioweapon attacks by the
depopulationists.

But contrary to any logical construct, and in the face of the
recent deception that resulted in millions of vaccine-adverse reaction
deaths and disabilities, medical "scientists" assure us that
during public health emergencies, experimenting with vaccines
that may cause more harm than good is perfectly ethical.[157] No,
that statement did not come from the lying mouth of Fauci, but
from The Conversation, a site that touts its "academic rigor." Its
May 8, 2023 post is titled, "Gain-of-function research is more than
just tweaking viruses—it's a routine an essential tool in all biology
research."[158] But again, rest assured, the next release of experimental
"vaccines" will be even safer than the last ones, according
to the American Medical Association.[159] Oh wait, that assurance

---

[156] Jerome R. Corsi, *COVID-20: The Coming Killer Coronavirus* (out of print), (JRC Publishing LLC, 2020), 3.

[157] Michael J. Selgelid, "Gain-of-Function Research: Ethical Analysis," *Science and Engineering Ethics*, August 8, 2016, https://link.springer.com/article/10.1007/s11948-016-9810-1.

[158] Seema Lakdawala and Anice Lowen, "Gain-of-function research is more than just tweaking risky viruses—it's a routine and essential tool in all biology research," The Conversation, May 8, 2023, https://theconversation.com/gain-of-function-research-is-more-than-just-tweaking-risky-viruses-its-a-routine-and-essential-tool-in-all-biology-research-202084.

[159] Archana Asundi, MD, and Nahid Bhadelia, MD, "Making Emergency Use of Experimental Vaccines Safer," *AMA Journal of Ethics* 22, no. 1 (2020): E43-49, https://journalofethics.ama-assn.org/article/making-emergency-use-experimental-vaccines-safer/2020-01.

was made in January 2020, at the same time the bioweapon was coming to America. I retroactively feel much safer now, don't you?

On top of that, at the time the shots were being mandated and otherwise forced upon the public at large, the NIH promised us that those experimental vaccines would protect us against multiple coronaviruses.[160] A litany of never-ending emergency plagues were planned, of course. So relax, mRMA vaccines are not just the latest craze; there has been a long history of the development and release of these vaccines. I gained this knowledge having watched numerous synthetic RNA and DNA experimental vaccines used in my family's needle-free injector over the previous twenty years. Yet, an authority no less than the Johns Hopkins Bloomberg School of Public Health is proud of its decades-long development program.[161] (Yes, that Bloomberg—"public health *champion*" Mike Bloomberg.[162] The billionaire who ended his 2020 run for president of the United States by endorsing Joe Biden.) You're in good hands with Mike. Yet, there are a number of potential health implications of mRNA vaccines, including those cited by the state surgeon general of Florida, Joseph A. Ladapo.

---

[160] Brian Doctrow, "Experimental vaccine protects against multiple coronaviruses," NIH Research Matters, US Department of Health & Human Services, July 20, 2021, https://www.nih.gov/news-events/nih-research-matters/experimental-vaccine-protects-against-multiple-coronaviruses.

[161] "Johns Hopkins Bloomberg School of Public Health Again Ranked #1 by Peers in U.S. News & World Report," Johns Hopkins, Bloomberg School of Public Health, April 9, 2024, https://publichealth.jhu.edu/2024/johns-hopkins-bloomberg-school-of-public-health-again-ranked-1-by-peers-in-us-news-world-report.

[162] "Mike Bloomberg," Johns Hopkins Bloomberg School of Public Health, https://publichealth.jhu.edu/about/history/mike-bloomberg.

In 2007, the FDA published guidance on regulatory limits for DNA vaccines in the Guidance for Industry: Considerations for Plasmid DNA Vaccines for Infectious Disease Indications (Guidance for Industry). This Guidance for Industry highlights important considerations for vaccines that use novel methods of delivery regarding DNA integration:

- DNA integration could theoretically impact a human's oncogenes—the genes which can transform a healthy cell into a cancerous cell.
- DNA integration may result in chromosomal instability.
- The Guidance for Industry discusses biodistribution of DNA vaccines and how such integration could affect unintended parts of the body including blood, heart, brain, liver, kidney, bone marrow, ovaries/testes, lung, draining lymph nodes, spleen, the site of administration and subcutis at injection site.[163]

---

[163] Joseph A. Ladapo, Letter to the U.S. Food and Drug Administration and the Centers for Disease Control and Prevention, Florida Health, December 6, 2023, https://www.floridahealth.gov/about/_documents/12-06-2023-DOH-Letter-to-FDA-RFI-on-COVID-19-Vaccines.pdf?utm_source=floridahealth.gov&utm_medium=referral&utm_campaign=PressRelease&utm_content=Florida%27s_Future_Budget&url_trace_7f2r5y6=Press_Release_Template_fry_2023_alt.docx.

Pregnancy and childbirth

IDSA, the Infectious Diseases Society of America, is currently monitoring the spread of mpox in several African nations.[164] According to the IDSA, "mRNA vaccines do not cause birth defects, infertility, or other problems related to pregnancy or childbirth."[165]

The IDSA cannot be wrong, right? Well, maybe. Long-term studies will be needed to confirm the assumption that no harm is being done. We actually discovered in the Department of Defense (DOD)'s trial run of the poison shots (Protocol Number C4591001) that forty-four thousand service members and their families unknowingly served as laboratory test animals. These dedicated warriors and their family members were treated as mere lab rats, developing 1,291 new diseases that did not exist in them prior to the phase one, two, and three clinical trials, as previously mentioned. As troubling as it is to have all phases of safety studies done all at the same time and humans substituted for test animals, it is even more disturbing to know that Pfizer's own after-action results demonstrated a huge hidden mortality and an 82 percent spontaneous abortion rate. The laundered test results were used as the basis for the "emergency use authorization," the "safe and effective" scam with full knowledge of the dire consequences of the shots to humans. The DOD had already tested the efficacy of their bioweapon before flying the shots around the world in

---

[164] "Mpox: What You Need to Know," Infectious Diseases Society of America, December 13, 2024, https://www.idsociety.org/public-health/Mpox/.

[165] "mRNA Vaccines: What to Know," Infectious Diseases Society of America, March 4, 2024, https://www.idsociety.org/covid-19-real-time-learning-network/vaccines/mrna-vaccines-what-to-know/#/+/0/publishedDate_na_dt/desc/.

their military transport aircraft with the DOD's uniformed and more subtle plain-clothes Defense Health Agency officials leading the charge.

But, who needs children, let alone healthy ones? After all, the holders of the keys to enlightenment, the high-learned ones pushing or going through transgender procedures and/or living the LGBTQXYZ lifestyle know what is best for the future of society. Isn't it time we just listen and follow the experts instead of believing in God's creation and plan? I vote no. Hell, *no*!

At present, mRNA vaccines are classified as "gene therapy." Of course, the "gene modification" component is not included in the description of the vaccine. This devious action was taken since the synthetic programming agents effect genes and are actually therapeutics. "Gene therapy" was more amorphous to fool the masses into "voluntarily" forever changing their genomes, evolving them to a new species—a state of being the NASA Langley Research Center–termed "Borg."

Stefan Oelrich, head of Bayer's pharmaceuticals division, said the following at the World Health Summit in 2021, according to the Armstrong Economics website:

> Two years ago, 95% of the people would have refused to take the gene therapy. But COVID made it possible.[166]

---

[166] Martin Armstrong, "Bayer President: The mRNA Vaccines Are Gene Therapy," ArmstrongEconomics, March 5, 2022, https://www.armstrongeconomics.com/international-news/vaccine/bayer-president-the-mrna-vaccines-are-gene-therapy/.

Absorb that poison pill slowly and without an adult beverage. The leader of one of the pharmaceutical industry's most prestigious companies clearly stated that the shots bridged the gap between treating an illness and transforming the patient. Humans whipped into a state of panic, fearing for their lives, are deceived into accepting, on faith, an injection promoted as curative. When in reality, they are being tricked into entering a life-altering transition into another species.

Add to that dark reality the fact that many people smelled a rat, were legitimately skeptical, or otherwise predisposed to refuse the injection, but out of the threat of termination of employment or other coercive measures, they swallowed hard and complied. Martin Armstrong, the author of the Armstrong Economics article, sums this hard-to-swallow reality up nicely:

> The mRNA vaccines for covid are a form of gene therapy. This fact has not been hidden from the public. Unfortunately, many are unwilling to accept that they forcibly took a vaccine that may come with long-term consequences as they were unknowingly the first live sample trial on the global population.[167]

Yet, in Europe, lobbyists are pushing hard for that general classification to be changed, arguing that only mRNA vaccines that actually modify the genome should be classified as such.[168] I

---

[167] Armstrong, "Bayer President."

[168] "Lobbies calling for mRNA vaccines not to be classified as gene therapy," European Parliament, last updated February 9, 2024, https://www.europarl.europa.eu/doceo/document/E-9-2024-000355_EN.html.

guess we need a genome semanticist to sort this out for the lobby. There are many significant legal and ethical issues surrounding vaccine mandates, including the case of *Robert v. Austin*. A number of violations of constitutional and human rights took place and are still in motion.

In conclusion, the broader agenda of depopulation and remnant control through medical interventions is unfolding before our eyes.

In December of 2023, I presented testimony to the Croatian Parliament on the topic "The Weaponization of Public Health." In collaboration with retired Lt. Col. Peter Chambers, DO, we explored the legal framework for global depopulation. What we learned shocked us, and we knew we needed to share the information with the world.

Project BioShield was initiated after the anthrax scare following the 9/11 terrorist attacks in 2001. Letters laced with white powder, many identified as anthrax, were found in mail around the country. Five people died from contact with the deadly substance, and seventeen became severely ill.

In response, the federal government created a task force code-named "Amerithrax,"[169] lead by the Federal Bureau of Investigation. What was sold as a means to protect America from further attack, BioShield, morphed into a scheme to bring about world depopulation. The sinister wheel was set into motion with

---

[169] "Amerithrax or Anthrax Investigation," US Federal Bureau of Investigation, https://www.fbi.gov/history/famous-cases/amerithrax-or-anthrax-investigation.

the turning point Project BioShield Act of 2003.[170] The four major events are shown in the graphic below:

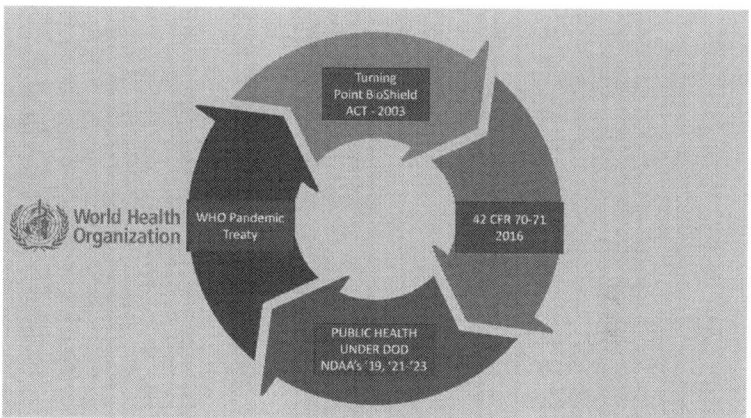

The website of the medical countermeasures division of the US government has this to say about Project BioShield:

> The objective of Project BioShield is to accelerate the research, development, procurement, and availability of effective medical countermeasures against biological, chemical, radiological, and nuclear (CBRN) agents.

> On July 21, 2004, the President signed into law the Project BioShield Act of 2004 (Project BioShield) as part of a broader strategy to

---

[170] Philip K. Russell, "Project BioShield: What It Is, Why It Is Needed, and Its Accomplishments So Far" in "Tribute to Ted Woodward," eds. Phil Mackowiak, Dick Hornick, and Bert DuPont, Supplement, *Clinical Infectious Diseases* 45, no. S1 (2007): S68–S72, https://doi.org/10.1086/518151.

defend America against the threat of weapons of mass destruction. The purpose of Project BioShield is to accelerate the research, development, purchase, and availability of effective medical countermeasures against biological, chemical, radiological, and nuclear (CBRN) threats. HHS [US Department of Health and Human Services] provides Congress with an annual report on its progress in the implementation of Project BioShield.[171]

One feature of the BioShield Act is quarantine procedures. These procedures are quantified in the previously noted parts 70 and 71 of the 2011 Code of Federal Regulations.[172] Under the auspices of the Public Health Service Act, regulations "to prevent the introduction, transmission and spread of communicable diseases from foreign countries into the [United States]" were put into place.[173]

The quarantine regulations were followed by DOD's National Defense Authorization Acts and additional public health orders in 2019, 2021, 2022, and 2023. The required annual issuance of the National Defense Authorization Acts was used to perpetuate the increased mandates and control procedures.

---

[171] "Project BioShield," Administration for Strategic Preparedness and Response, US Department of Health & Human Services, Medical Countermeasures, https://medicalcountermeasures.gov/barda/cbrn/project-bioshield/.

[172] *Interstate Quarantine*, 42 C. F. R. § 70 (2000); *Foreign Quarantine*, 42 C. F. R. § 71 (1985).

[173] *Quarantine and Inspection*, 42 U. S. C. § 264 (2011).

A critical next component of the depopulation plan was to codify global authority for the plan's execution. The key element being activating the WHO under the authority of the United Nations. The WHO pandemic treaty is the Owners' weapon of choice to bring all of its global governance goals to a head. The result would be biblical.

Think of how all of this madness is coming together. A vast empire having power and great authority is forming. given to him by Satan himself as described in Revelation 13:2.[174] This ruler receives worship from "all the world" (Revelation 13:3–4 KJV) and will have authority over "every tribe, people, language and nation" (Revelation 13:7 NIV). This person will truly be the leader of a one-world government that is recognized as sovereign over all other governments. We see nations today willing to give up some of their sovereignty to combat climate change; it's easy to imagine that the disasters and plagues described in Revelation 6–11 would create such a monumental crisis that the nations of the world will embrace anything and anyone who promises a solution.

The wheel spun 360 degrees, resulting in firmly established military authority to ensure the success of the democidal mission to eradicate or radically transform seven billion people around the globe.

We defeated the DOD's plan to use COVID as the driver to unilaterally deliver the kill shots. However, the Owners just took that failure in stride, as other wheels were in motion. For example,

---

[174] "Revelation 13:2," BibleRef, https://www.bibleref.com/Revelation/13/Revelation-13-2.html.

they created a plan to develop and release a plague.[175] Dr. Long and I have uncovered their mission to release the plague as it was demonstrated in Pfizer's six-month post-marketing report in the appendix.[176] The appendix lists 1,291 serious and deadly diseases caused by the shots. A list that massive would have taken years of planning and subsequent testing to compile.

In response, our group has launched a subsidiary project in Eastern Europe in association with Dr. Anatoli Brouchkov. Dr. Brouchkov witnessed teams of Communist Chinese and other scientists roaming around Europe and Siberia digging up ancient corpses, trying to find an incurable plague—in the name of science, of course. Dr. Brouchkov has been studying an ancient bacteria he located in 2009.[177] His expertise has enabled us to develop a supplement that repairs a person's DNA and defends against electromagnetic fields and all forms of radiation to counteract the Owners' evil democidal pursuits. Issmaeel Ansari of Queen Mary University of London and other researchers expresses concerns about the deliberate release of plague.

> We discuss the likelihood of a deliberate release of
> plague and the feasibility of obtaining, isolating,

---

[175] Issmaeel Ansari, Gareth Grier, and Mark Byers, "Deliberate release: Plague – A review," *Journal of Biosafety and Biosecurity*, Volume 2, Issue 1, March 2020, https://www.sciencedirect.com/science/article/pii/S2588933820300017.

[176] *5.3.6 Cumulative Analysis Of Post-Authorization Adverse Event Reports Of Pf-07302048 (Bnt162b2) Received Through 28-Feb-2021*, PHMPT.org, April 30, 2021, https://phmpt.org/wp-content/uploads/2021/11/5.3.6-postmarketing-experience.pdf.

[177] Mae Rice, "A Russian Scientist Injected Himself With 3.5-Million-Year-Old Bacteria," Discovery, August 1, 2019, https://www.discovery.com/science/a-russian-scientist-injected-himself-with-3-5-million-year-old-b.

culturing, transporting and dispersing plague in the context of an attack aimed at a westernized country. The current threat status and the medical and public health responses are reviewed. We also provide a brief review of the potential prehospital treatment strategy and vaccination against *Y. pestis* [the bacteria that causes plague]. Further, we discuss the plausibility of antibiotic resistant plague bacterium, F1-negative *Y. pestis*, and also the possibility of a plague mimic along with potential strategies of defense against these. An extensive literature search on the MEDLINE, EMBASE, and Web of Science databases was conducted to collate papers relevant to plague and its deliberate release. Our review concluded that the deliberate release of plague is feasible but unlikely to occur, and that a robust public health response and early treatment would rapidly halt the transmission of plague in the population. Front-line clinicians should be aware of the potential of a deliberate release of plague and prepared to instigate early isolation of patients. Moreover, front-line clinicians should be weary of the possibility of suicide attackers and mindful of the early escalation to public health organizations.[178]

---

[178] Issmaeel Ansari et al., "Deliberate release: Plague – A review," *Journal of Biosafety Biosecurity* 2, no. 1 (2020): 10–22, https://doi.org/10.1016/j.jobb.2020.02.001.

Todd S. Callender, J.D., Jerome R. Corsi, Ph.D., and Craig D. Campbell, Ph.D.

Much of the article is based upon the speculation of these medical professionals. If their warnings were to be widely spread, I am sure they would be labeled alarmists at the least and at worst, naturally, the throwaway term "conspiracy theorists." However, if their research and conclusion sound like the script for an *X-Files* episode, consider the following.

Since the 1950s, our US Department of Energy (DOE) has created, patented and sold (online), 470,000 pathogens, including Marburg, Ebola, Zika, and every other imaginable disease. Many of those pathogens are contained in our medications, food, and water, including "death domain-associated protein 6," a.k.a. gene ID 1616, a.k.a. kinase. We, of course, downloaded and saved this data in multiple locations and shared this information in a publicly available database. I believe the government has since closed access to the data.

The DOE controls many things, but it is the energy and radiation we are concerned about here. Their genome project collection started back in the late '50s, early '60s. It consists of organisms that have been contaminated with cesium 137, a radioactive element.

Thanks to the tireless research and reporting of Lisa McGee, another whistleblower turned warrior, we discovered that the DOE has labs at Savannah River in South Carolina, Washington state, Arizona, and other locations throughout the United States. Their experimentation included intentional contamination of cesium 137 into the environment and cleanups from accidental spills. Cesium 137 mimics potassium, so it's water soluble and just spreads into the environment like water.

The specimens came from the soil specimens, aquatic life, and land-based wildlife. The specimens became the foundation of the collection contained in the DOE's database. The specimens were then mutated along with additional viruses and organisms, and gamma-irradiated. They now compromise all categories of bio-weapons, with two to four bioweapons listed globally. They are all in their database, they are digital, and they all have IP addresses.

The DOE's activities represent but another vector of doom, death, and destruction that God has tasked us with stopping. One of the ways we intend to halt this additional attempt to depopulate the world is by alerting the public to its existence through this book. You, the reader, will not be surprised that we now know of the other mass poisonings our government conducted involving innocent and unknowing citizens like those who suffered the results of the Tuskegee Experiment.[179]

Crossing the Rubicon with Replicon

On January 10, 49 BC, Roman General Julius Caesar crossed the Rubicon River back into the north of Italy from the Roman province of Gaul (modern-day France), of which he was governor.[180] He returned to his native land a hero to the people, having expanded Rome's territory in Europe to Britannia. Caesar was the catalyst of impending dramatic and irreversible change,

---

[179] See Ada McVean, "40 Years of Human Experimentation in America: The Tuskegee Study," McGill Office for Science and Society, January 25, 2019, https://www.mcgill.ca/oss/article/history/40-years-human-experimentation-america-tuskegee-study.

[180] National Geographic Society, "Jan 10, 49 BC: Caesar Crosses the Rubicon," National Geographic Society, last updated October 19, 2024, https://education.nationalgeographic.org/resource/caesar-crosses-rubicon/.

and he knew it. Actually, the Rubicon is just a stream that separated Rome from the province of Gaul that Caesar governed on Rome's behalf. The stream was a natural barrier, the crossing of which violated Roman law. Roman legions were prohibited from crossing the Rubicon without permission of the Roman senate. The prohibition prevented the Republic from being threatened by rogue forces of its own, as a Roman army could not proceed toward the capital without the ruling class being assured of peaceful intent. In this case, peace was not the intent, and Julius Caesar was as rogue as they come.

Caesar did not come in peace; crossing the Rubicon as he did started a five-year civil war that ended the Roman Republic and began the Roman Empire, a dictatorship. Caesar was victorious and declared himself emperor and "Caesar" became synonymous with "supreme leader."

"Crossing the Rubicon" has become a popular idiom to describe a purposeful breach of protocol, making a decision that cannot be reversed and from which there is no return. Such action symbolizes "burning one's bridges."

Today, scientists in Japan are preparing to cross the Rubicon and burn all of humanity's bridges. They have reached a modern-day Rubicon in the form of the development of an experimental potential global-killer "replicon" concoction they have named "Kostaive." The term "replicon" refers to a new type of gene therapy in which the mRNA vaccine amplifies by self-duplicating throughout the patient's body. Prudent forces are attempting to thwart the crossing. Humanity itself is at stake. Buckle up.

The Replicon Agenda: Another Dose of Bioterrorism?

On Thursday, October 3, 2024, on my *Truth be Told*, Vaxxchoice channel, on CloutHub, we recorded an episode of *In the Lion's Den with Dr. Bill Lionberger* called "The Replicon Agenda: Another Dose of Bioterrorism?" with guest Dr. Ana Maria Mihalcea, MD, PhD, and our researcher extraordinaire, Lisa McGee.

Replicons were the topic for that epic broadcast during which Dr. Mihalcea exposed the dangers of world vaccine injury with the potential for it to spread worldwide, literally unchecked. Any host, human or animal, could be a mass spreader, with disastrous effect.

A replicon has the ability to cross between species and alphavirus to permanently introduce artificial genes into the entire ecosystem.

So just what exactly is a "replicon"? Sounds like Omicron, remember that one? Well, it is a genetic element that can replicate independently within a cell. It is a self-amplifying technology, an RNA vaccine that has an innate ability to make copies of itself. What could possibly go wrong? Well, how about total depopulation?

The potential of a replicon plus influenza or a replicon plus coronavirus super virus can potentially transmit as a multi-species alphavirus with the capability to cause deadly harm to humans.

Dr. Mihalcea sees it from the perspective of self-assembling and self-replicating nanotechnology, because that is exactly what it is: nanotechnology gone wrong. This aspect of nanotechnology poses a direct danger to humanity and the animal kingdom, the potential extinction of all species. The possibility for this outcome was discussed as a possibility twenty or thirty years ago, and must be avoided at all costs.

It is even in Ray Kurzweil's book,[181] in which he warns us that the singularity is near. Specifically, he says that if nanotechnology builds self-assembling machines and those machines can self-replicate, unchecked and uncontrolled by the manufacturer, it creates "a grey goo" scenario. As Sabil Francis explains in the online *Britannica* encyclopedia:

> Grey goo [is] a nightmarish scenario of nanotechnology in which out-of-control self-replicating nanobots destroy the biosphere by endlessly producing replicas of themselves and feeding on materials necessary for life.[182]

In such a scenario, the machines run amok…they have no soul, no ethics—merely a coded mandate to perpetuate their own existence. They would mindlessly use up all the energy of all the material the world possesses, and thereby exterminate all life on earth. The machine will just execute its instructions; the human will not be able to stop the extinction event. Deep thinkers like Kurzweil and researcher Dr. K. Eric Drexler[183] (who focuses on nanotech) are aware that unchecked, nanotech is predisposed

---

[181] Ray Kurzweil, "The Singularity Is Near: When Humans Transcend Biology," Singularity.com, January 1, 2005, https://www.singularity.com/aboutthebook.html.

[182] *Britannica*, "grey goo," last updated August 1, 2016, https://www.britannica.com/technology/grey-goo.

[183] "K. Eric Drexler," National Space Society, https://nss.org/national-space-society-governor-k-eric-drexler-biography/.

to evolve in that destructive direction. So, machines can become "biological" machines. The fusion of synthetic biology and nanotechnology enables the creation of artificial machines from organic material, from RNA and DNA. In this context, our very species is in grave danger.

The liposome,[184] the encapsulation of these replicons themselves, can self-replicate, which is visible in blood samples. A significant mRNA problem existed even before the current injections. In the past four years, many research teams analyzed vials of blood but did not find mRNA. In other studies, researchers found no phosphorus or nitrogen in human blood samples. However, they did find elements of self-assembling nanotechnology.[185] The inclusion of such large vectors of mRNA in the millions of doses that were manufactured may not have even been feasible. However, if mRNA can be made to self-replicate, that just adds another layer of danger to the equation.

Basically, it appears that what we have experienced is nanotechnological self-assembling weapons deployed on a mass nanoscale. The "fact checker" diversion tactic is to repeat over and over that self-replication and the potential for injury is low as the shots are injected into the arm and stay in the muscle. Fat chance—the last time I looked, the arm bone is connected to the shoulder bone, and the connections continue throughout the body. Blood circulates, making the entry point moot.

---

[184] See Benedette Cuffari, "What is a Liposome?" News-Medical.net, last updated January 29, 2019, https://www.news-medical.net/life-sciences/What-is-a-Liposome.aspx.

[185] Olga V. Morozova et al., "Self-assembling amyloid-like nanostructures from SARS-CoV-2 S1, S2, RBD and N recombinant proteins," *Archives of Biochemistry and Biophysics* 752 (February 2024): 109843, https://doi.org/10.1016/j.abb.2023.109843.

Anyway, we are dealing with a digitalized machine-driven computer operational system, and these protein sequences are bacterial based. The ingredients all have IP addresses that link to the Department of Energy supercomputer and a plethora of others. We are dealing with software platforms that when booted, operate, are updated, rebooted ("boosted"), and recalibrated to function at the next level.

The nanobots are self-assembling, triggered, and programmed to take command of the body by electromagnetic fields. This is when 5G rears its ugly head, as 5G, the Owners' next emerging weapons platform, chooses targets using their IP addresses.

There is one thought that comes to mind, one of "look at all the obedient servants." The Owners are creating their slave army, financed by absorbing the needed resources from the unknowing donor class. These are government entities and NGOs...you know, Satan's very own public-private partnership. Satan's minions are all working together, one giant World Wide Web of power and control.

The components of this global operation are programmed to detonate with military-grade precision when the time comes. A triggering mechanism, peer-reviewed, and in circulation, is the use of a pulsed and modulated 18 gigahertz signal (5G), a range of frequencies monopolized by the United States Department of Defense first exhibited in Operation Desert Storm using voice to skull technology (V2K) to convince Iraqi soldiers that Allah commanded them to surrender. The countdown clock is ticking; time for humanity is running out. Keep in mind that Wuhan China was the first 5G city in the world when they turned on ten thousand microwave transmitters on Halloween night 2019. COVD immediately followed and it is the testimony of Dr. Lee Vliet that every malady known to mankind.

During manufacture, these "vaccines" travel along an assembly line to the end point, then packaged and shipped to the assembling facilities. Those facilities, run by Pfizer, Moderna, and others, each receive their allotted shipments. The ingredients are purposely coming from a plethora of different third-party vendors, including government agencies. In a scheme this complex and dark, compartmentalization is key. The government coordinates chemical companies and other component providers, each operating in their own silo—merely links in a long conga line to hell.

The individual "components" are barcoded and digitized and thereby no longer possess an organic foundation. The bacteria has been converted into a protein sequence software platform. A next step is to infuse them with chemical compounds that are registered on the Environmental Protection Agency's environmental contaminant list.

An IP address is then assigned, and they are output as vaccines and patented viruses. The vaccines are just carriers for these patented viruses. Most viruses discovered in the last thirty or forty years are patented and have become software platforms. Do not tell anyone! This is one of the most widely held, hide-in-plain-sight, "smile, you are on a conveyor belt to the pit," "you will find out when it is too late" secrets.

Melissa McAtee, Pfizer whistleblower and producer of Vaxxchoice's CloutHub and other alt-media channels, is a crucial witness in two current suits against Pfizer by attorneys general in Kansas and Missouri. Melissa worked in a Pfizer factory near Wichita, Kansas, as a quality assurance auditor. At the factory, she witnessed unknown, unmarked, and unlabeled bags of glowing fluid enter the Pfizer factory. That liquid was bottled in vaccine vials and sent out for delivery without any knowledge of the actual ingredients or contents being provided (not sold) as COVID-19 vaccines. In other words, the "safe and effective" contents of the vaccines were wholly unknown to the people bottling, packaging, and delivering poison injectables, which included anti-freeze, otherwise known as polyethylene glycol, a substance never before used intravenously in humans.

On November 28, 2023, Meiji Seika Pharma proudly made an announcement. The news release indicated that the Japanese pharma giant had received the manufacturing and marketing approval of the self-amplifying mRNA vaccine against COVID-19. The rollout of the vaccine was scheduled for October 2024.

What we have explained is the new trend in biotechnology, the rise of the RNA machine, self-amplification, and mRNA vaccine design. As described in a *Trends in Biotechnology* review, "Delivery of replicons is achieved with virus-like replicon particles (VRPs), or in nonviral vehicles such as liposomes and lipid nanoparticles."[186] Liposomes are small, spherical vesicles made of lipids that can encapsulate and transport drugs and other molecules to specific sites in the body.[187] Lipids are "a broad group of organic compounds which include fats, waxes, sterols, fat-solu-

---

[186] See Jerome D.G. Comes et al., "Rise of the RNA machines – self-amplification in mRNA vaccine design," *Trends in Biotechnology* 41, no. 11 (2023): 1417–1429, https://www.cell.com/trends/biotechnology/fulltext/S0167-7799(23)00154-3?_returnURL=https://linkinghub.elsevier.com/retrieve/pii/S0167779923001543?showall%3Dtrue.

[187] Hamdi Nsairat et al., "Liposomes: structure, composition, types, and clinical applications," *Heliyon* 8, no. 5 (May 2022): e09394, https://www.cell.com/heliyon/fulltext/S2405-8440(22)00682-X.

ble vitamins (such as vitamins A, D, E and K), monoglycerides, diglycerides, phospholipids, and others. The functions of lipids include storing energy, signaling, and acting as structural components of cell membranes."[188] Virus-like replicon particles (VRPs) are not true viruses. VRPs are structures unique to synthetic biology that use nanotechnology to engineer biological mechanisms at the molecular cell level. Lipids were used in this instance to cloak the nanobot bombers with pathogenic payloads that are capable of delayed or triggered delivery.

Now enter the research that Dr. Mihalcea has conducted. Self-replication exists in the vials; she has demonstrated that to be true.

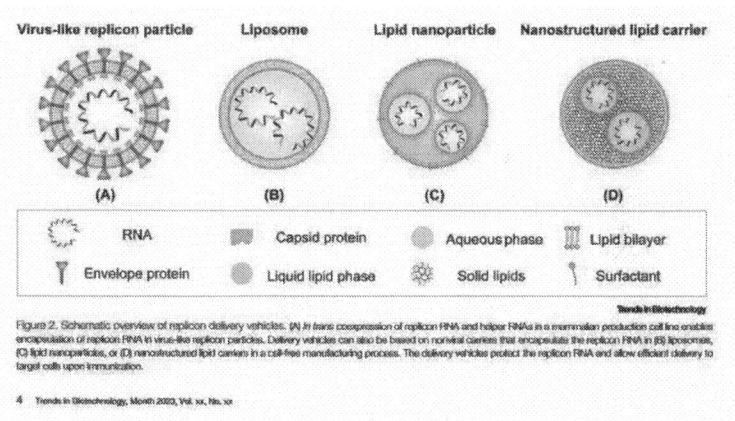

Figure 2. Schematic overview of replicon delivery vehicles. (A) In trans coexpression of replicon RNA and helper RNAs in a mammalian production cell line enables encapsulation of replicon RNA in virus-like replicon particles. Delivery vehicles can also be based on nonviral carriers that encapsulate the replicon RNA in (B) liposomes, (C) lipid nanoparticles, or (D) nanostructured lipid carriers in a cell-free manufacturing process. The delivery vehicles protect the replicon RNA and allow efficient delivery to target cells upon immunization.

4   Trends in Biotechnology, Month 2023, Vol. xx, No. xx

The graphic above depicts the virus-like replicon particle on the left. To the right, you see liposomes and nanostructured lipid carriers. They are all part of an alternative version of this replicon mechanism. In the Moderna patent, it discusses that these

---

[188] "Lipid," Wikipedia, https://en.wikipedia.org/wiki/Lipid.

Todd S. Callender, J.D., Jerome R. Corsi, Ph.D.,
and Craig D. Campbell, Ph.D.

nanoparticles are polymer-based, self-assembled nanoparticles that are fully programmable, meaning they are really self-propelled and autonomous computers (computers that work in series or in parallel).

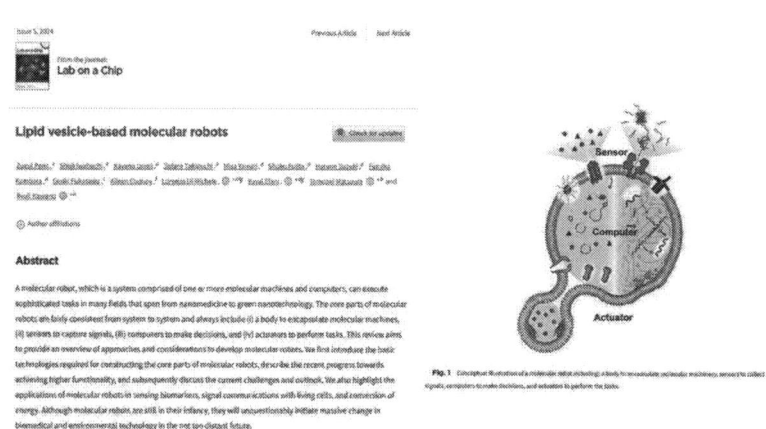

Issue 5, 2024   Previous Article   Next Article

From the Journal:
Lab on a Chip

Lipid vesicle-based molecular robots

Abstract

A molecular robot, which is a system comprised of one or more molecular machines and computers, can execute sophisticated tasks in many fields that span from nanomedicine to green nanotechnology. The core parts of molecular robots are fairly consistent from system to system and always include (i) a body to encapsulate molecular machines, (ii) sensors to capture signals, (iii) computers to make decisions, and (iv) actuators to perform tasks. This review aims to provide an overview of approaches and considerations to develop molecular robots. We first introduce the basic technologies required for constructing the core parts of molecular robots, describe the recent progress towards achieving higher functionality, and subsequently discuss the current challenges and outlook. We also highlight the applications of molecular robots in sensing biomarkers, signal communications with living cells, and conversion of energy. Although molecular robots are still in their infancy, they will unquestionably initiate massive change in biomedical and environmental technology in the not too distant future.

Fig. 1   Conceptual illustration of a molecular robot including a body to encapsulate molecular machines, sensors to collect signals, computers to make decisions, and actuators to perform the tasks.

Shown above is a lipid vesicle-based molecular robot. It is a software-driven system with biological sensors, using DNA as a computing platform and actuators. These molecular robots are consistent from system to system. They include a body to encapsulate the molecular machine, a sensor to capture signals, computers inside of them to make decisions, and actuators, which are like robotic arms to perform tasks.

Molecular robots go hand in hand with biological computers, accepting inputs that are translated into appropriate outputs. Due to the advances in synthetic chemistry and biology, these molecules, such as DNA and proteins, have become readily available, leading to the development of these biological computers. Their computational speed is up to 109 transitions per second as an input-responsive matter.

In Israel, a team of scientists adapted DNA molecules to act as a tiny molecular computing device. The Guinness World Records certified their prototype as the smallest biocomputer to date. These robotic computers can self-assemble membranes into tissue-like structures, disassemble, and reassemble in response to input at lightning-fast speeds.

> A team of scientists led by Ehud Shapiro of the Weizmann Institute of Science (Israel) have adapted molecules of DNA to act as tiny molecular computing devices. Two DNA molecules and a molecule called an enzyme react together, acting as input, software, hardware, and power supply. Experiments have shown that a microlitre of salt solution, containing 3 trillion self-contained DNA computing devices can perform 66 billion operations per second, with the necessary power/fuel for the computations provided by the DNA itself as it is cleaved by the hardware enzyme. The results were announced on 24 February 2003 in the Proceedings of the National Academy of Sciences. The team consisted of Yaakov Benenson, Rivka Adar, Tamar Paz-Elizur, Zvi Livneh, and Ehud Shapiro (all Israel).[189]

---

[189] "Smallest biological computing device," Guinness World Records, February 20, 2023, https://www.guinnessworldrecords.com/world-records/smallest-biological-computing-device.

Professor Ian F. Akyildiz, perhaps the world's foremost expert on nano-computers, brags in 2018 about using mRNA nanobots to transform living tissue and a whole body (alive or dead) into a cloud-computing node.[190] He even indicates, in that year, that this mRNA technology was being used actively in vaccines. In fact, the technology was so mature and robust that the Institute of Electrical and Electronics Engineers (started in 1884) generated international standards (standard 1906.1) on their use in 2017.

These tiny machines can reshuffle materials, or they can be created with membranes that release "cargo." The cargo can be triggered by frequencies, light, temperature, magnetic fields, or biomarkers.

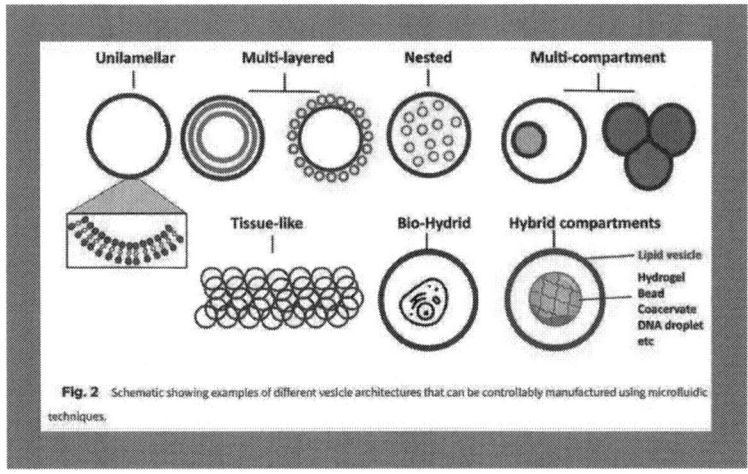

Fig. 2 Schematic showing examples of different vesicle architectures that can be controllably manufactured using microfluidic techniques.

---

[190] Free Your Mind Videos, "mRNA Vaxx EXPOSED: mRNAs Are Nothing More Than Programmed Nanoscale Machines | Prof. Ian F. Akyildiz," video, Rumble, January 2025, https://rumble.com/v63212b-mrna-vaxx-exposed-mrnas-are-nothing-more-than-programmed-nanoscale-machines.html.

The graphic above is a visual representation of various structures that can be formed using these machines. For example, liposomes containing cargo, or tissue-like structures, are created through self-replication.

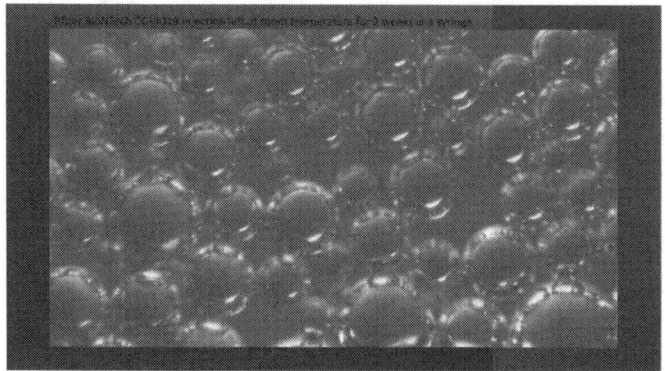

The graphic above is a microscopic picture of liposomes. Dr. Mihalcea left a few drops of the contents from a COVID-19 vaccine vial in a syringe. After two weeks, when examined under a microscope with no cover slide, it was discovered that the contents of the vial had self-replicated, creating these liposomal structures. The structures have other smaller structures, connecting the larger structures to each other.

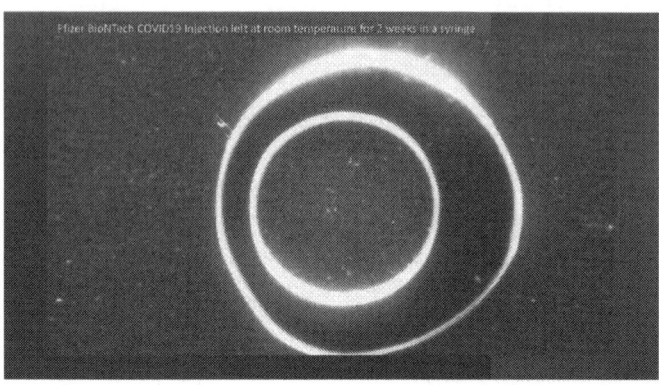

The graphic above is a closeup of a structure taken after a slide cover was placed on the liposomes. The self-assembling nanoparticles are visible on the outside of the rings of the two membrane walls. The self-replicating nanoparticles were swarming inside the inner wall. The nanobots were deployed in the COVID-19 bioweapon.

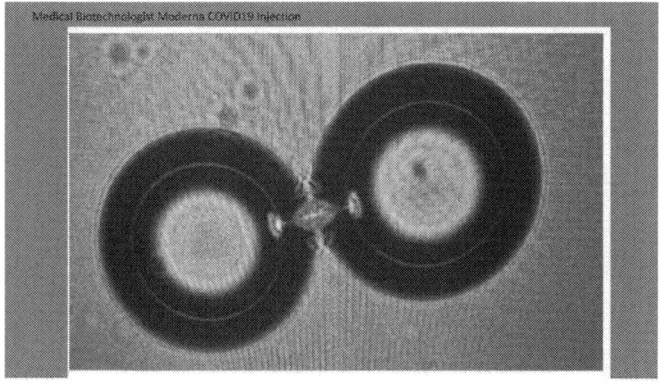

The slide above was taken by a medical technologist from Puerto Rico studying Moderna vaccines. This computerized image shows that a nanoport developed and self-assembled. The connecting structure is visible under the microscope and enables the two structures to communicate, transmit cargo, and then self-assemble.

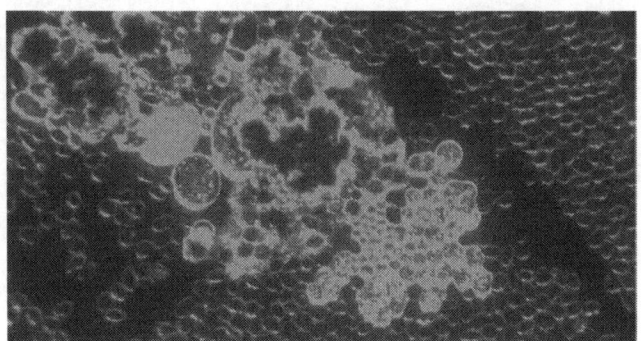

The slide above is from embalmed blood. The liposomes were actually still self-assembling in the blood of a dead body.

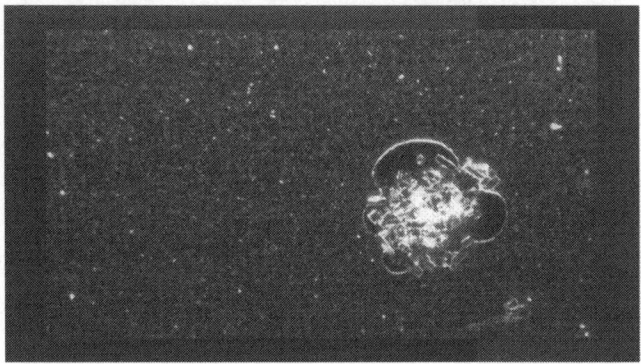

The graphic above is from a vial containing the Pfizer-BioNTech vaccine. Nano and microrobots are building structures using computerized-chip technology. The structures are sending IP addresses or MAC addresses to the cloud.

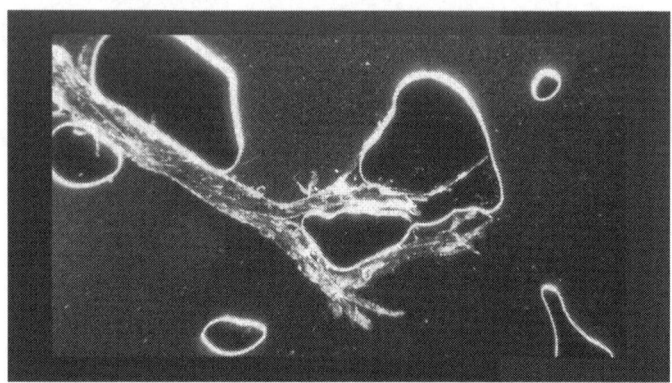

The graphic above clearly shows the self-assembly and building of liposomes as filamental structures in the blood.

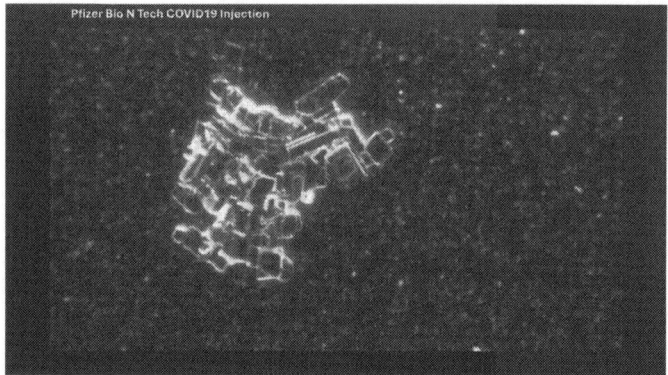

In the graphic above, the previous structures that are under high magnification definitely show microchips and microtechnology in action.

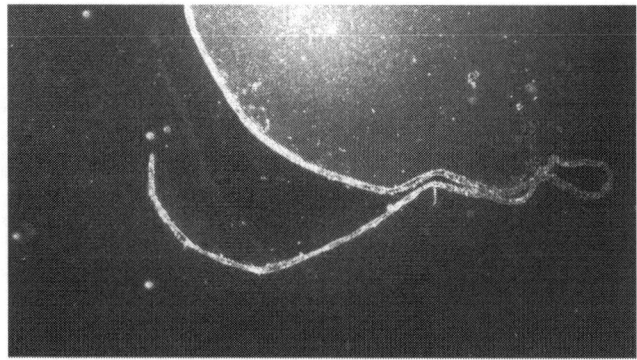

The graphic above shows the contents of the vial after six days and demonstrates a fusion between advanced biology and technology. It is evident that filamental structures are being built.

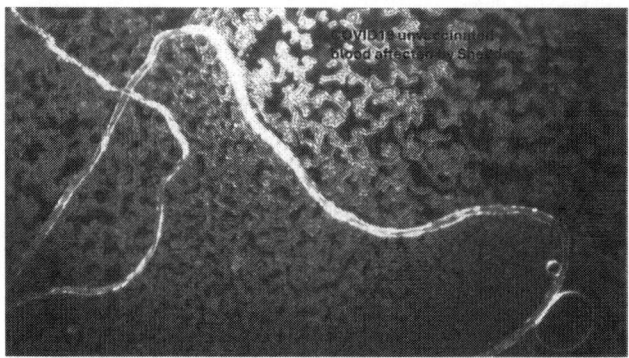

The graphic above shows structures that self-assembled through self-replication in human blood. Electricity from the human blood is "hijacked," and polymerization has occurred through that self-replication and self-assembly. These filaments have enormous microchips adjacent to them, and then they build mesogens. A mesogen is "a compound that displays liquid crystal properties. Mesogens can be described as disordered solids or ordered liquids because they arise from a unique state of matter that exhibits both solid- and liquid-like properties called the liquid crystalline state."[191]

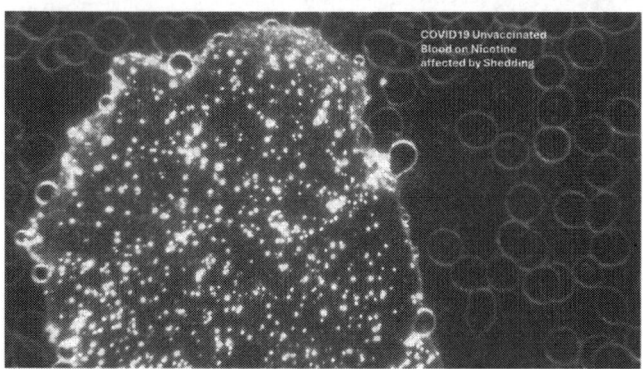

This graphic shows a mesogen brain chip in unvaccinated blood.

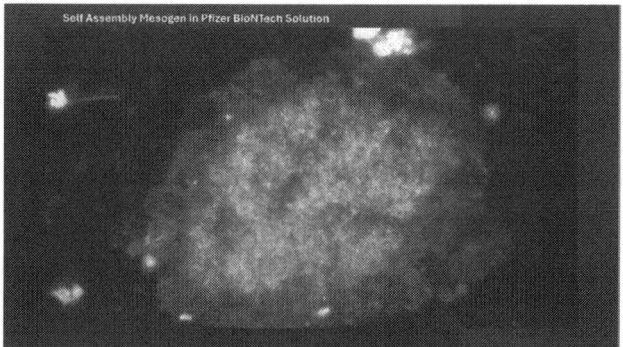

---

[191] "Mesogen," Wikipedia, https://en.wikipedia.org/wiki/Mesogen#:~:text= A%20mesogen%20is%20a%20compound,called%20the%20liquid%20 crystalline%20state.

The structure in the graphic above looks exactly like what grew in the COVID-19 vials. This represents extreme technology, enabling the self-assembly of mesogens. All of the nanoparticles are self-assembling and self-replicating to build this microchip-like structure (computer).

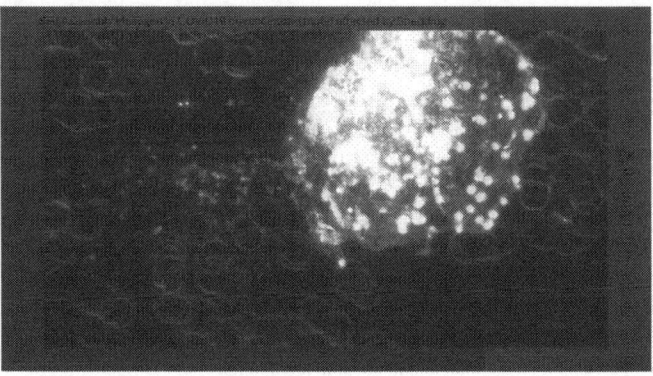

The graphic above, of unvaccinated blood, shows self-replication. Nanoparticles are self-assembling, which represents an important aspect of self-replication.

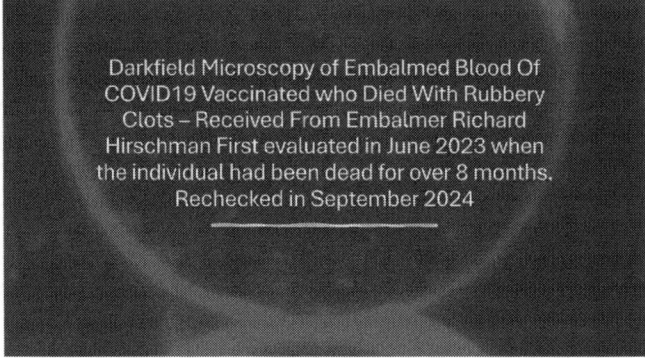

Darkfield Microscopy of Embalmed Blood Of COVID19 Vaccinated who Died With Rubbery Clots – Received From Embalmer Richard Hirschman First evaluated in June 2023 when the individual had been dead for over 8 months. Rechecked in September 2024

The graphic above is from a blood sample from someone who died with the rubbery clot, provided by embalmer Richard Hirschman.

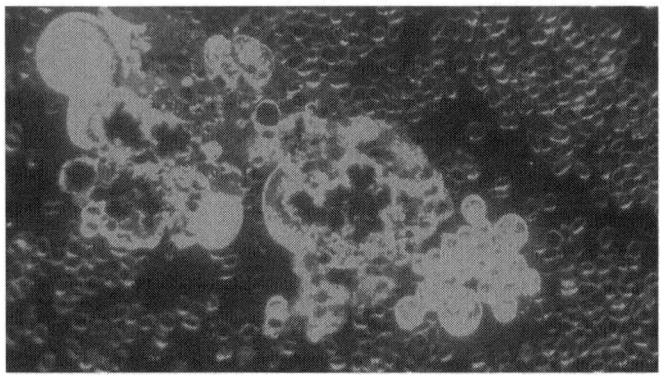

The graphic above was taken over eight months after the person had died after vaccination. The structures continue self-replicating.

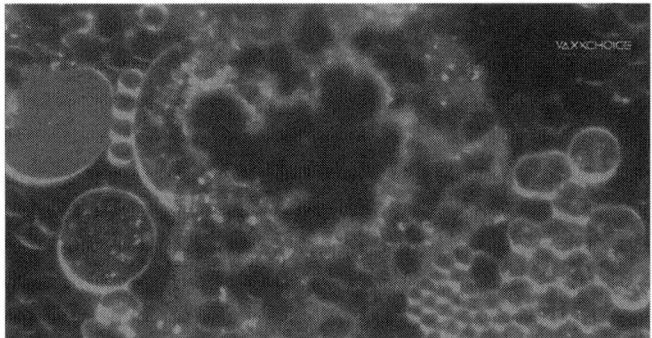

The bubbles are liposomes with the cargo; they continue to self-assemble and self-replicate.

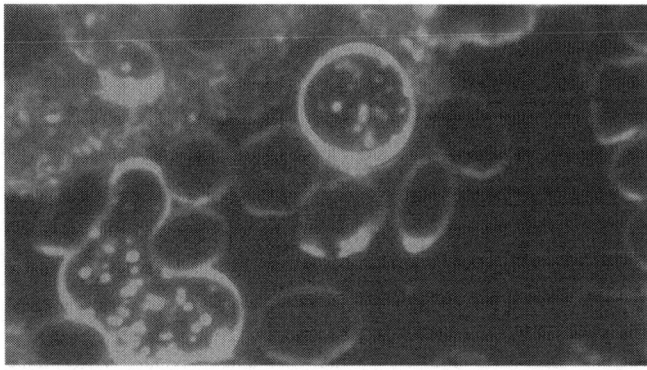

The graphic above is the same blood as in the previous slide but under larger magnification. The nanobots are inside of the structures.

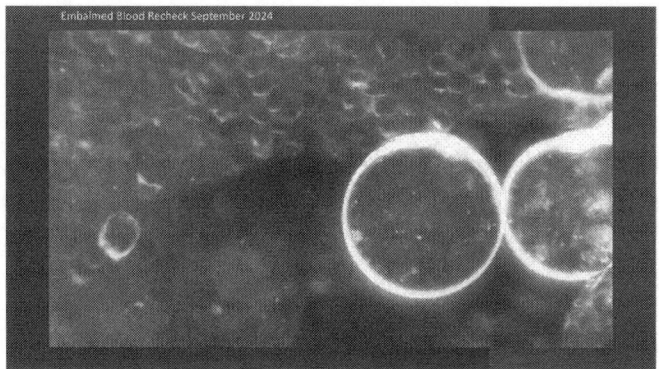

The graphic above is of the same blood viewed again the following September. In the upper right corner, there is evidence that self-replication is continuing, over two years after death.

Dr. Lionberger asked Dr. Mihalcea to pause in her presentation to discuss his observations. Specifically, he was concerned about the comparison in size of these self-assembled structures to that of the inner walls of the capillaries. Normal functioning red blood cells in the human body are two microns in diameter. The diameter of the inner wall of a capillary is between four and five microns. The structures we see in the above graphics are much, much larger than the opening of a capillary, making it impossible for the structures to travel through the blood stream without blocking the passages.

The pathogenic implications are catastrophic to the human biome. The structures are so large that they cannot travel through the capillaries—the result being a backup of the rubbery clots. Microclots such as these attract other fibren components that result in giant clots that invade blood vessels and lung tissue, inter alia, which eventually kill the host. Microclots then grow into killer clots.

Dr. Mihalcea agreed with that assessment. The rubbery clots had been analyzed. They were made from polyvinyl alcohol, polyamides, and polyethylene. Those polymers, assembled by this technology, created clots that were temperature and light dependent. They could be dependent upon electromagnetic fields, a result of the fusion between biology and technology. What had been observed are self-replicating machines. They were robotic computer systems being sold to the public as vaccines supposedly to prevent or kill a virus. That deception could not be more clear, misleading most people to take something that is ultimately lethal instead of curative.

Dr. Lionberger has seen information regarding replicon, indicating that it may create a supermagnetic field as part of its process. The human system is affected by magnetism[192] as it is bioelectric.[193]

Dr. Mihalcea agreed, as the magnetic field is critical to the self-replication technology. The process is controlled through magnetic fields and light, specifically in the functioning of the brain. For example, to build a parallel processing platform in the brain through nanotechnology, the carbon nanotubes that self-assemble there are as large in diameter as a microtubule.

Microtubules are microscopic hollow tubes made of the proteins alpha and beta tubulin that are part of a cell's cytoskeleton, a network of protein filaments that extends throughout the cell, gives the cell shape, and keeps its organelles in place. Microtubules are the largest structures in the cytoskeleton at about 24 nanometers thick. They have roles in cell movement, cell division, and transporting materials within cells.[194] In the brain, the microtubule processes consciousness. The technology can literally create or insert thoughts by building this parallel

---

[192] "That many animals sense and respond to Earth's magnetic field is no longer in doubt, and people, too, may have a magnetic sense. But how this sixth sense might work remains a mystery. Some researchers say it relies on an iron mineral, magnetite; others invoke a protein in the retina called cryptochrome." From Eric Hand, "The body's hidden compass—what is it, and how does it work?" *Science*, June 23, 2016, https://www.science.org/content/article/body-s-hidden-compass-what-it-and-how-does-it-work.

[193] "Your cells crackle with electric signals that guide embryonic development and heal wounds. If we can learn to tweak this "bioelectric code", we might be able to prevent cancer and even grow new limbs." From Sally Adee, "The amazing ways electricity in your body shapes you and your health," NewScientist, February 22, 2023, https://www.newscientist.com/article/2360290-the-amazing-ways-electricity-in-your-body-shapes-you-and-your-health/.

[194] BD Editors, "Microtubule," Biology Dictionary, last updated April 28, 2017, https://biologydictionary.net/microtubule/.

brain. Cyrus Parsa, founder of The AI Organization, sued the US government arguing that this technology has the potential to hack human neural networks through mind control, thus endangering and enslaving all of humanity; Professor Yuval Noah Hirari calls us "hackable animals."

> Cyrus Parsa has warned the world about the threats of AI takeover for several years now. He has an excellent way of explaining how humanities bio-field and neural networks are being hacked and mind controlled by Big Tech companies. Many people are in complete denial of the technological dangers of AI and why this is intimately linked to my [Dr. Mihalcea] work in exposing the nanotechnology and synthetic biology in the human blood. The Radio-frequency sensor tag on the nanoparticles connect to Wifi and transmit biometric data to the cloud and supercomputers that then are in charge of developing the digital human twin in the metaverse. If you have not yet seen what I have found in peoples blood, please look at these microscopy videos of C19 unvaccinated blood. Self assembly bio sensor nano particles **SHED** and enter the human via the skin and we also inhale them.[195]

[195] Ana Maria Mihalcea, "Cyrus Parsa's Lawsuit from 2019 – Excellent Summary of The Dangers Of AI And Big Tech Mind Control," Reasonable Faith Honolulu, November 11, 2023, https://reasonablefaithhonolulu.org/cyrus-parsas-lawsuit-from-2019-excellent-summary-of-the-dangers-of-ai-and-big-tech-mind-control/.

Dr. Mihalcea added that an important aspect of the self-replicating nanotechnology is that if, for example, someone has already received a vaccination, and thus a vector of this material, that person becomes a spreader. The end result over time is the infection of the entire world. Replication starts slowly in an individual's body but then it has an exponential growth curve.

An extinction-level event may begin within minutes. The math of self-replication is exponential, a geometric progression.

An alphavirus is the foundational template of a replicon vaccine. Lisa and other researchers found that the Venezuelan equine encephalitis virus (VEEV),[196] as indicated in the Federal Register, is the vector of that patented virus. She found that the DOD had several patented viruses from that particular VEEV, as it has been mutated several times—and not just the DOD, also the Department of Energy, and Health and Human Services.

Lisa and her team found several entries for patented vaccines/ viruses. VEEV had been added as a bioagent, and thus a new strain was developed. The procedure was repeated, and voilà, the replicon vaccine, the VEEV strain TC-83 (A3G). This particular vaccine was put into the virocell,[197] and into the virocell line. This vaccine was one of the WHO's virocells inside the replicon. It was also in the Pfizer and Moderna mRNA COVID-19 shots and made it into the Federal Register in 2022 as a registered bioagent. It was then laced into the virocells that are present in the replicon.

---

[196] Brianna Crosby and Maria E. Crespo, "Venezuelan Equine Encephalitis," National Library of Medicine, July 3, 2023, https://www.ncbi.nlm.nih.gov/ books/NBK559332/.

[197] Patrick Forterre, "Manipulation of cellular syntheses and the nature of viruses: The virocell concept," *Comptes Rendus Chimie*, Volume 14, Issue 4, 2011, 392–399, https://www.sciencedirect.com/science/article/pii/ S1631074810001724.

Is it any wonder that public health autorities define humans as an "experimental subject"? Lisa also found that there are several formulas of WHO's virocell lines that are infused within this patented mRNA. That replicon is being used for the replicon vaccine.

The material safety sheet for the Vero E6 cell line indicates the liquid is to be used for research only. It has been amplified in radiation and includes several other "viruses," platforms that have been added. Vero E6 cells are cells isolated from the African green monkey that are used for the synthetic production of viruses. VEEV has been mutated several times, and it is a zoonotic virus. As defined by *Britannica* online:

> A zoonotic disease [is] any of a group of diseases
> that can be transmitted to humans by nonhuman
> vertebrate animals, such as mammals, birds, rep-
> tiles, amphibians, and fish. A large number of
> domestic and wild animals are sources of zoo-
> notic disease, and there are numerous means of
> transmission. Public health veterinarians have a
> critical role in zoonotic disease surveillance, pre-
> vention, and control, but risk reduction increas-
> ingly requires multidisciplinary teams and a uni-
> fied concept of medicine in humans and other
> animal species.[198]

These substances have been deceptively called vaccines and viruses to traffic humanity's illnesses and diseases to everyone,

---

[198] Millicent Eidson, "zoonotic disease," *Britannica*, last updated February 15, 2025, https://www.britannica.com/science/zoonotic-disease.

contaminated with DNA. It is very deceiving because they are not vaccines; they are software systems. It is a forced evolution: being converted into chronic disease and illness supply-and-demand units. We are being harnessed for energy, through the blood, and then also harnessed through this bacteria-based residual-waste product. We are harnessed by waste products that we generate from these substances. They absolutely are computerized platforms. This is a system to convert humans and evolve them into units of energy and commodity.

Dr. Lionberger questioned the concept of the alphavirus and this ability to transcribe it. Not only can it infect humans, but it can also infect animals and insects. Did the alphavirus have the ability to cross species?

Dr. Mihalcea answered that, biologically, the alphavirus does have the ability to be transmitted from one species to another. It was obvious that the powers that be recognize that fact and are promoting its development. For example, the 2024 presidential budget on nanotechnology specifically listed the development of replicon vaccines in the United States as a priority.

Replicon vaccines are being discussed, and there are Ebola-HIV platforms to be used as biological weapons systems. They have already been designed and appear in the related literature. If deployed, and it sheds, the shedding process meaning it is transmissible from person to person. It can potentially affect all life: humans, animals, and insects. In such a case, this would create a biological warfare scenario leading to an extinction event eliminating all life on planet earth.

Lisa boiled the issues down to the essence: We are in a spiritual war and to fully understand what is going on, one has to understand that, whether you are spiritual or not, the goal is the transmutation of the biological system into something entirely different.

We are witnessing an attempt to completely alter God's design of creation. The goal is to reset the very mechanisms of our biological system. With the onslaught of mutated vaccines and viruses, humans are being converted into bioweapons, batteries, power sources, transmitting devices, transducers, and cloud-computing nodes as indicated in Microsoft's patent number WO2020060606.[199]

The Owners say that they are protecting us, while in truth it is just one global power grab. The evil forces need us to blindly comply in order for them to continue to control us. Their current weapons of choice are created viruses, followed by toxic liquids to inject into our bodies, falsely labeled as vaccines.

Again, these liquids contain computer software systems, with other substances that cause physical reactions from our biological systems as byproducts: infections, tumors, cancer, and autoimmune diseases.

The byproducts are used to develop the next advanced strain or mutation. The dark forces have created a supply-and-demand apparatus, and we are but units in that supply chain. We are manipulated into supplying the demand and demanding the supply, a vicious circle.

These implications of a self-replicating vaccine creating autoimmune reactions are even greater than ever before. There is no

---

[199] Microsoft Technology Licensing, LLC, "WO2020060606 – Cryptocurrency System Using Body Activity Data," March 26, 2020, Patentscope, WIPO, https://patentscope.wipo.int/search/en/detail.jsf?docId=WO2020060606.

shut-off mechanism. Once launched, the elements just continue to replicate, utilizing the human or animal hosts as an energy supply until the energy is depleted. When our engine runs out of fuel, in our case blood, then it is lights out.

We have seen what is happening through the microscope. Yet, critics unfamiliar with science maintain that if they cannot see it (the nanotechnology) with the naked eye, then it does not exist. Of course, they cannot see air but that does not mean air does not exist. The typical microwave oven emits frequencies that are undetectable, yet effective in cooking food; 5G are microwave frequences. Ask them why they waste their time breathing. Regardless of the skepticism, we know what we see and what is being built by the process.

Nanoparticles are so small, they are like a gas, entering through the skin or inhalation. The blood of the host is contaminated, and the contamination spreads. The replicating process takes place within and without, from person to person.

Pfizer documents indicate that upon receiving a COVID-19 shot, the vaccinated person can pass the vaccine to others. An unvaccinated person inhales the air around a vaccinated individual, and the transfer can take place. The evil ones have covered all the bases. Injected or not, we all become victims to the shots and shoot others. Over time there is no escape. It's insidious criminal genius planning, and designed to terminate or transform humanity en masse.

If the self-amplifying mechanism is merely present, there is more death. The massive death caused by the original form of the virus/vaccine may soon be greatly exceeded. When the engine of self-replication is amped up, we will see even more myocarditis, tubal cancers, vaccine-induced AIDS, and blood clotting in a geo-metrically accelerating fashion.

Lisa added that the trauma to our already over-stressed immune systems will just result in more illness and death. She questioned if there will be different outcomes for people only receiving the initial mRNA shot versus people accepting boosters as well. Will people who survived the shots adapt to the harshness and corrosiveness of these chemicals and develop resistance? Please recall the DOD's own clinical trial data (C4591001) of the Pfizer shots revealed that the 44,000 test subjects (victims) went home from the trial with one or more side effects of 1,291 new diseases Pfizer characterizes as "Serious Adverse Events of Special Interest."

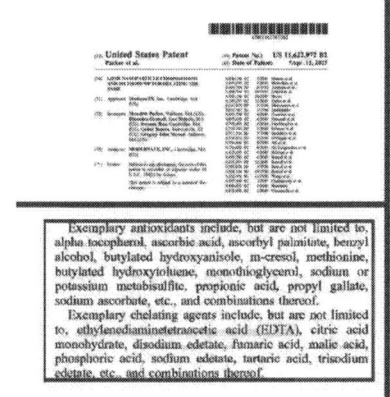

The graphic above is a page from the Moderna patent. It deals with lipid nanoparticle composition and the "methods of formulating the same." It states that there are methods for inhibiting the formation of the lipid nanoparticle that encapsulates as a liposome. Using a "chelating agent" with a "reducing agent" will stop the process.

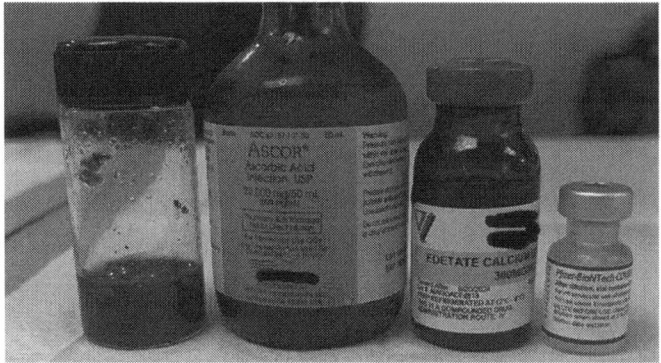

The photo above shows a blood sample on the left and on the right ascorbic acid, EDTA (or ethylenediaminetetraacetic acid), and the Pfizer vial.

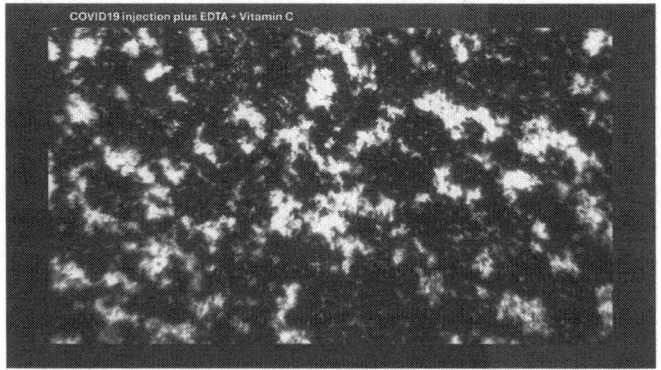

The graphic above shows the result after the addition of EDTA and vitamin C. The effect is immediate and complete; all of the nanoparticles have been destroyed.

According to Dr. Lionberger, EDTA has a high affinity for metals. When it comes into contact with nanotech, it disassembles and destroys the nanotech. Dr. Mihalcea added that fifty-four undeclared metals were found in the sample vials, making the substance metal rich.

Dr. Mihalcea then stated that EDTA also inhibits polymerization. The hydrogel, a kind of polymer called polyvinyl, which can be used to extract aluminum and titanium, is needed for the self-assembly as a start signal. Per Google AI (accessed January 30, 2025), "Polyvinyl refers to a polymerized vinyl compound, resin, or plastic. Polyvinyl chloride (PVC) and polyvinyl alcohol (PVA) are examples of polyvinyl." A chelating agent prevents the start signal and thereby stops the polymerization process. The microrobots, which are actually quantum dot-like structures in their centers, have a piece of metal. Attacking that structure stops the robots.

An added bonus is protection from other dark technology being used against us, such as geoengineering.

> Geoengineering is the artificial modification of Earth's climate systems through two primary ideologies, Solar Radiation Management (SRM) and Carbon Dioxide Removal (CDR).[200]

"Chemtrails" are real. Take it from former CIA Director John Brennan in his speech at the Council on Foreign Relations on June 29, 2016:

---

[200] Dane Wigington, "Radio Show: Climate Engineering – A Clear Danger," GeoEngineering Watch, August 26, 2015, https://www.geoengineering watch.org/radio-show-climate-engineering-a-clear-danger.

Another example is the array of technologies, often referred to collectively as geoengineering, that potentially could help reverse the warming effects of global climate change. One that has gained my personal attention is stratospheric aerosol injection, or SAI, a method of seeding the stratosphere with particles that can help reflect the sun's heat in much the same way that volcanic eruptions do.[201]

When Brennan speaks, the demons listen. Self-appointed earth saviors have been spraying the skies with reflective nanomaterials in aerosol form to reflect sunlight before it reaches the earth. Those sprays may include barium, strontium, and/or aluminum.

The takeaway is good news. In their own literature, the vaccine manufacturers admit that EDTA and vitamin C shut down the nanomachines.

Dr. Mihalcea has been using EDTA plus vitamin C for three years. She has seen it work on people with symptoms like heart palpitation or brain fog. If they take a chelation, they feel better immediately. But everyone must do their own research and make their own decisions regarding anything they put in their bodies.

If any of these self-activating, self-replicating, vaccines/viruses are released and go cross species, the implications are deadly for patient zero and will quickly go worldwide. The VEEV has protein sequences of Marburg and Ebola.

---

[201] John O. Brennan, "John Brennan on Transnational Threats to Global Security," Council on Foreign Relations, June 29, 2016, https://www.cfr.org/event/john-brennan-transnational-threats-global-security.

Those shots have been given to livestock and that may just be a test population. Again, if it has the ability to go cross species, that has greater implications than just cows and horses. Think about the gases, the shedding of the animals. All the animals are shedding as well.

Dr. Mihalcea recalled that in 2013, a DOD document was declassified regarding a project called "Nano Domestic Quell."[202] The DOD had infected 87 percent of the US population through the water supply and beverages such as Coca-Cola, Pepsi, and Dasani water with dormant nanoparticles. So, what was their explicit purpose?

The dormant nanotech was to be activated later, launching an influenza-like illness that could kill people within ten days. It sounds like another one of those conspiracy theories; however, nanoparticles have actually been found in these beverages. The activator could be a high frequency signal such as from a 5G tower. It is a ticking time bomb of a biological weapon agent for sure.

Yes, the Owners declared war on us decades ago, and we are just now waking up, or at least a few of us are waking up. They are even going after our kids with CDC-recommended childhood vaccines.

This is all part of an elaborate system, a poisonous tree with a multitude of branches. There is a war going on for our biological systems, and when the assault is activated, we will be

---

[202] Ana Maria Mihalcea, "Is Nano Domestic Quell Government Project Still Going On? How Long Have Our Bodies Been Loaded With Nano Particles In Food, Drinks And Water Supply? Are We Now Part Of The World Wide Sensor Network?" Humanity United Now – Ana Maria Mihalcea, MD, PhD, Substack, December 4, 2023, https://anamihalceamdphd.substack. com/p/is-nano-domestic-quell-government.

converted into the bioweapons from which they say that they're protecting us.

It is all about depopulation and control of the remnants. Think of it as a nuclear bomb detonated from within humanity itself. *We* are the ticking time bombs.

These agents that we have been discussing are called "causative agents" for a reason. They are programmed agents incapable of independent thought or resistance. We are in the age of genetic bioterrorism. The terrorists are using their nanobot agents to terrorize us. One of the most terrorizing and often used movie images is a scene in which a person is attacked from within. Take, for example, that scene in *Alien* when the creature hatches from the chest of its human host. Does John Hurt still have nightmares from filming that scene? I would.

Nanobot technology has been developing over decades in preparation of being employed. Why are they being employed? What is their future intent? What are these structures going to assemble into at the end stage?

Does the typical family physician have any idea what he or she is recommending? No, they have no idea. The network doctor just reads the literature passed down from above and follows the established protocols. They have been told not to think independently, question instructions, and not to say anything or its out to the scary world of private practice.

The Owners want to eliminate seven billion people—whether that be by biological weapons attacks under the cover vaccination, geoengineering, whatever works best. Two years' worth of rain dumped on Dubai in twenty-four hours or fires in northern California, Maui, and Wyoming. Hurricane Helene, then

Milton. We are in a war worldwide on every level of existence. Weather modification is actually codified in United States law as the National Weather Modification Act of 1976 (15 USC 330, et seq.).[203]

Dr. Mihalcea then discussed quantum dots. Nano quantum dots are smaller than twenty nanometers. These particles also self-assemble to form larger structures. Dark-field microscopes increase magnification up to four thousand times, enabling her to expand the dots to about five hundred nanometers in diameter for the human eye to see. Because of light emission, they appear slightly larger than they are in reality. The dots are self-assembling nanotechnology that we only see on the extreme microscopic scale.

Even if it takes an electron microscope, studying this technology from the nanobot-scale to microbot-scale is important. If the dot disappears on the microscale, then that gives us really a reason for hope.

An IBM supercomputer, vintage 1972, was the Department of Energy's very first computer upon the DOE's creation in 1977. They now have additional computers, and there are other systems, but the chemical compounds, protein sequences, and software platforms all have IP addresses to IBM.

These "vaccines" have been put into Vero cells (refer to prior mention earlier in this chapter) registering as a cell, gene, protein, and enzyme, when it is actually the Venezuelan equine encephalitis virus (VEEV) that was mentioned earlier. Venezuela? That South American coastal paradise? America is being invaded

---

[203] Public Law 94-490, October 13, 1976, https://uscode.house.gov/statutes/pl/94/490.pdf.

across our southern border by Venezuelans.[204] At the same time, our bodies are being invaded internally by millions of nanobots with a Venezuelan ingredient. In addition, there are strong indications that Dominion Voting Systems machines were used over a decade ago to ensure then-communist dictator Hugo Chávez of Venezuela would stay in office.[205] Did that system invade the US to steal our elections? The trifecta of destruction.

On a side note, just how evil is the communist regime in Venezuela? In September 2024, Patrick Byrne, former CEO of Overstock and outspoken Trump supporter, was informed by a Drug Enforcement Administration agent that Venezuela had placed a $25 million bounty on his head. Byrne has since fled to Dubai.[206] Back to our internal threat. For more information on the health and survival issues we are facing, go to Dr. Mihalcea's Substack: https://substack.com/@anamihalceamdphd. Also, you can read the books she wrote in a two-part series called *TransHuman*: The first is *The Real COVID Agenda* and the next is *Overcoming the Global Depopulation Agenda*.

Justin Leslie, another Pfizer whistleblower, worked directly on this product. And he said the only thing scarier than mRNA is siRNA (small interfering RNA). Per Google AI (accessed January

[204] Sarah Matusek, "Is a Venezuelan gang growing in the US? Colorado feels the threat." The Christian Science Monitor, September 13, 2024, https://www.csmonitor.com/USA/2024/0904/venezuelan-gang-tren-de-aragua-colorado.

[205] Tim Golden, "U.S. Investigates Voting Machines' Venezuela Ties," *New York Times*, October 29, 2006, https://www.nytimes.com/2006/10/29/washington/29ballot.html.

[206] Andrew Stanton, "Trump Ally Says Venezuela Has $25M Bounty on His Head, Flees US for Dubai," *Newsweek*, October 10, 2024, https://www.newsweek.com/patrick-byrne-trump-ally-flees-us-venezuela-1966745.

30, 2025), siRNA is a type of non-coding RNA molecule, typically 20–24 base pairs in length, that plays a role in the RNA interference (RNAi) pathway.

In a 2022 preprint (not yet peer-reviewed) study, some medical researchers believe replicon RNA shots may induce "durable protective immunity from SARS-CoV-2 in nonhuman primates after neutralizing antibodies have waned."[207]

Over the past months, the Japanese truth community sounded the alarm over a new type of vaccine that was released en masse into the Japanese population in the fall of 2024, perhaps as early as October 2024. The Japanese government allowed Meiji Seika Pharma to be one of the first pharmaceutical giants to roll out replicon; with heavy protests, it is unclear whether any Japanese citizens received the shots.

Meiji is a major Japanese food and pharmaceutical conglomerate based in Tokyo, with operations in India and the US. Meiji is chomping at the bit to take their vaccine business to the next level. Per the Meiji website on their vaccines as of January 30, 2025:

> Demand for vaccines is on the rise worldwide, and Meiji is responding on several fronts. As well as our approved influenza, hepatitis and Japanese encephalitis vaccines, we continue to develop new vaccines for emerging threats such as coronaviruses and Dengue fever. We also manufacture combined vaccines and single-supply

---

[207] Megan A. O'Connor et al., "A Replicon RNA vaccine induces durable protective immunity from SARS-CoV-2 in nonhuman primates after neutralizing antibodies have waned," preprint, bioRxiv, August 9, 2022, https://doi.org/10.1101/2022.08.08.503239.

products for which no alternative products are available.[208]

Shionogi Inc. "a discovery-based pharmaceutical company," entered the race as well. Per the Shionogi website, Shionogi Inc. is "committed to identifying unmet needs and harnessing the full potential of science to treat challenging human disease."[209]

The Bible tells us that in the end times evil will be portrayed as good and good as evil. We are also warned that man's hubris and sinful nature has consequences. Whether these Japanese scientists are blinded by their desire to be first with a ground-breaking discovery or by the enormous profit potential for the pharmaceutical interests they represent or they just innocently believe they are saving humanity, the potential disastrous results are within easy reach. Lord, help us all.

Isaiah 5:20 (ESV)

Woe to those who call evil good and good evil, who put darkness for light and light for darkness, who put bitter for sweet and sweet for bitter!

To go back to the Shionogi website mission—"unmet medical needs"? It seems that every biologist who knows how to use an incubator and microscope is ready to meet every viral need imaginable and unimaginable. It is a boom industry, a thriving job market, and the profit potential is unlimited.

---

[208] "Vaccines," Meiji, https://www.meiji.com/global/pharmaceuticals/vaccines.html.

[209] Shionogi website, https://www.shionogi.com/us/en/.

TODD S. CALLENDER, J.D., JEROME R. CORSI, PH.D.,
AND CRAIG D. CAMPBELL, PH.D.

The Japanese government-funded biotech startup VLP Therapeutics Japan, according to *The Japan Times*, is "developing a self-amplifying RNA vaccine that is safer and can be delivered in much smaller doses compared with current mRNA vaccines."[210] The new type of vaccine is known commonly in Japan as a replicon.

As self-amplifying, subgenomic viral RNAs, replicons can "enter a target cell and undergo limited transcription and translation to synthesize encoded proteins but will not produce infectious progeny."[211] As a "self-amplifying" RNA "vaccine," it makes copies of itself, allegedly before producing the proteins for which the patient is supposed to make antibodies. A replicon performs differently than the current spike protein mRNA "vaccines" from Pfizer and Moderna, which have become notorious for their side effects. These deadly side effects range from blood clots to cancer, as predicted in November 2021 by Daniel Nagase, MD.[212] The current COVID-19 mRNA injections do not officially have the ability to self-replicate unless they are integrated into a person's DNA. If the Pfizer or Moderna mRNA is reverse transcribed and alters a cell's DNA, only then does it attain the ability to repli-

---

[210] Tomoko Otake, "Japan has a new vaccine research funding unit for future pandemics — is it up to the task?" *The Japan Times*, May 18, 2023, https://www.japantimes.co.jp/news/2023/05/18/national/science-health/japan-funding-unit-future-pandemics/.

[211] Juliet Morrison and Stanley Plotkin, "Chapter 19 – Viral Vaccines: Fighting Viruses with Vaccines," in *Viral Pathogenesis*, 3rd ed., ed. Michael G. Katze, Marcus J. Korth, G. Lynn Law, and Neal Nathanson (Elsevier, 2016): 253–269, https://www.sciencedirect.com/topics/biochemistry-genetics-and-molecular-biology/replicon.

[212] Dnagase, "Dr. Nagase Nov 3, 2021 Genetic Damage mRNA," video, Rumble, October 12, 2022, https://rumble.com/v1nqjqw-dr.-nagase-nov-3-2021-genetic-damage-mrna.html?e9s=src_v1_upp.

cate through cell division. Every time a gene-altered cell divides, it makes a copy of the Pfizer or Moderna gene(s).

The new "self-amplifying" replicon vaccines are different in that they have the innate ability to make copies of themselves without altering a cell's DNA, even though reverse transcription and DNA alteration can happen as well.

The full magnitude of the dangers of a replicon's "self-amplifying" technology cannot be over emphasized. The choice of alphaviruses as the foundation template of replicon vaccines made it not only possible but likely that the new man-made genes in replicon vaccines, if ever introduced into people, would also spread to not just other humans, but also other species.

Alphavirus[213] is a family of viruses that can infect humans and animals. Some species are transmitted by mosquitoes. Alphavirus species are often very sturdy in that they can survive outside in the environment for extended periods of time, still remaining infective. Their extended life enables them to multiply and spread again. Dr. Nagase sums up the issues:

> While I knew that a self-replicating vaccine was dangerous, I initially thought that if people had pre-existing antibodies to naturally occurring Alphaviruses (that the self-replicating vaccine is based upon), healthy people might be able to carry enough Alphavirus antibodies to neutralize any self-replicating RNA shed from people who took the Replicon or other self-amplifying RNA

[213] "Alphavirus Infection," ScienceDirect, https://www.sciencedirect.com/topics/medicine-and-dentistry/alphavirus-infection.

"vaccines." Obtaining natural alphavirus antibodies would be most easily done by frequent
natural exposures to mosquito bites. However,
my thoughts about natural ways to protect
against the replicon "vaccines" only looked at
a part of the problem. There was another much
greater danger that only occurred to me in the
past couple days.[214]

Add to this witches' brew the prospect of interspecies transmission, also referred to as cross-species transmission. The prospects are not only real, but planned and deployed, warranting a
chapter or more in most virology texts. For example, in the scientific journal *Current Opinion in Virology*, an entire issue is devoted
to interspecies viral transmission.[215] Alphaviruses are named as
one of the paradigmatic viruses of this phenomenon, particularly
with respect to their ability to activate an immune response.

Interspecies transfer refers to a virus infecting more than one
species. Just how many species are there? There are about 2.16
million species as of 2022.[216] It may be possible to develop a virus
that no longer suffers from self-extinction by killing off its host

---

[214] "Dr. Nagase Nov 3, 2021 Genetic Damage mRNA."

[215] Sander Herfst, Martin Ludlow, Heather D. Hickman, and Mehul Suthar,
eds., "Emerging viruses: intraspecies transmission – Viral Immunology,"
in *Current Opinion in Virology* 28 (February 2018), https://www.
sciencedirect.com/journal/current-opinion-in-virology/vol/28/suppl/C.
See also: Francisco Dominguez et al., "Alphavirus-based replicons
demonstrate different interactions with host cells and can be optimized to
increase protein expression," American Society for Microbiology, *Journal
of Virology* 97, no. 11, https://journals.asm.org/doi/10.1128/jvi.01225-23.

[216] Hannah Ritchie, "How many species are there?" Our World in Data, November
30, 2022, https://ourworldindata.org/how-many-species-are-there.

species. If it is modified to infect another species (can you say gain of function?) and another, it continues on its way. By surviving indefinitely in other host species, the high, or even total, mortality in one or more species does not end that virus's reign of terror. In addition, the evolutionary pressure to not damage the host disappears when a virus is able to infect multiple species.

The presence of such a virile alphavirus would result in sickness and death among humans as long as the virus was able to infect other host species. For example, the eastern equine encephalitis alphavirus may exist in healthy birds but can cause deadly harm if transmitted to humans.[217] A replicon consists of a virus genome that has been engineered to insert a new protein. But where? And why? By deleting some of the genes of the parent virus, it behaves like CRISPR.[218] CRISPR has the ability to easily and precisely edit DNA. According to the "replicon" entry from the *Molecular Virology of Human Pathogenic Viruses*, "Such genomic constructs often lack the genes for their envelope spike, and are transfected into packaging cell lines that provide a viral envelope in trans. This permits the assembly of a virus-like particle with the cellular specificity associated with the envelope."[219]

---

[217] See "Transmission of Eastern Equine Encephalitis Virus," US Centers for Disease Control and Prevention, May 15, 2024, https://www.cdc.gov/eastern-equine-encephalitis/php/transmission/index.html.

[218] See McKenzie Prillaman, "Stanford explainer: CRISPR, gene editing, and beyond," Stanford Report, June 10, 2024, https://news.stanford.edu/stories/2024/06/stanford-explainer-crispr-gene-editing-and-beyond. (Note: CRISPR is a gene editing technology that is supposed to allow researchers to modify the DNA of living organisms. It is supposedly based on a bacterial defense system that protects against viruses.)

[219] Morrison and Plotkin, "Chapter 19 – Viral Vaccines."

For an explanation of this process, read the footnoted article.[220] To quote Roger Rabbit, "Jumping without a parachute? Kinda dangerous, ain't it?"

How does one go about testing for that substance? Supposedly, replicons cannot spread beyond the cells that they initially "infect" and are a lower-risk platform than recombinant viruses. Lower risk? But still risky. I repeat, "Kinda dangerous, ain't it?" But, according to the literature, the self-replicating RNA can spread to other cells. They can exploit the attributes of many wild-type viruses that would be unacceptable for use as an infectious recombinant virus.

Back to the name—the word choice does not exactly promote confidence. But on the other hand, humans, having sold their souls to demonic forces, often promote their wares openly to spite the followers of the light.

"Replicon" sounds like an Autobot subspecies of the evil Decepticons from the *Transformers* movie series. Since deception is a primary weapon of the Owners, this may point to the genesis of the name. Deception coupled with transformation fits like a glove.

Japan being the launchpad for this endeavor is equally concerning from a different pop-cultural point of view…first Godzilla, then Rodan, and now Replicon? Straight out of a science fiction movie and even more destructive? Leave it to the Japanese.

The Japanese government launched this unproven substance in the form of a vaccine in October of 2024. The replicon shots

---

[220] Andrzei Palucha et al., "Virus-Like Particles: Models for Assembly Studies and Foreign Epitope Carriers," *Progress in Nucleic Acid Research and Molecular Biology* 80 (2005): 135–168, https://www.sciencedirect.com/science/article/pii/S0079660305800042?via%3Dihub.

may have an irreversible never-ending impact on our species. If anyone receiving the shot procreates or swaps bodily fluids with others who do procreate, the results could cascade through the world's population. This means global human extinction, unless the Owners possess immunity or a magical elixir.

This effort is clearly aimed at genetically modifying our species and making such an adaptation permanent among future generations, if there are any.

How does the Japanese government justify ordering so much when there is not a well-established public health threat that I could ascertain?

The vaccine itself sounds really scary, but I'm not seeing a logical run-up to convincing anyone to get it, and Japan doesn't make sense as the country that would lead the uptake of this new abomination.

The human race is at risk by the genetic remapping taking place as of this moment. We know the Owners of this world own our governments, so analyzing the Japanese government's motives is less important than their ability to launch this unproven concoction.

The project leaders do not require a large application of the shots to achieve their goal.

The goal may be to race toward some deadline for the mutation of our species. We do not have to guess whether they are willing to do this as they have already knowingly poisoned their population. Japan had all the same materials as the US DOD, after we sued the DOD to stop the mandated COVID-19 shots.

In short, I do not believe we can afford to make the assumption that Japan will not release such a thing—and fool their people into taking it. What will stop them from putting this material into lidocaine and insulin as has already taken place with hydrogel and mCherry?[221]

Dr. Daniel Nagase, who was born in Japan and now residing in Canada, has been vocal regarding his attempt to save lives during COVID-19 plandemic.[222] He had been a doctor for over fifteen years, ten of which were in emergency rooms, and prescribed ivermectin to patients. The reaction by the medical authorities was swift and draconian. He has been stripped of his medical license. It is hard to believe the Japanese now trust a new self-amplifying RNA vaccine[223] after the COVID-19 shot debacle. Also, Japan was, and may still be, among the countries that shy away from vaccinating babies. There is also no microbiological proof of these viruses. However, that has not stopped mad scientists from faking them. It is unclear exactly what they are vaccinating against. This situation is evolving into another potential lab leak story, now with an insect vector. (An insect vector is an insect that transmits disease-causing pathogens to humans or other animals. These pathogens can be viruses, bacteria, or parasites.)

---

[221] See "mCherry," FPbase, last updated August 18, 2022, https://www.fpbase.org/protein/mcherry/. (Note: mCherry is a red fluorescent protein (RFP) that is used to study cells and molecules. It is a member of the mFruits family of proteins and is derived from the DsRed protein found in Discosoma sea anemones.)

[222] See John Gideon Hartnett, "Dr. Daniel Nagase: A Courageous Doctor Speaks Out," Bible Science Forum, October 6, 2021, https://biblescienceforum.com/2021/10/06/dr-daniel-nagase-a-courageous-doctor-speaks-out/.

[223] See Frank Bergman, "Leading Japanese Experts Warn: 'Self-Amplifying mRNA Vaccines' Will Trigger Worldwide Disaster," "Exposing the Darkness" Substack, September 22, 2024, https://lionessofjudah.substack.com/p/leading-japanese-experts-warn-self.

But, really, is the threat of this "alphavirus" enough to create the demand for this dangerous-sounding vaccine? However, it goes without saying that this ambiguity will not prevent the WHO from declaring another "public health emergency of international concern." If countries continue to follow the "science" of an organization run by a terrorist-affiliated failure, only death will result. Again, that is the plan—or rather plandemic: panic, knee-jerk response, slavish obedience, denial of obvious adverse effects. Decimation of the human population.

In 2021, the PCR testing for COVID-19 was questioned.[224] In 2023, the PCR kits were recalled by the CDC due to harmful bacteria contamination.[225] Demonstrations were conducted that the kits produced positive COVID-19 results in cases in which a papaya or cola produced a positive indication. What test will the "experts" propose using to "prove" people have an alphavirus? Will the results be equally as uncertain? It is remarkable how these "COVID-19 PCR test kits" were made available, financed and sold to governments around the world starting in 2017. The "19" in "COVID-19" indicates that the disease only arrived on earth in 2019.[226] How is that possible, one might ask. Perhaps it's man-made?

---

[224] Emily Anthes, "C.D.C. Virus Tests Were Contaminated and Poorly Designed, Agency Says," *New York Times*, December 15, 2021, https://www.nytimes.com/2021/12/15/health/cdc-covid-tests-contaminated.html.

[225] Alexander Tin, "Thousands of COVID tests recalled over bacteria risk, FDA warns," CBS News, May 5, 2023, https://www.cbsnews.com/news/covid-tests-recall-bacteria-fda-roche-biosensor/.

[226] "Coronavirus/COVID-19 Facts and FAQs," California Department of Corrections and Rehabilitation, https://www.cdcr.ca.gov/covid19/wp-content/uploads/sites/197/2020/03/R_CORONAVIRUS-FACTS.pdf.

Now, spin the "benefit" of this self-amplifying vaccine in a single person, let alone the benefit of the vaccine components spreading to others. I dare you. If a known and declared side effect is present, there is a distinct legal issue. Add to the mix the spread, the "secondhand smoke" component, and another class of potential litigants.

But of course, if the harm to people takes place in a country in which litigation is limited or prevented by the style of governance and lack of personal rights, such as in a communist dictatorship, culpability is not an issue.

Take for example, the Socialist Republic of Vietnam. As of this writing, Vietnam is conducting human trials.[227] Over nine thousand Vietnamese were infected with the alphavirus-based replicon "vaccine." That trial is in phase one, two and three of human studies. It may be possible that there has already been leakage of genetic material from the ARCT-154, a self-amplifying mRNA COVID-19 vaccine, into animals and insects in Vietnam. But I'm sure they are taking strong preventive measures, perhaps following the Wuhan lab protocols. After all, faithful communists and evil scientists share information.

If someone outside of the study group contracts a cold or flu with the ARCT-154 gene present, it may indicate that the virus is already on the loose. If we find those genes in the natural populations of alphaviruses that infect animals and insects, is it already too late?

---

[227] Nhân Thi Hồ et al., "Safety, immunogenicity and efficacy of the self-amplifying mRNA ARCT-154 COVID-19 vaccine: pooled phase 1, 2, 3a and 3b randomized, controlled trials," *Nature Communications* 15 (2024): 4081, https://www.nature.com/articles/s41467-024-47905-1.

Is Vietnam's viral endeavor a by-product of the WHO's scheme to promote "virus sharing"?

> Influenza virus sharing is vital to global pandemic preparedness. The sharing of viruses facilitates pandemic risk assessment, the development of candidate vaccine viruses, updating of diagnostic reagents and test kits, and surveillance for resistance to antiviral medicines.[228]

Of course, by describing its efforts to ensure that every mad scientist on the planet has the means and motivation to concoct a global extinction candidate, the WHO is killing many birds with one stone: the die-off of the human race, the promotion of minions willing to facilitate in the extinction, and a means to bring the few survivors to their knees. A healthy remnant will be needed as the slave class for the elites as they emerge from their underground shelters after the viral apocalypse.

We used to trust government medical scientists. Before 2020, we believed that we could rely upon this highly touted group of selfless, health-ensuring superstars to use their superior talents and brain power to protect us. That trust has been destroyed following the COVID-19 plandemic. We discovered that many, even most of them, to be under performing, self-serving, power hungry, wealth, and fame-absorbed snakes. As a mere extension of their pharma masters, they were revealed as willing and eager minions with an uncanny penchant to lie, obfuscate, and even promote

---

[228] "Virus Sharing," World Health Organization, https://www.who.int/initiatives/global-influenza-surveillance-and-response-system/virus-sharing.

human suffering. They were unrepentant even upon exposure as frauds. They were presented naked to the public for their spreading of wholly unscientific mask mandates, social-distancing edicts, lockdown assurances, and insistence on forced injections.

It only takes a single instance of an artificial gene present in the environment to pose significant potential harm. Think of the consequences of birds or insects as viral delivery mechanisms. The WHO would swoop in with another "public health emergency of international concern" declaration.

All weapons in the Owners' health "protection" arsenal would be deployed. To prevent the spread, the quarantines and other mandates would be enforced—at the point of a gun, literally. Imagine people in solitary confinement, animals (including pets) slaughtered, and insects eradicated. Quarantines would be immediate, incontestable, and indeterminate. Otherwise, the man-made gene could spread around the world, across multiple species, and nearly impossible to eliminate. Seemingly harsh measures such as eradication would be promoted and even accepted as completely necessary.

CHAPTER 6

THE UNITED NATIONS AGENDA 2030: THE SUSTAINABILITY ENTRAPMENT GAMBIT

W e are facing a global coup d'état, pursued with the most efficient organization and spread across all sectors of public administration. The common denominator of this ideological warfare is the aversion to natural law and the monetization—that is, the transformation into commodities—of all aspects of human life. This darkness is the combination of death and money that is repeated in all the programmatic points of the United Nations' 2030 Agenda, so that even those who do not share its crazy ideas have an economic interest in going along with them or cooperating in their implementation.

The United Nations (UN)'s *2030 Agenda for Sustainable Development* was adopted by all of its member states in 2015.

Originally, the agenda was called "Agenda 21."[229] The UN has promoted the agenda as the blueprint for "peace and prosperity" for everyone,[230] focusing on the themes of sustainability, poverty eradication, and environmental protection. Per the United Nations Department of Economic and Social Affairs Sustainable Development Goals website:[231]

> At its heart are the 17 Sustainable Development Goals (SDGs), which are an urgent call for action by all countries—developed and developing—in a global partnership. They recognize that ending poverty and other deprivations must go hand-in-hand with strategies that improve health and education, reduce inequality, and spur economic growth—all while tackling climate change and working to preserve our oceans and forests.[232]

While the seventeen enumerated goals sound like the solution for all failed human endeavors on our planet, the reality is quite the opposite, as their sinister intention is to eliminate all private property rights, borders, and seven billion people. The Owners intend to enslave the remnant of humanity and live blissful lives

---

[229] "Agenda 21," Sustainable Development Goals Knowledge Platform, December 2022, https://sustainabledevelopment.un.org/outcomedocuments/agenda21.

[230] "The 17 Goals," United Nations, Department of Economic and Social Affairs, https://sdgs.un.org/goals.

[231] United Nations, "Transforming our World: The 2030 Agenda for Sustainable Development," https://sustainabledevelopment.un.org/content/documents/21252030%20Agenda%20for%20Sustainable%20Development%20web.pdf?ref.

[232] "The 17 Goals."

without the useless eaters getting in the way. The seventeen pro-
pagandized goals are as follows:

Goal 1: End poverty in all its forms everywhere

Goal 2: End hunger, achieve food security and
improved nutrition and promote sustainable
agriculture

Goal 3: Ensure healthy lives and promote well-
being for all at all ages

Goal 4: Ensure inclusive and equitable quality
education and promote lifelong learning opportunities for all

Goal 5: Achieve gender equality and empower
all women and girls

Goal 6: Ensure availability and sustainable management of water and sanitation for all

Goal 7: Ensure access to affordable, reliable, sustainable and modern energy for all

Goal 8: Promote sustained, inclusive and sustainable economic growth, full and productive
employment and decent work for all

Goal 9: Build resilient infrastructure, promote inclusive and sustainable industrialization and foster innovation

Goal 10: Reduce inequality within and among countries

Goal 11: Make cities and human settlements inclusive, safe, resilient and sustainable

Goal 12: Ensure sustainable consumption and production patterns

Goal 13: Take urgent action to combat climate change and its impacts

Goal 14: Conserve and sustainably use the oceans, seas and marine resources for sustainable development

Goal 15: Protect, restore and promote sustainable use of terrestrial ecosystems, sustainably manage forests, combat desertification, and halt and reverse land degradation and halt biodiversity loss

Goal 16: Promote peaceful and inclusive societies for sustainable development, provide access to justice for all and build effective, accountable and inclusive institutions at all levels

Goal 17: Strengthen the means of implementation and revitalize the Global Partnership for Sustainable Development[233]

Coming from a business background, my immediate question in reaction to this fanciful wish list is, how does anyone measure any of these goals to determine true progress let alone ultimate achievement? Some nations are sure to fall short of achieving one or more of these dreams. How will we know? What is to be believed from member states ruled by tyrants with a track record of being less than honest? Let's just throw out a wild example—Communist China. And since I'm pitching, let me throw out just one not-so-random example of Communist Chinese Party lies—the origin of COVID-19. Sounds related, yes?

Even the World Health Organization is led by the Chinese Communist Party (CCP)-anointed Tedros Adhanom Ghebreyesus,[234] who parroted every false report and notion put out by the CCP regarding the bioweapon. Communist China has set him up as the fall guy for covering up the leak.[235] Your veracity must be pretty shot when even your own puppet master rats you out. Monarchies and dictatorships were the norm for national leadership until the United States created a constitu-

---

[233] "The 17 Goals."

[234] Peter Hasson, "China Helped Put This Man In Charge Of the World Health Organization—Is It Paying Off?" The National Interest, March 23, 2020, https://nationalinterest.org/blog/buzz/china-helped-put-man-charge-world-health-organization%E2%80%94-it-paying-136002.

[235] Joe McDonald, "China health officials lash out at WHO chief, defend search for origin of COVID-19," PBS News, April 8, 2023, https://www.pbs.org/newshour/world/china-health-officials-lash-out-at-who-chief-defend-search-for-origin-of-covid-19.

tional republic.[236] Speaking of veracity, we had to scour through dozens of search results to find one that properly defines the US as a republic, not today's popular false notion of a pure democracy. The 2030 Agenda creates the new framework for a return to governance of, by, and for the autocrats. The Owners are salivating at the prospect. In regards to the sustainability goals, it should go without saying, but things that cannot be measured cannot be obtained. Call it Todd's "Rule of the Obvious."

The 2030 Agenda is more likely to lock nations into a cycle of dependency and control than liberate them and generate prosperity for all. The UN agenda is reminiscent of the CCPs "Belt and Road Initiative."[237] That new silk road was promoted by the CCP as a gift to the world, a glorious and noble global infrastructure development program. Emperor Xi's international sales force painted visions of skies replete with rainbows and butterflies. Just sign here; you'll just need to agree to it and read it later. Trust us.

In reality, the "Belt and Road" railroad was merely a thinly veiled entrapment scheme, consummated with bribes,[238] bathed in false promises, awash with resulting structural collapse and numerous uncompleted projects, and culminating in bankrupt

---

[236] See "Republic vs Democracy," U.S. Constitution.net, May 4, 2024, https://www.usconstitution.net/republic-vs-democracy/.

[237] Nectar Gan and Simone McCarthy, "China is celebrating a decade of the Belt and Road Initiative. What is it about?" CNN, October 16, 2023, https://www.cnn.com/2023/10/16/china/china-bri-explainer-xi-jinping-intl-hnk/index.html.

[238] Jonathan E. Hillman, "Corruption Flows Along China's Belt and Road," Center for Strategic and International Studies, January 18, 2019, https://www.csis.org/analysis/corruption-flows-along-chinas-belt-and-road.

and enslaved nations.[239] The now many bridges to nowhere, crippling debt, and domestic workforce now ruled by nasty Mandarin-speaking whip-crackers may be a disappointment to the peasants but at least the leaders of the now entrapped nations received generous retirement packages. The growing gulag of CCP slaves bow to their new master, the ever-smirking Pooh Bear of Beijing, Xi Jinping. The UN model may be different, but the results will surely be the same, only on a grander scale. According to the UN, the SDGs are the "heart" of the 2030 Agenda. Unfortunately for the Owners, they only have hearts of stone, and by extension, their UN weapon is equally devoid of true caring.

All of their initiatives, programs, and pleas to the world are mere siren calls to lure our ships onto the rocks of destruction. Yet, the people of the world are awakening to their schemes for ultimate power and control. God willing, we will muster the courage, strength, and means to end this madness and defeat the Owners once and for all. It is time to get out the stakes and drive them through the very heart of this darkness.

Each goal has been created with specific targets and timetables. The targets are divided into sub-targets. Progress reports are filed annually. In order to understand the lengths to which the Owners have plotted out our futures to the last detail, let us go through the SDGs one at a time.

---

[239] Yoshihisa Komori, "China's Grandiose 'Belt and Road' Initiative Has Flopped," Japan Forward, November 3, 2023, https://japan-forward.com/chinas-grandiose-belt-and-road-initiative-has-flopped/.

Goal 1: End poverty in all its forms everywhere.[240]

According to the UN, global efforts to eradicate extreme poverty have faced significant setbacks by the COVID-19 pandemic and a series of major shocks during 2020–22. The pandemic caused extreme poverty to increase in 2020 for the first time in decades, reversing global progress by three years. "Recovery has been uneven, with low-income countries lagging behind."[241] With the ongoing polycrisis (pandemics, economic turmoil, etc.), ending poverty by 2030 appears increasingly out of reach, particularly in regions that lack the fiscal capacity to cope with economic stresses.

The lack of success, based upon the UN's own tracking of this impossible goal, demonstrates the fact that it was an ill-conceived notion created to fail in its stated goal but highly successful in its real goal—the transfer of wealth from donor nations to the UN's fleet of nongovernmental organizations.

Target 1.1: Extreme poverty levels returned to pre-pandemic levels in most countries by 2022, except in low-income countries where recovery has been slower. In 2022, 9% of the world's population or 712 million people were living in extreme poverty, an increase of 23 million people compared to 2019. If current trends continue, 590 million people, or 6.9% of the

---

[240] "Goal 1: End poverty in all its forms everywhere," Sustainable Development Goals, United Nations, https://www.un.org/sustainable development/poverty/.

[241] "1 No poverty," United Nations Statistics Division, https://unstats.un.org/sdgs/report/2024/Goal-01/.

world's population will still live in extreme poverty by 2030....

Target 1.2: Though data covering the period of COVID-19 are limited, the pandemic is likely to have slowed progress made in halving national poverty rates. Given historical trends, less than 30% of countries worldwide will have halved poverty by 2030.

Target 1.3: In 2023, only 28.2% of child globally received child cash benefits, compared to 22.1% in 2015, leaving 1.4 billion children aged 0–15 without coverage. To guarantee at least a basic level of social protection for all children, upper- and lower-middle-income countries would need to invest an additional US$98.1 billion and US$88.8 billion, respectively, while low-income countries would require an additional US$59.6 billion.

Target 1.5: Economic losses due to disasters remained stubbornly high in recent years and showed no sign of alleviation. Between 2015 and 2022 direct economic loss has been reported to exceed more than $115 billion per year worldwide, which amounted to 0.3% of the GDP of the reporting countries.

Target 1.a: Data from approximately 100 countries show that the proportion of total government spending on essential services (education, health and social protection) is approximately 50%, with an average of 60% amongst advanced economies and 40% amongst emerging market and developing economies. While this indicator trends slightly upward for both groups over the past two decades, the gap between them remains stable at approximately 20 percentage points.[242]

In an overview on this SDG, the UN describes the goal's importance.

Eradicating extreme poverty for all people everywhere by 2030 is a pivotal goal of the 2030 Agenda for Sustainable Development. Extreme poverty, defined as surviving on less than $2.15 per person per day at 2017 purchasing power parity, has witnessed remarkable declines over recent decades.

However, the emergence of COVID-19 marked a turning point, reversing these gains as the number of individuals living in extreme poverty

---

[242] "Progress and info, 2024," Goal 1, Department of Economic and Social Affairs, United Nations, https://sdgs.un.org/goals/goal1#progress_and_info.

increased for the first time in a generation by almost 90 million over previous predictions.[243]

So the 2030 Agenda is being derailed by the "Great Die-Off"? Or instead, straight out of the blocks, we are already learning that the seventeen SDGs are merely the public relations ploys of the Owners to fool the public into thinking that the UN is not merely another division of the "Army of Darkness." Please refer back to page one of the Owners' plan: step 1—depopulation, step 2—the remnant will own nothing and be happy, and step 3—we own you, shut up and obey.

The UN ends their commentary on their own little war on poverty with the following obvious conclusion:

> Poverty has many dimensions, but its causes include unemployment, social exclusion, and high vulnerability of certain populations to disasters, diseases and other phenomena which prevent them from being productive.[244]

As the UN states, "The share of the world's working population living in poverty has steadily decreased, from 8.4% in 2015 to 6.9% in 2023. However, nearly 241 million workers globally were still living in extreme poverty in 2023 and little positive change is expected in 2024."[245] This target will never be achieved, and in fact, poverty will only increase due to the negative effects of the other initiatives being forced upon the world by the Owners.

---

[243] "Goal 1: End poverty in all its forms everywhere."
[244] "Goal 1: End poverty in all its forms everywhere."
[245] "Progress and info, 2024," Goal 1.

TODD S. CALLENDER, J.D., JEROME R. CORSI, PH.D.,
AND CRAIG D. CAMPBELL, PH.D.

Goal 2: End hunger, achieve food security and improved nutrition and promote sustainable agriculture

Globally, hunger persists with nearly 1 in 10 of the world's population facing it in 2022, while 2.4 billion people experienced moderate to severe food insecurity. In the same year, nearly 60 per cent of countries worldwide saw significant increases in food prices due to conflicts and disrupted supply chains. Achieving zero hunger requires intensified efforts to transform food systems towards sustainability, resilience, and equity. Furthermore, accelerating improvements in diets, nutrition, health, and hygiene is crucial to meeting the SDG target of halving the number of children suffering from chronic undernutrition.[246]

So, just how is the UN and their meals-on-our-wheels program working?

Target 2.1: After a sharp increase following the COVID-19 pandemic, global hunger stabilized at around 9.2% of the population from 2021 to 2022. Between 691 and 783 million people faced hunger in 2022. Considering the midrange

---

[246] "Progress and info, 2024," Goal 2, Department of Economic and Social Affairs, United Nations, https://sdgs.un.org/goals/goal2#progress_and_info.

(735 million), 122 million more people faced hunger in 2022 than in 2019, when the prevalence stood at 7.9%. Additionally, an estimated 29.6% of the global population—2.4 billion people—were moderately or severely food insecure in 2022.

Target 2.2: Globally in 2022, an estimated 22.3% of children under age 5 (148 million) were affected by stunting, down from 24.6% in 2015 and 26.3% in 2012 (baseline year of WHO nutrition targets). Based on current trends, 1 out of 5 (19.5%) children under age 5 will be affected by stunting in 2030. Overweight affected 37.0 million children under age 5 (or 5.6%) and wasting affected 45 million (or 6.8%) in 2022.

Target 2.3: The income gap between small-scale and non-small-scale food producers remains significant. In 95% of countries with available data, the average annual income of small-scale producers is less than half that of nonsmall-scale producers. Among small-scale food producers, units headed by men typically generate higher incomes compared to those headed by women.

Target 2.a: In 2022, global public expenditures reached $36 trillion, of which $749 billion went towards agriculture—an all-time high. Agriculture represented 2.1% of total government expenditure, a recovery from the pandemic, and is only marginally below the 2019 level. Government expenditure on agriculture relative to the agriculture sector's contribution to GDP, measured in terms of the agriculture orientation index, declined from the 2015 baseline of 0.50 to 0.43 in 2021, but rebounded to 0.48 in 2022.

Target 2.b: Total notified annual agriculture export subsidy outlays fell from its peak of \$ 6.7 billion in 1999 to \$33 million in 2022. As of 1st January 2024, only least developed countries (LDCs) and net food importing developing countries are allowed to use certain forms of export subsidies.

Target 2.c: In 2022, the share of countries facing moderately to abnormally high food prices reached a new record-high of 58.1% after falling by more than half in 2021 from the previous historical peak of 48% in 2020. The 2022 share represented a nearly four-fold increase from the 2015–19 average levels of 15.2%. Major disruption to logistics and food supply chains, following the breakout of the war in Ukraine, resulted in higher food and energy prices, particularly during the first half of 2022."[247]

---

[247] "Progress and info, 2024," Goal 2.

In an overview on this SDG, the UN describes the goal's importance as follows:

> Goal 2 is about creating a world free of hunger by 2030. The global issue of hunger and food insecurity has shown an alarming increase since 2015, a trend exacerbated by a combination of factors including the pandemic, conflict, climate change, and deepening inequalities....
>
> It is projected that more than 600 million people worldwide will be facing hunger in 2030, high-lighting the immense challenge of achieving the zero hunger target....
>
> Investment in the agriculture sector is critical for reducing hunger and poverty, improving food security, creating employment and building resilience to disasters and shocks.[248]

Investment in the agriculture sector is essential to reduce hunger and poverty, improve food security, increase employment, and save us from the shock of disasters? Investment? By whom? Let us explore the change in land ownership in the US. Who is buying the land? Why, those saviors of mankind, the benevolent and ever helpful Bill Gates and the CCP. We are in safe hands to be sure.

---

[248] "Goal 2: Zero Hunger," Sustainable Development Goals, United Nations, https://www.un.org/sustainabledevelopment/hunger/.

Yes, Bill Gates has become the largest private land owner in America. According to *The Land Report*, Gates is numero uno:

> With almost 250,000 acres of highly produc-
> tive farm ground spread out over 17 states,
> the co-founder of MICROSOFT ranks as the
> nation's largest private farmland owner. Much
> of Gates's acreage was bought in huge tranches,
> including a group of farmland assets owned by
> the Canada Pension Plan Investment Board that
> was acquired in 2017 and the 2018 acquisition
> of the 100 Circles acreage in the Horse Heaven
> Hills of Eastern Washington. Those two pur-
> chases alone total an investment of more than
> $690 million in farmland assets.[249]

But is Gates buying up all that land in the US to reduce hunger and poverty? Let us hear an explanation from the Farmer Bill himself on a November 2023 episode of Trevor Noah's podcast:

> The decision to buy this land was made by peo-
> ple who help manage my money so that we get
> a good return, so that the Foundation can buy
> more vaccines.[250]

---

[249] "Bill Gates," *The Land Report*, https://landreport.com/land-report-100/bill-gates.

[250] Trevor Noah, host, *What Now? with Trevor Noah*, podcast, "Bill Gates Doesn't Need to Track You," Spotify Studios, November 21, 2023, https://open.spotify.com/episode/5WyKalyhN5XAr1mIqG4czh.

Really? Farmland is the best "investment" out there and the key to his prosperity? Not precious metals or crypto but dirt, and lots of it. Then we are to believe that Gates has no idea or input on the use of his fortune, and a crack team of accountants and estate planners are running the show? Sure. Nothing to see here, move on. Farmer Bill has spoken; it must be true. So let it be written, so shall it be done. Hail Pharoah Gates. I smell fish, stinking, rotting fish...wrapped in a hidden agenda that may not be discovered until the real reason the pharaoh traded in his asp collection to become Farmer Bill.

Goal 3: Ensure healthy lives and promote well-being for all at all ages

Achieving global health goals faces significant challenges, with progress slowing since 2015 in areas like maternal mortality, premature deaths from major noncommunicable diseases, and access to essential healthcare. Inequalities persist, especially among vulnerable populations, exacerbated by the climate crisis. To meet the SDG 3 targets by 2030, substantial investment and focus are needed to address these challenges, including tackling inequality and environmental factors. Urgent action is required to protect vulnerable groups and regions with high disease burdens.

Target 3.1: The global maternal mortality ratio marginally declined from 227 maternal deaths per 100,000 live births in 2015 to 223 in 2020. Reaching the global maternal mortality rate target of 70 per 100,00 live births will require an annual rate of reduction of 11.6% between 2021 and 2030. Two regions, subSaharan Africa and Southern Asia, accounted for around 87% (249,000) of the estimated global maternal deaths in 2020. Globally, skilled birth attendance rose from 80% in 2015 to 86% in 2023. There are, however, significant regional disparities, particularly in sub-Saharan Africa where the rate was just 73% in 2023.

Target 3.2: In 2022, global under-five deaths was 4.9 million, down from 9.9 million in 2000 and 6.0 million in 2015. The under-five mortality rate fell to 37 deaths per 1,000 live births in 2022—51% lower than in 2000 and a 14% decline since 2015. Similarly, the global neonatal mortality rate fell to 17 deaths per 1,000 live births in 2022, a 44% and 12% decrease from the 2000 and 2015 levels, respectively.

Target 3.3: Mixed progress is observed towards the SDG target of ending communicable diseases a). There were an estimated 1.3 million new HIV infections in 2022, 27% fewer than in 2015, and 38% fewer than in 2010. Increased access to HIV treatment has averted almost 20.8 million AIDS-related deaths in the past three decades. b). The reported global number of people newly diagnosed with TB was 7.5 million in 2022, the highest since 1995. On the other hand, the annual number of people who died from TB decreased in 2022 after two consecutive years of increase due to COVID-19 pandemic. c). In 2022, there were an estimated 249 million malaria cases globally, exceeding the pre-pandemic level of 233 million in 2019. d). In 2022, 1.62 billion people required interventions and care for neglected tropical diseases (NTDs), a 26.1% of decline from 2010. As of December 2023, 50 countries, territories and areas have eliminated at least one NTD.

Target 3.5: Global drug-related treatment coverage has decreased from approximately 11% in 2015 to under 9% in 2022. Alarmingly, treatment coverage for women consistently lags behind that for men across all regions. In 2022, over 13% of men with drug use disorders received treatment globally, while less than 6% of women did. Moreover, data on treatment coverage for alcohol use disorders vary widely, ranging from a mere 0.3% to a maximum of 14% in reporting countries.

Target 3.7: The proportion of women of reproductive age (aged 15–49 years) who have their need for family planning satisfied with modern methods increased slightly from 76.5% to 77.6% between 2015 and 2024. This corresponds to an increase of 75 million women of reproductive age using modern methods since 2015. The adolescent birth rate has globally declined from 47.2 births per 1,000 girls and women aged 15 to 19 years in 2015 to 40.7 in 2024.

Target 3.8: The proportion of the population not covered by essential health services decreased by about 15% between 2000 and 2021, with minimal progress made after 2015. In 2021, about four and a half billion people were not covered by essential health services.

Target 3.a: In 2022, the global prevalence of current tobacco use among the population aged 15+ was estimated at 20.9%. This translates to around 1.25 billion adult tobacco users in the world. The prevalence has declined since 2015 when it was 23.9%, and the number of users has decreased by 50 million.

Target 3.b: Coverage of the third dose of vaccine protecting against diphtheria, tetanus, and pertussis (DTP-3) recovered to 84% in 2022, an improvement from 81% in 2021 but still below the 2019 level of 86%. In 2022, 20.5 million children remained vulnerable to vaccine-preventable diseases. The current 2-dose measles vaccine coverage of 74% is insufficient to prevent outbreaks. HPV vaccine declined significantly during the pandemic, but 2022 saw the first encouraging signs of recovery in vaccination with 15% full scheduled coverage among girls.

Target 3.c: While a recent study shows that the projected global shortage of health workers by 2030 has reduced from 18 million to 10 million, the aging of the population induces an increased health need and further widens this gap. An additional 1.8 million health workers are needed in fifty-four countries (mostly from high-income countries) just to maintain the current age-standardized density of health workers.[251]

The UN also gives this overview for the goal:

Sustainable Development Goal 3 of the 2030 Agenda for Sustainable Development is to "ensure healthy lives and promoting well-being for all at all ages". The associated targets aim to reduce the global maternal mortality ratio; end preventable deaths of newborns and children; end the epidemics of AIDS, tuberculosis, malaria and other communicable diseases; reduce mortality from non-communicable diseases; strengthen the prevention and treatment of

---

[251] "Progress and info, 2024," Goal 3, Department of Economic and Social Affairs, United Nations, https://sdgs.un.org/goals/goal3#progress_and_info.

substance abuse; halve the number of deaths and
injuries from road traffic accidents; ensure universal access to sexual and reproductive healthcare services; achieve universal health coverage;
and reduce the number of deaths and illnesses
from hazardous chemicals and pollution.[252]

The UN's assessment of their 2023 goal progress indicates
this about the influence of the pandemic: "The pandemic and
other ongoing crises are hindering progress in achieving SDG3,
exacerbating existing health inequalities and threatening progress
towards universal health coverage. As a result, 68 million children
are known to be un- or under-vaccinated as of 2022 from TB and
malaria increased."[253]

So, is being unvaccinated or under-vaccinated a bad thing or
a good thing? Based on the prior chapter in this book, I vote for
the latter.

The World Bank is fully dedicated to the success of the seventeen SDGs and especially the one that concentrate on health.
In measuring the progress of SDG3, the World Bank supports
the findings of the Center for Global Health, which reports the
following:

---

[252] "Health and population," Department of Economic and Social Affairs,
United Nations, https://sdgs.un.org/topics/health-and-population.
[253] "Progress and info, 2024," Goal 3.

SDGs reinforce health as a political priority and
set an ambitious agenda [254]

- The 2030 Agenda for Sustainable Development has rein-
forced global health as a political priority.
- Healthy populations are critical to sustainable development.
- Health is also an outcome and indicator of progress that
reflects the success of many goals and the 2030 Agenda
as a whole.[255]

So, the World Bank is involved in the SDGs? It's more than
involved with promotion of the SDGs; the World Bank Group
entered into a treaty with the UN back during the UN's founding:

> The World Bank Group has a treaty-based rela-
> tionship with the United Nations (UN) that
> dates back to its founding, and through that rela-
> tionship, works to build a partnership that sup-
> ports Member States and contributes to effective
> development outcomes while preserving the dis-
> tinct mandates of each institution. Over the years,
> the WBG has collaborated with the UN in nearly

---

[254] Stefano Vella MD, "Measuring Progress in SDGs," Center for
Global Health (Istituto Superiore di Sanità), https://thedocs.
worldbank.org/en/doc/274691605003514448-0050022020/original/
12ISSMEASURINGPROGRESSINSDG3HEALTH.pdf.

[255] Stefano Vella MD, "Measuring Progress in SDGs," Center for Global Health
(Istituto Superiore di Sanità), https://thedocs.worldbank.org/en/doc/
274691605003514448-0050022020/original/12ISSMEASURING
PROGRESSINSDG3HEALTH.pdf.

every region and sector, and its engagement has deepened since the adoption of the Millennium Development Goals (MDGs), and now with the Sustainable Development Goals (SDGs).[256]

It sounds like a partnership. The World Bank is heavily invested in the UN and SDG. Who is the majority partner? I am guessing the one with the vault.

Goal 4: Ensure inclusive and equitable quality education and promote lifelong learning opportunities for all

SDG4 is a key enabler of most other SDGs. Unfortunately, global progress in education has not been fast enough. Only 58% of students worldwide achieved at least the minimum proficiency level in reading at the end of primary schooling in 2019. A large share of countries is moving backwards in learning outcomes at the end of lower secondary school. Improvement in upper secondary completion rate has slowed since 2015. Some regions, including sub-Saharan Africa, are facing teacher shortages, high student-teacher ratios, and inadequate training and lack of professional development opportunities for teachers. Accelerating progress towards SDG

---

[256] "World Bank Group and the 2030 Agenda," World Bank Group, https:// www.worldbank.org/en/programs/sdgs-2030-agenda.

4 should be prioritized as it will have a catalytic impact on achieving the overall 2030 Agenda.

Target 4.1: Completion rates in primary and lower secondary level education continue on an upward curve while the percentage of young people completing upper secondary school increased from 53% in 2015 to 59% in 2023. This increase, however is at a slower pace relative to progress in the preceding eight year period and such improvements do not always result in positive learning outcomes. Between 2018 and 2022, based on learning outcomes at the end of lower secondary school across 81 OECD and partner countries, mean performance in mathematics fell by a record 15 points while in reading fell 10 points. However, reading and mathematics scores had been declining for these countries prior to 2015, suggesting that COVID-19 explains only part of the decline. A complex set of factors affect the education systems of upper-middle income and high-income countries.

Target 4.2: Data from 76 mainly low- and middle-income countries from 2015 to 2023 shows that approximately two-thirds of young children are developmentally on track, with no significant gender differences. However, there are wide variations among countries and regions. In 2022, globally, 7 out of 10 children participated in organized learning one year before reaching official primary school age. Despite a 1.5 percentage point decline during the COVID-19 pandemic, participation levels have started to recover and return to pre-pandemic levels.

Target 4.3: In countries with recent data, around one-sixth of individuals aged 15–64 have participated in education and training. Participation is significantly higher among youth aged 15–24 compared to those aged 24–55, with an average participation rate of nearly 50% across most regions. However, less than 3% of older adults aged 25–55 engage in education and training in most regions.

Target 4.5: Socioeconomic disparities are prevalent in education, affecting various indicators. Global and regional parity ratios may hide gender inequalities within countries, disadvantaging either girls or boys. Disparities based on location or household wealth are more pronounced, with rural or less affluent families facing greater challenges. These gaps widen at higher education levels, leading to increased dropout rates and fewer opportunities for those from disadvantaged backgrounds.

Target 4.a: Only half of all primary schools have the basic infrastructures and materials to provide an adequate schooling experience to pupils with disabilities and one in five primary schools globally does not have single-sex sanitation facilities. On average, 44% of primary schools, 56% of lower secondary schools and 69% of upper secondary schools had access to Internet in 2022, almost double the rates in 2021. At the upper secondary level, 91% of schools have access to electricity, 81% have computers for pedagogical use and 69% of schools are connected to the internet.[257]

Let me offer one disclaimer before diving into this one. I know it goes without saying, but just to avoid confusion: In regards to "equitable education for all," behind the closed doors at the UN whispers were heard as they drafted this little nugget. Naturally, "all" does not include the American poor, white, rural Christians in areas like the Appalachians. Again, that goes without saying, so let us proceed, undaunted:

Quality education and lifelong learning opportunities for all are central to ensuring a full and productive life to all individuals and to the realization of sustainable development. Despite considerable progress in school enrolment, millions

---

[257] "Progress and info, 2024," Goal 4, Department of Economic and Social Affairs, United Nations, https://sdgs.un.org/goals/goal4#progress_and_info.

of children remain out of school, especially where educational systems struggle to keep up with population growth. Even when more children are enrolled, many do not acquire the basic skills. Quality education is hampered by the lack of trained teachers and adequate school facilities. Achieving this Goal will require intensified efforts, particularly in sub-Saharan Africa and Southern Asia, targeted to vulnerable populations, specifically persons with disabilities, indigenous people, refugees and the rural poor.[258]

"Intensified efforts." A focus on refugees. It is hard not to focus on the intensified effort it takes to deal with the alarming and increasing numbers of "refugees" flooding into the Western world from other places. If the flow were to be caused by regulated and legal processes—requests filed and considered, needs of the individual and country balanced, and resettlement of those legally admitted handled in an orderly way—it would work.

However, providing equitable quality education to an invading hoard, a veritable army made up of a combination of needy, desperate, criminal, violent, and crazy elements is difficult to regulate. The Migration Policy Institute's press release goes into more detail:

The increase in the number of immigrant-background children in U.S. schools over the last

---

[258] "Goal 4: Ensure inclusive and equitable quality education and promote lifelong learning opportunities for all," United Nations Statistics Division, https://unstats.un.org/sdgs/report/2017/goal-04/.

decade has challenged K-12 educators to expand their capacity to serve students who may have unique characteristics and particular needs.

School systems tend to focus on children through the lens of their English proficiency level, which has meant a limited scope and availability of data on immigrant students as a distinct group. But these data limitations can hinder the ability of educators and policymakers to improve instruction and services for recently arrived immigrant students, many of whom arrive with limited or interrupted education and have experienced trauma. They also are more likely than their peers to live in low-income and linguistically isolated households, which are factors associated with academic struggle."[259]

So, some people receive more equal treatment than others. Take the case of "migrants" and "refugees." Illegal border crossers into Western nations have quickly morphed since January 21, 2021, into a full-blown invasion by the unvetted masses. From the Middle East to North Africa, to South and Central America, the floodgates were opened and those regions exported their "less fortunates," without control. For example, the communist country of Venezuela, and other rogue nations, took full advantage of

---

[259] "As School Systems Receive Growing Numbers of Recently Arrived Immigrant Students, Better Data Are Needed on Characteristics of this Group," press release, Migration Policy Institute, October 19, 2023, https://www.migrationpolicy.org/news/recently-arrived-immigrant-students.

complicit Western leaders, and opened their prisons, mental institutions, and poverty centers and promoted waves of movement to the United States and Europe.

Aided and abetted by the UN and its International Organization for Migration, along with a plethora of "charitable organizations" and other NGOs, the invasion grew in scope and continued until January 20, 2025. With the new American administration, the US borders are being secured, legal citizens are again being protected, and the illegals are being returned to their countries of origin, whether they like it or not. Equal treatment under the law is being restored after four years of lawlessness.

Goal 5: Achieve gender equality and empower all women and girls

> Progress towards gender equality is clearly off track. Harmful practices like child marriage and female genital mutilation are decreasing, but not fast enough to keep pace with population growth. Gender parity, especially in women's participation in public life and managerial roles, remains distant. At the current rate, achieving gender parity in managerial positions will take 176 years. Many women still lack control over their sexual and reproductive health, and violence against women persists. Urgent action is needed to challenge biased social norms, eliminate harmful practices, and change discriminatory laws. Increasing women's leadership roles

and investments in gender equality are crucial at national, regional, and global levels.

Target 5.1: Based on data collected in 2022 in 120 countries, 55% of the countries lacked non-discrimination laws that prohibit direct and indirect discrimination against women and half of the countries continued to lack quotas for women in the national parliament.

Target 5.3: Globally, around 640 million girls and women were married before age 18, with India accounting for one-third. While progress has reduced child marriage, still, one in five young women (19%) are married before 18, down 22% in 2013. Despite averting 68 million child marriages in this period, the pace isn't sufficient to eliminate the practice by 2030.

Over 230 million girls and women worldwide are estimated have undergone female genital mutilation as of 2024, an increase of 30 million compared to the last estimate in 2016.

Target 5.4: On an average day, women spend about 2.5 times as many hours in unpaid domestic and care work as men, according to the latest data between 2000 and 2022.

Target 5.5: Progress in women's political participation remains slow. As of January 1, 2024, women held 26.9% of seats in national parliaments worldwide, marking a modest increase of 4.6 percentage points since 2015 (22.3%). In local governments, the participation was higher at 35.5% as of 1 January 2023. While global employment sees nearly 40% representation from women, they only held 27.5% of management positions in 2022, a notable decrease from 28.5% in 2021.

Target 5.a: In one in three of the 49 countries with data, less than 50% of women and men have ownership or secure rights over agricultural land. Furthermore, there is a notable disparity between women and men's agricultural land ownership, with men owning land at least twice as often as women in almost half of the countries. Legal protections for women's land rights are low or not existent in approximately 58% of the reporting countries.

Target 5.b: In 2023, 78% of the global population aged 10 and above owned a mobile phone. Women were approximately 8% less likely to own a mobile phone than men in 2023, a decrease from 10% in 2020.

Target 5.c: Data from 105 countries and areas for the period 2018–2021 show that 26% of countries globally have comprehensive systems to track and make public allocations for gender equality, 59% have some features of a system, and 15% do not have minimum elements of these systems.[260]

Did you know that the world is not on track to achieve gender equality goals by 2030?! So, what exactly is gender equality anyway? God-based humanity on two distinct genders, male and female, period.

Genesis 1:27 (ESV)

So God created man in his own image, in the image of God he created him; male and female he created them.

But, according to Shaziva Allarakha, MD, in her/his/its article, "What are the 72 Other Genders?" published on MedicineNet,[261] God may have started with two genders, but the doctor and the rest of the all-knowing among us believe that there may be seventy-two more. What is a gender identity?

---

[260] "Progress and info, 2024," Goal 5, Department of Economic and Social Affairs, United Nations, https://sdgs.un.org/goals/goal5#progress_and _info.

[261] Shaziya Allarakha, "What Are the 72 Other Genders?" MedicineNet, February 9, 2024, https://www.medicinenet.com/what_are_the_72_other_ genders/article.htm.

In today's age, one does not need to fit in with regards to their choices, including their gender identity.

- Gender is no more regarded as a binary concept where one can either be a male or a female.
- It has emerged as a continuum or spectrum where one can identify themselves as any of the gender identities.

The term gender identity means how a person identifies themselves concerning their gender. It may be regardless of their anatomy or genetics. Thus, a person may identify themselves as male, female, none, both, or some other category independent of their genitals.

The idea is to make everyone feel comfortable in their skin irrespective of what gender they were assigned at birth.

I am so confused. How are the UN's gender equality goals to be realized if we now have to equalize seventy-two variations? It was a herculean task with just two, but with six dozen total? Now to set the record straight for the imagineers of new genders: There are only two, and they will never be equal. But they are complimentary, designed with magnificent differences, and those differences combined make God's master plan ingenious.

Goal 6: Ensure availability and sustainable management of water and sanitation for all

None of the SDG 6 targets are on track to be met. As of 2022, 2.2 billion people were without access to safely managed drinking water and 3.5 billion lacked access to safely managed sanitation. Between 2002 and 2021 droughts affected more than 1.4 billion people. As of 2022, roughly half of the world's population experienced severe water scarcity for at least part of the year, while one quarter faced 'extremely high' levels of water stress. Climate change worsens these issues, posing significant risks to social stability. While transboundary river and lake basins are home to approximately 40% of the world's population and are shared by 153 countries, less than a fifth of these countries have operational arrangements for cooperation in place for all their transboundary waters. Coordinated global action on integrated water management, addressing the impacts of climate change on water resources, and better management of shared waters are key to restoring focus on the Goal.

Targets 6.1 and 6.2: Between 2015 and 2022, the population using safely managed drinking water increased from 69% to 73%, the population using safely managed sanitation increased from 49% to 57% and the population using basic

hygiene services increased from 67% to 75%.
Achieving universal coverage of safely managed drinking water, safely managed sanitation,
and basic hygiene services by 2030 will require
respective increases of 6x, 5x, and 3x in the current global rates of progress.

Target 6.3: Among the 73 countries reporting on
both total wastewater generation and total wastewater treatment in 2022, 76% of total wastewater
flows received at least some treatment. Of the 42
countries that specified the level of treatment,
60% of total wastewater flows were safely treated
(i.e. at least secondary treatment). In all world
regions, many rivers, lakes and aquifers are still in
good condition—as of 2023, 56% of water bodies assessed in 120 countries have good water
quality. However, countries that implement the
most extensive monitoring programmes show
that water quality is degrading since 2017.

Target 6.4: Water use efficiency rose from $17.4/
m3 in 2015 to $20.8/m3 in 2021, a 19% increase.
At the global level, the water stress level reached
an average level of 18.6% in 2021 but it hides
large regional variations as some regions in the
world show critical water stress levels which may
compromise their economic and social development. Globally, water stress level has slightly
increased by 3% from 2015 to 2021.

Target 6.5: Global progress on implementing integrated water resources management remains slow—49% in 2017, 54% in 2020, 57% in 2023, not on track to reach the 2030 target (91%). Only 43 out of 153 countries have operational arrangements in place for 90% or more of their shared transboundary waters (rivers, lakes and aquifers), and more than 20 countries have no operational arrangements in place for any of their transboundary waters. Since 2020 only around ten new arrangements for transboundary water cooperation have been adopted.

Target 6.6: The world has experienced a net increase in permanent surface water between 2005 and 2022, much of which resulted from climate change and reservoir filling. While this global net gain is positive, it is important to recognize that the data also include losses of permanent water in some regions linked to droughts and increased water demands.

Target 6.a: ODA [official development assistance] disbursements to the water sector increased between 2021 and 2022 by 10% to $8.5 billion, reversing a declining trend seen over the past five years."[262]

---

[262] "Progress and info, 2024," Goal 6, Department of Economic and Social Affairs, United Nations, https://sdgs.un.org/goals/goal6#progress_and_info.

Todd S. Callender, J.D., Jerome R. Corsi, Ph.D.,
and Craig D. Campbell, Ph.D.

With respect to the water-related goals, we focus on two primary violators of water rights: Communist China and the current US administration.

First, Communist China and the CCP's exploitation of Tibet. In the article "China's Weaponization of Water in Tibet: A lesson for the Lower Riparian States," published in the *Journal of Indo-Pacific Affairs*, authors Neeraj Singh Manhas and Dr. Rahul M. Lad detail what rarely makes the news.

> Tibet, dubbed "Asia's water tower," boasts eight major transboundary river systems, including the Brahmaputra, Indus, and Mekong rivers, vital to three billion people in South and Southeast Asia. As an upper riparian state, China has contemplated dam construction and river diversion since 1989. Driven by internal economic motives and aspirations for regional dominance, China seeks to control water flow, impacting lower riparian states such as India, Bangladesh, Nepal, Bhutan, Myanmar, Thailand, Cambodia, Laos, and Vietnam. With approximately 87,000 dams built, China poses a historic threat, having already dammed most internal rivers. This article examines China's potential weaponization of Tibetan water, offering insights for lower

riparian states to prepare for contingencies and devise long-term strategies.[263]

Goal 7: Ensure access to affordable, reliable, sustainable and modern energy for all

In 2022, global electricity access declined for the first time in a decade, primarily due to disruptions from COVID-19 and the Ukraine conflict. Despite improvements in energy intensity and renewable energy growth, international financial flows for clean energy in developing countries remain insufficient. At the current rate, 660 million people will still lack electricity and 1.8 billion will not have access to clean cooking by 2030. To achieve universal access to energy by 2030, we need to expedite electrification efforts, boost investments in renewable energy, enhance energy efficiency, and establish supportive policies and regulatory frameworks.

Target 7.1: In 2022, global electricity access remained at 91%, but the number without access increased by 10 million from 2021 to 685 million people. Factors such as COVID-19 and the Ukraine conflict disrupted progress. Projections

---

[263] Neeraj Singh Manhas and Dr. Rahul M. Lad, "China's Weaponization of Water in Tibet: A Lesson for the Lower Riparian States," *Journal of Indo-Pacific Affairs*, March 12, 2024, https://www.airuniversity.af.edu/JIPA/Display/Article/3703876/chinas-weaponization-of-water-in-tibet-a-lesson-for-the-lower-riparian-states/.

suggest that by 2030, 660 million will still lack electricity. Sub-Saharan Africa accounted for 83% of deficit in 2022. However, Central and Southern Asia reduced their gap from 235 million in 2015 to 33 million in 2022. Annual progress slowed to 0.4% between 2020 and 2022, requiring a 1.08% increase until 2030 to meet the target.

In 2022, around 74% of the world used clean fuels for cooking. Yet, about 2.1 billion still relied on polluting fuels and technologies such as charcoal, coal, crop waste, dung, kerosene, and wood. The global access deficit decreased from 36% to 26% since 2015. However, current trends suggest a 21% shortfall in achieving universal access by 2030, leaving 1.8 billion without access to clean cooking by 2030.

Target 7.2: In 2021 the global share of renewable sources in total final energy consumption stood at 18.7%. Excluding traditional use of biomass, the share of modern renewable sources rose gradually from 10% in 2015 to 12.5% in 2021. The electricity sector led the charge with renewables, contributing 28.2% to total final electricity consumption. However, insufficient progress in the heat and transport sectors underscores the need for stronger conservation measures and policy actions. Tripling world's installed renewable energy generation agreed at the COP28 is an important step aligning with the SDG7.

Target 7.3: In 2021, the primary energy intensity improved by 0.8%, falling below both the 1.2% five-year average and the SDG 7.3 target of 2.6%. To meet the 2030 target, annual improvements must now average around 4%. The robust economic recovery in 2021 led to the largest annual rise in energy consumption in 50 years, exceeding 5%. This surge was driven by a shift towards energy-intensive industries and the resurgence of other demand sectors after lockdowns were lifted.

Target 7.a: In 2022, international public financial flows supporting clean energy in developing countries rose to $15.4 billion, a 25% increase from 2021 but still half of the 2016 peak of $28.5 billion. However, in 2023, it was anticipated a decrease in global five-year average flows by $450 million. The decreasing trend in these flows may hinder SDG 7 achievement, especially for LDCs, LLDCs and SIDS.

Target 7.b: Installed renewable energy capacity is on the rise worldwide, reaching 424 watts per person globally in 2022. Developed nations averaged 1,073 watts per person, while developing countries averaged 293 watts per person.

This represents an 8.5% increase from 2021, maintaining a steady compound annual growth rate of 8.1% over five-year periods.[264]

A perfect energy storm is developing. The expansion of data centers, AI, bitcoin mining, pot growing, and electric vehicle energy demands are increasing dramatically, and the sky is not the limit; it is only a launchpad. A Category 6 hurricane is brewing, and tech is the vortex.

> After more than 30 years of falling or flat demand for electricity, electric utilities are forecasting the nation will need the equivalent of about 34 new nuclear plants, or 38 gigawatts, over the next five years to supply power for data centers, electrification and new industry according to filings made to the Federal Energy Regulatory Commission and compiled by Grid Strategies....

> And those estimates don't necessarily include the growth of hard-to-track but disproportionately energy-hogging cryptocurrency or cannabis farming, which are estimated to be using up to 2.3% and 1%, respectively, of the nation's electricity. Energy demand in these industries has skyrocketed as the popularity of cryptocurrency and the legalization of marijuana have spread....

---

[264] "Progress and info, 2024," Goal 7, Department of Economic and Social Affairs, United Nations, https://sdgs.un.org/goals/goal7#progress_and_info.

The issue is also a global one, as a recent International Energy Agency report says electricity for data centers, including for AI and cryptocurrency, could double by 2026.[265]

Goal 8: Promote sustained, inclusive and sustainable economic growth, full and productive employment and decent work for all

Progress towards SDG 8 faces challenges from COVID-19 aftermath, trade tensions, rising debts in developing nations, conflicts, and geopolitical strains, collectively threatening global economic growth. While labour markets have shown resilience, uneven pandemic recovery, the declining protection of labor rights and emerging vulnerabilities erode social justice prospects. The report foresees a worsening labour market outlook, with higher unemployment and sluggish growth in 2024, exacerbating income inequality and jeopardizing equitable pay for women and decent work for young people. Achieving SDG 8 mandates policies fostering economic growth with a focus on social justice and inclusive employment.

---

[265] Kristi Swartz and Pam Radtke, "Data centers, bitcoin and EVs send utilities scrambling for more power," Canary Media, March 19, 2024, https://www.canarymedia.com/articles/electrification/data-centers-bitcoin-and-evs-send-utilities-scrambling-for-more-power.

Target 8.1: After a sharp 3.9% decline in 2020 due to the COVID-19 pandemic, the global economy rebounded with a 5.3% increase in real GDP per capita in 2021. However, growth slowed to 2.2% in 2022 and is forecasted to slow down further to 1.0% in 2023, before picking up slightly to 1.8% and 1.5% in 2024 and 2025, respectively. For LDCs [least-developed countries], real GDP growth dropped from 5.1% in 2019 to 0.7% in 2020, then recovered to 3.8% in 2021 and 4.6% in 2022. Growth is expected to rise to 4.4% and 5.5% in 2023 and 2024. However, it's projected to slow down to 4.9% in 2025.

Target 8.2: Productivity growth stagnated in 2022 and 2023, remaining below 0.5%. This sluggish trend stands in stark contrast to the pre-pandemic period of 2015 to 2019, where the rate exceeded 1.5%. The pandemic sharply interrupted this trend, with 2020 registering a marked decline as output fell faster than employment—though this was fully offset by a short-lived rebound of productivity during 2021. The recent slow productivity growth poses a risk to economic development and living standards, given its crucial role as a driver of growth.

Target 8.3: In 2023, over 2 billion workers globally were employed informally, accounting for

58.0% of the global workforce. This figure is expected to see a marginal decrease to 57.8% in 2024. The decline of the informality rate by less than a percentage point since 2015 is far too slow for widespread formalization to occur anytime soon.

Target 8.5: In 2023, the global unemployment rate not only rebounded, dipping below its pre-pandemic level, but also achieved a historic low since 2000, settling at 5.1%. However, projections indicate a slight increase in global unemployment in 2024, with approximately 2 million more individuals unemployed, leading to a 5.2% unemployment rate. Women and youth continue to experience higher unemployment rates compared to their male and adult counterparts worldwide and across most regions.

Target 8.6: In 2023, the global NEET (not in education, employment, or training) rate for young people was 21.7%, showing a significant decrease since 2020 and nearing the 2015 baseline of 21.8%. This rate is expected to persist through 2025. There is a critical need to intensify initiatives aimed at reducing NEET rates among youth, especially focusing on young women. Globally, young women are still more than twice as likely as young men to be NEET.

TODD S. CALLENDER, J.D., JEROME R. CORSI, PH.D.,
AND CRAIG D. CAMPBELL, PH.D.

Target 8.8: Globally, many workers face significant risks in their workplaces, and work accidents remain prevalent. In 11 out of 93 countries with data, more than 10 work-related fatalities per 100,000 workers were reported. Additionally, in half of the 96 countries with available data, the number of non-fatal injuries per 100,000 workers exceeded 641.

From 2015 to 2022, the global average level of national compliance with labor rights declined by 7%. This decline is observed across both developed and developing countries and has become more pronounced in all regions since 2020. Recent data indicates that ongoing crises have led to an increase in violations of labour rights in practice and, alarmingly, by violations of fundamental civil liberties of workers, employers, and their organizations.

Target 8.9: In 2022, tourism rebounded to 82% of its 2019 level, contributing 3.1% to global GDP. Lifted travel restrictions and pent-up demand drove this recovery, but regional differences persist. Oceania excluding Australia and New Zealand and SIDS still faced challenges, with tourism economic performance at 68% and 43% of pre-pandemic levels respectively.

Target 8.10: Since 2015, global access to finance has increased, but recent years show changes in access methods. The number of ATMs per 100,000 adults declined from 64.6 in 2015 to 63.9 in 2022, while commercial bank branches dropped from 15.0 to 13.7 per 100,000 adults. The COVID-19 pandemic has accelerated the shift towards digital financial access. This reflects a global decline in bank branches, except in Central Asia, Southern Asia, and sub-Saharan Africa.

Target 8.10: The Global Findex 2021 reports that despite 76% of adults having a financial account, 41% lack financial resilience. Financial resilience means being unable to access extra funds equivalent to 5% of their country's gross national income within 30 days of a financial shock like a health emergency or job loss. This varies by region, with South Asia being the least financially resilient (only 32%) and East Asia the most (77%).

Target 8.b: In 2023, less than half of the reporting countries (36 out of 87) had implemented a national strategy for youth employment. About one-third of these countries possess a strategy but lack clear evidence of its implementation, while one-fifth are in the process of developing one.[266]

Once again, the UN's purposely beyond-lofty stated goals fail as their real goal of wealth transfer continues on unimpeded by logic, accountability, or common sense.

Goal 9: Build resilient infrastructure, promote inclusive and sustainable industrialization and foster innovation

Since 2022, the manufacturing sector has faced stagnation, attributed to geopolitical instability, inflation, logistical challenges, rising energy costs, and a broader global economic slowdown. Globally, manufacturing's share in employment has regressed. While there has been progress in reducing CO_2 intensity in manufacturing, it falls short of 2030 target values. To expedite progress towards SDG 9, efforts should prioritize accelerating the green transition, strategically prioritizing sectors, and addressing inequalities in digital and innovation sectors.

Target 9.2: The manufacturing sector rebounded strongly in 2021 post-COVID, but growth has

---

[266] "Progress and info, 2024," Goal 8, Department of Economic and Social Affairs, United Nations, https://sdgs.un.org/goals/goal8#progress_and_info.

plateaued at around 2.7% since 2022, expected to continue in 2024. Despite this, global manufacturing value added per capita rose by 16% from 2015 to 2023, reaching $1,922 per capita. Regional gaps are stark, with Europe and Northern America hitting a record $4,986 per capita, contrasting with stagnant levels of $163 in sub-Saharan Africa.

Since 2015, global manufacturing employment has fluctuated. Starting at 14.3% in 2015, it dipped to 14.2% in 2020 but saw a marginal recovery in 2021. However, by 2022, it declined to 14.1%, with notable regional disparities. While sub-Saharan Africa and Central and Southern Asia saw slight increases, other regions experienced declines, with Australia and New Zealand recording the highest fall of 0.5 percentage points from 2021 to 2022. These trends highlight the ongoing impact of crises on manufacturing employment growth.

Target 9.3: Small enterprises face heightened vulnerability, particularly in low income countries. According to survey data spanning from 2006 to 2023, only 16.9% of small-scale manufacturing industries in sub-Saharan Africa had access to loans or lines of credit, compared to 45.4% in Latin America and the Caribbean. This underscores how global uncertainty hampers investment flow and financial access for small businesses, hindering their resilience and adoption of new technologies.

Target 9.4: Globally, CO2 emissions per unit of GDP have steadily declined by 11.5% from 2015 to 2021, with a reduction of 16% observed in the manufacturing sector. Despite these positive trends, global CO2 emissions from fuel combustion hit a record high of 33.6 gigatonnes in 2021, with manufacturing emissions also reaching their highest level since 2014 at 6.1 gigatonnes. These figures highlight the insufficient rate of reduction in CO2 emissions intensity to achieve a significant overall decrease in worldwide CO2 emissions.

Target 9.5: After a slowdown in 2020, global research and development (R&D) expenditure appeared to return to pre-pandemic levels in 2021, climbing from 1.72% of GDP in 2015 to 1.93% in 2021. However, many developing economies have R&D expenditure relative to GDP below 1%.

Target 9.5: The number of researchers per million inhabitants globally increased from 1,143 in 2015 to 1,352 in 2021, with Europe and Northern America, and Australia and New Zealand employing three times higher than the global level (i.e. 4,050 and 4,696 respectively in 2021). On the other hand, sub-Saharan Africa has been substantially lower, standing at 96 researchers per million inhabitants. Additionally, women remain underrepresented, comprising only 31.5% of all researchers worldwide in 2021.

Target 9.b: The gradual upward trend of medium and high-tech manufacturing value added in total value added, rising from 46.3% in 2015 to 46.9% in 2019, was briefly interrupted by the COVID-19 pandemic in 2020, dropping to 46.8%. Despite uncertainties and economic challenges, the sector displayed resilience with a slight decline of 0.67 percentage points in 2021. In Eastern and South Eastern Asia, this sector accounted for approximately 50.6% of total manufacturing in 2021, whereas in sub-Saharan Africa, it represented just 18.3%.

Target 9.c: Mobile broadband (3G or higher) is accessible to 95% of the world's population, up from 78% in 2015. In most developing countries, this type of access is the main way—and often the only way—to connect to the Internet. However, addressing the remaining 5% coverage gap poses challenges. Notably, in Oceania (excluding Australia and New Zealand), the gap remains significant at 31%. Although the gap in sub-Saharan Africa is shrinking, it still stands relatively high at 17%, particularly impacting central and western Africa.[267]

The use of the term "Oceania" to describe one of the geographic areas of the earth is particularly telling. In George Orwell's epic *1984*, "Oceania" is one of the three superstates comprising all areas on the planet. Is the UN showing its hand regarding its true rulership intentions on behalf of the Owners?

Goal 10: Reduce inequality within and among countries

Incomes of the poorest 40% of the population have generally grown faster than the national average in many countries and financial transfers during the pandemic boosted shared prosperity. However, over the past five years, the gap in per capita income growth between the poorest and richest countries has widened. In addition, discrimination based on age, gender, religion, race, or belief affects one in six people globally. The year 2023 marked a record high of 35.8 million refugees, and over 8,000 migrant deaths were recorded globally. Addressing both within- and between-country inequality necessitates equitable resource distribution, investment in education and skills development, implementation of

---

[267] "Progress and info, 2024" Goal 9, Department of Economic and Social Affairs, United Nations, https://sdgs.un.org/goals/goal9#progress_and_info.

social protection measures, combating discrim-ination, supporting marginalized groups, and fostering international cooperation for fair trade and financial systems.

Target 10.1: Among 124 countries with avail-able data, more than half have achieved income growth for the bottom 40% of the population at a rate higher than the national average. However, there are notable regional disparities. In 78% of countries in Northern America and Europe, the bottom 40% experienced faster income growth than the national average, while only 30% of countries in Central Asia and Southern Asia demonstrated this trend. Limited data from the pandemic period suggests that in most regions, financial transfers boosted shared prosperity in many countries by supporting the income growth of disadvantaged populations.

Target 10.3: The number of countries reporting on discrimination has increased by 37% since 2022. However, one person in six continues to encounter discrimination. Racial discrimination and discrimination based on age, gender, reli-gion or belief remain pervasive. While 7% of the population surveyed report being discriminated on the ground of social origin or socio-economic status, only less than a fifth of countries monitor this ground.

Target 10.4: The share of economic output earned by workers decreased from 54.1% in 2004 to 52.7% in 2021, amounting to an average decline of $568 (PPP) per worker. The pandemic exacerbated this situation, with economic output and labour income in 2021 still below 2019 levels in many regions. As earnings from work are crucial for the less well-off and vulnerable, the long-term decline in labour income share represents an upward pressure for inequality.

Target 10.5: In 2022, banks improved their overall performance compared to 2015 amid ongoing COVID-19 recovery. The proportion of countries reporting a return on assets (ROA) above one percent increased to 77.2% from 70% in 2021, with the median ROA rising from 1.34% to 1.56%. Asset quality also improved, with the median nonperforming loans to total loans ratio decreasing from 4.07% in 2021 to 3.52% in 2022. However, the capital buffer remained stable, with the median Tier 1 capital to risk-weighted assets at 16.8% in 2022, compared to 17% in 2021.

Target 10.7: In 2023, there were 8,177 migrant fatalities globally, marking the deadliest year on record, per data from IOM [International Organization for Migration]'s Missing Migrants Project. This underscores the urgent need for safe migration pathways, as people continue to risk their lives on irregular routes due to limited alternatives.

Target 10.7: At mid-2023, 35.8 million refugees under UNHCR's mandate, including other people in need of international protection, remained forcibly displaced due to war, conflict, persecution, human rights violations, and events seriously disturbing public order. This figure represents the highest total recorded to date and reflects increases due to new situations and no progress in resolving protracted refugee situations. In 2015, there were 213 refugees per 100,000 people worldwide, but by mid-2023, this figure doubled to 441 refugees per 100,000 people.

Target 10.c: The global average remittance costs as a proportion of the amount remitted dropped from 7.42% in 2016 to 6.18% in 2023. Corridors offering costs below 5% increased from 23% in 2016 to 75% in 2023. While progress is evident, sustained efforts are needed to meet the target 10.c.[268]

---

[268] "Progress and info, 2024" Goal 10, Department of Economic and Social Affairs, United Nations, https://sdgs.un.org/goals/goal10#progress_and_info.

Todd S. Callender, J.D., Jerome R. Corsi, Ph.D.,
and Craig D. Campbell, Ph.D.

Alas, the age-old conundrum: equality of opportunity versus equality of outcome, or in today's terms—equality versus equity.

Goal 11: Make cities and human settlements inclusive, safe, resilient and sustainable

More than half the world's population currently reside in cities. However, cities are grappling with a multitude of complex issues, made more difficult by rising global urban poverty levels in the wake of COVID-19. From rising slum populations, insufficient public transport, city expansion outpacing population growth to threats to critical infrastructure and disruption of basic services by disasters, it is essential that cities are equipped to adequately handle these challenges. As the world turns more urban, with nearly 70% of the global population projected to reside in cities by 2050, critical infrastructure, affordable housing, efficient transport and essential social services are crucial for creating resilient, sustainable cities for all.

Target 11.1: In 2022, 24.8% of the urban population lived in slums or slum-like conditions, slightly lower than 25% in 2015, but higher than 24.2% in 2020. The total number of slum dwellers was 1.12 billion in 2022, 130 million more than in 2015. Over 85% of slum dwellers were concentrated in Central and Southern Asia (334 million), Eastern and South-Eastern Asia (362 million), and subSaharan Africa (265 million). Sub-Saharan Africa has the highest percentage of urban population living in slums, at 53.6%. Projections suggest that sub-Saharan Africa will experience the greatest proportional increase in slum dwellers, with an additional 360 million expected by 2030. This emphasizes the urgent need for a comprehensive approach to address the urban housing crisis, including providing varied housing options and equitable access to basic services.

Target 11.2: Data collected in 2023 from 2,039 cities across 188 countries shows that 6 out of 10 urban residents globally have convenient public transport access, with notable gaps between developed and developing regions. In LDCs, only 4 out of 10 people have access, compared to 8 out of 10 in more developed regions. Urgent investments are needed to expand access, especially in impoverished urban areas in developed countries.

Target 11.3: Data from 1217 cities across 185 countries shows that cities are sprawling faster than they are densifying. Between 2000 and 2020, cities expanded up to 3.7 times faster than they densified. Globally, sprawl averaged 5.6% annually, while densification was only 1.5%.

Despite a slight decline in sprawl rates from 2010 to 2020, they still exceeded densification rates, displacing ecologically valuable lands. Balancing people, prosperity, and the planet by 2030 requires concerted efforts to curb urban sprawl locally, sub-nationally, and nationally.

Target 11.5: On average, 104,049 critical infrastructure units and facilities were destroyed or damaged by disasters annually from 2015 to 2022. Furthermore, disasters disrupted over 1.6 million basic services, including educational and health services, each year.

Target 11.6: A comparison of air pollution five-year average before and after the development of the SDGs showed a significant decrease of 9% in fine particulate matter global levels and current alignment with the WHO Air Quality Guideline (AQG) Interim Target 1 value of 35 ug/m3.

Target 11.7: Data from 1,365 cities across 187 countries reveals that access to open public spaces is notably deficient in LDCs, where fewer than 3 in 10 people can conveniently reach such areas. Conversely, in high-performing regions like Australia and New Zealand, North America, and Europe, approximately 6 to 7 out of 10 urban residents enjoy convenient access to open public spaces, highlighting the prevalent global challenge.

> Target 11.b: In 2023, local-level risk governance has improved in recent years, with 106 countries cumulatively reporting having local disaster risk reduction strategies in place and in line with national strategies. On average, 72% of the local governments in reporting countries have specified having local disaster risk reduction strategies.[269]

The UN is trying very hard to make the Western world "inclusive." By importing the rest of the world into the West makes that half very inclusive. Now how is the UN going to make the East inclusive? Well, that is not part of the plan.

As for the use of the descriptor "human settlements," is the UN inferring that there are going to be inhuman settlements after the human ones are inclusive, safe, resilient, and sustainable? Perhaps these fifteen-minute cities will be occupied in whole by the transhuman remnant of slaves the Owners need to empty their trash after the depopulation plan is complete?

As for "safe," I dare you to make the argument that the UN-forced migration, a military invasion operation in every sense of the word, has promoted safety. From desperate mothers dying in the Darién Gap, to child and drug trafficking, to the Venezuelan gang deployment, safety is not a word that comes to mind. Of

---

[269] "Progress and info, 2024" Goal 11, Department of Economic and Social Affairs, United Nations, https://sdgs.un.org/goals/goal11#progress_and_info.

course, the Owners are safe in their bunkers and walled off estates as we, the little people, are anything but safe.

"Resilient" is an interesting word to describe the UN's goal. The UN defines resilience as "the ability of a system, community, or society to resist, absorb…and recover from…a hazard in a timely and efficient manner."[270] It is another one of those self-inflicted wound kind of things. The Owners break something—a country, for example—and then the UN swoops down in a timely manner and efficiently does the Owners' bidding. This is where "Build Back Better" gets its practical application.

"Sustainable"? Sustainability will only be achieved if the UN is able to pull off this massive extinction event with a remnant control result and rosy future of the transhumans owning nothing while the Owners are happy. Here's wishing them bad luck.

Goal 12: Ensure sustainable consumption and production patterns

The crisis of unsustainable consumption and production patterns worldwide is fuelling the ongoing triple planetary crisis of climate change, nature loss and pollution. Domestic material consumption and material footprint continue to rise, some one billion meals worth of edible food are wasted every day in homes around the world and stockpiles of e-waste steadily grow. While countries are fulfilling their environmental

---

[270] "Definition: Resilience," Sendai Framework Terminology on Disaster Risk Reduction, United Nations Office for Disaster Risk Reduction, https://www.undrr.org/terminology/resilience.

agreement obligations and embracing comprehensive approaches to address environmental degradation, public funding supporting the production and consumption of fossil fuels has more than tripled since 2015, impeding the transition to net-zero emissions. Each stage of production or manufacturing presents an opportunity to reduce resource and fossil fuel use, foster innovation, conserve energy, cut emissions, and advocate for a circular economy approach.

Target 12.1: From 2019 to 2023, one-third of member states (63 countries) have reported 516 policy instruments related to sustainable consumption and production.

Target 8.4/12.2: From 2015 to 2022, Domestic Material Consumption (DMC) increased by 5.8%, and Material Footprint (MF) rose by 6.8%. Regional disparities between DMC and MF continue to grow, particularly between regions where MF is higher than DMC (Eastern and South-Eastern Asia, Europe and Northern America, Northern Africa and Western Asia) and those where MF is lower than DMC (Central and Southern Asia, Latin America and the Caribbean, Sub-Saharan Africa, Oceania), showing different patterns of material consumption and their corresponding environmental impact.

Target 12.3: In 2022, 19% of global food was wasted, totalling 1.05 billion tonnes, with household waste accounting for 60%. This waste generates significant greenhouse gas emissions, costing over $1 trillion annually, while 783 million people suffer from hunger. Addressing this issue is crucial for halving food waste by 2030, yet only 9 out of 193 countries have included food waste in their Nationally Determined Contributions as of 2022. Meanwhile, the percentage of food lost globally after harvest on farm, transport, storage, wholesale, and processing levels is estimated at 13.2% in 2021.

Target 12.4: Number of parties to international multilateral environmental agreements on hazardous waste, and other chemicals that meet their commitments and obligations in transmitting information as required by each relevant agreement:

Minamata Convention on Mercury: Most Parties have met their obligations, with 94% appointing National Focal Points and 95% submitting complete national reports in 2023.

Basel, Rotterdam, and Stockholm Conventions: Parties continue to make strides in meeting their obligations and in policy-making to keep pace with rapidly changing global circumstances, such as responding to the growing challenges created by contemporary waste streams such as plastic waste and e-waste, improving the procedure to control transboundary movements of wastes, and enlarging their scope with the listing of new chemical.

Montreal Protocol: Parties consistently fulfil reporting obligations on the production and use of ozone-depleting substances, with 156 out of 198 ratifying the Kigali Amendment by January 2024, demonstrating an increased commitment to mitigating climate change under the Protocol.

Targets 12.4 and 12.5: In 2022, e-waste generation rose to 7.8 kg per capita from 6.2 kg per capita in 2015, but only 1.7 kg per capita was properly managed. Mismanaged e-waste leads to resource loss, increased use of virgin resources, and environmental hazards, underscoring the urgency for improved and environmentally sound management.

Target 12.6: In 2021–2022, 73% of companies included in the sample published sustainability reports, with the number of companies tripling since 2016. This growth was observed in all regions in 2022.

Target 12.c: Fossil fuel subsidies hit a record high of $1.53 trillion in 2022, reversing the declining trend observed from 2012 to 2020. The post-COVID energy price surge inflated these subsidies, prompting some governments to introduce new support measures. Consequently, public funding for oil, coal, and gas production and consumption more than doubled from 2021 to 2022 and tripled since 2015, impeding progress towards net-zero transition.[271]

The UN and WEF continue to place the blame on the developed nations for being irresponsible consumers and producers. In most respects, nothing can be further from the truth. Take just one example, and the West is wooed into committing economic suicide by conforming to faux solutions such as climate accords and petroleum exploration restrictions, while rogue states such as Communist China exploit their own and the world's resources without restraint or complaint.

Goal 13: Take urgent action to combat climate change and its impacts

Climate records were shattered in 2023, with the world watching the climate crisis unfold in real time. Communities around the world are suffering the effects of extreme weather, which is

---

[271] "Progress and info, 2024," Goal 12, Department of Economic and Social Affairs, United Nations, https://sdgs.un.org/goals/goal12#progress_and_info.

destroying lives and livelihoods on a daily basis. The roadmap to limit the rise in global temperature to 1.5°C and avoid the worst of climate chaos cannot afford any delays, indecision or half measures by the global community. It demands immediate action for drastic reductions in global greenhouse gas emissions in this decade and the achievement of net zero by 2050.

Target 13.1: The number of disaster-related deaths and missing persons per 100,000 population (excluding COVID-19 deaths) has nearly halved from 1.62 in the decade 2005–2014 to 0.82 in 2013–2022. However, the absolute number remains high. Between 2013 and 2022, disasters worldwide claimed 42,553 mortalities each year. Further, the number of persons affected by disasters per 100,000 population has increased by over two-third, from 1,169 in 2005–2014 to 1,980 in 2013–2022.

In 2023, 129 countries reported the adoption and implementation of national disaster risk reduction strategies, increasing from 55 countries in 2015. Among these countries, 122 countries have reported promoting policy coherence and compliance with the SDGs and the Paris Agreement as a key element in the strategy.

Target 13.2: The year 2023 broke every single climate indicator and was the warmest year on record according to the World Meteorological Organization. Global temperatures rose to 1.45°C, dangerously close for the first time to the 1.5°C lower limit of the Paris Agreement on climate change. Despite some reduction in greenhouse gas emissions in developed countries, concentrations of greenhouse gases reached record high observed levels in 2022 and real-time data in 2023 show greenhouse gases continuing to increase. Carbon dioxide levels are 150% above pre-industrial levels.

Target 13.3: A study in 2023 of more than 530 grade 9 science and social science subject curricula found that 69% contained no reference to climate change and 66% made no mention of sustainability. However, three-quarters of countries reported they have plans to revise their curricula in the next three years to focus more on climate change and sustainability.

Target 13.a: Climate finance, reported by Annex I Parties as support provided to developing countries, has increased at a compound rate of 5% from 2015 to 2020, amounting to $41 billion. Although there are a range of estimates and a lack of an agreed accounting methodology on the $100 billion per year goal, the goal was not yet met as of 2021. However, recent progress made in the provision and mobilization of climate finance amounted to $89.6 billion in 2021."[272]

The climate change hoax and its "green new steal" are merely power and control tools used by the leftist globalist elites to end freedom and free markets. In the book *The Truth about Energy, Global Warming, and Climate Change: Exposing Climate Lies in an Age of Disinformation*,[273] Dr. Jerome Corsi uses a truly science-based approach to enable us to understand the reality of Earth's climate and false narratives that Green New Deal proponents spew as indisputable facts. The radical left can deny the facts, but Dr. Corsi shines the light on the darkness.

Goal 14: Conserve and sustainably use the oceans, seas and marine resources for sustainable development

Oceans cover over 70% of the Earth's surface and play a crucial role in providing food and livelihoods for more than 3 billion people as well as combating the effects of climate change. Yet, alarming trends from declining fish stocks, marine pollution, ocean acidification and habitat

---

[272] "Progress and info, 2024," Goal 13, Department of Economic and Social Affairs, United Nations, https://sdgs.un.org/goals/goal13#progress_and_info.

[273] Jerome R. Corsi, *The Truth about Energy, Global Warming, and Climate Change: Exposing Climate Lies in an Age of Disinformation* (Post Hill Press, 2022).

destruction threaten marine ecosystems and the livelihoods of coastal communities worldwide. Urgent action is needed to address these challenges and ensure the long-term health and sustainability of the ocean through sustainable fishing practices, marine conservation efforts, pollution reduction and global cooperation to safeguard marine life and ecosystems for future generations.

Target 14.3: Ocean acidification is increasing and will continue to do so if carbon dioxide emissions do not stop rising. An increasing number of countries and stations (from 178 stations in 2021 to 638 in 2024) highlights the growing capacity of countries to observe the continued decline of ocean pH in the global ocean as well as the strong regional differences in the pace of change.

Target 14.6: Illegal, unreported and unregulated (IUU) fishing threatens the social, economic and environmental sustainability of global fisheries, hindering countries' abilities to manage their fisheries effectively. The first binding international agreement to specifically target IUU fishing, the Agreement of Port State Measures, now has 102 States covered under the Agreement (from 25 in 2016), covering 63% of the world's coastal States. States have made good overall progress with close to 75% scoring highly in their degree of implementation of relevant international instruments in 2022 compared to 70% in 2018."[274]

Conserving the assets of the oceans in a way that provides the marine-based protein needed to support human beings while sustaining those same assets for the future is not easily accomplished. As in point—bad actors, such as the Communist Chinese, plunder the entire world's resources solely for its needs and ambitions alone. Claiming almost the entire South China Sea region for their own purposes is just a starting point for Xi Jinping's gangster regime. Xi believes the world is his oyster, and the raping of its watery resources are but one aspect of his regime's wanton disregard for the well-being of other countries. Neither the UN nor the WEF is willing or able to curtail Xi's maniacal ambitions, especially since those organizations are virtually owned by the CCP.

Goal 15: Protect, restore and promote sustainable use of terrestrial ecosystems, sustainably manage forests, combat desertification, and halt and reverse land degradation and halt biodiversity loss

SDG 15 underscores the critical importance of biodiversity as humanity's life-support system. Yet, the relentless depletion of forests, coupled with an alarming rate of species extinction and

---

[274] "Progress and info, 2024," Goal 14, Department of Economic and Social Affairs, United Nations, https://sdgs.un.org/goals/goal14#progress_and_info.

stagnation in safeguarding key biodiversity areas, jeopardizes the delicate balance of our ecosystems. To address the pressing global environmental challenges and crises, including climate change, biodiversity loss, and pollution, as well as desertification, land and soil degradation, drought and deforestation, it is imperative to intensify efforts in fulfilling our global environmental and biodiversity commitments.

Targets 15.1 and 15.2: The world's forest area continues to decline, albeit at a slightly reduced pace compared to previous decades. The proportion of forest cover to total land area decreased from 31.9% in 2000 to 31.2% in 2020 with agricultural expansion accounting for nearly 90% of global deforestation. However, there has been notable progress towards sustainable forest management, marked by an increase in the proportion of forests under management plans and within protected areas. Moreover, certified forest area, which had shown steady long-term growth, has experienced a significant decline in the last two years, attributed to suspension of certificates due to the conflict in Europe.

Targets 14.5, 15.1 and 15.4: Global protected and conserved area coverage of marine, terrestrial, freshwater and mountain key biodiversity areas showed substantial improvements prior to 2000, this growth has stagnated over the last two decades. Particularly worrying is Central, Southern and Western Asia, Northern Africa, and Oceania, where average protected and conserved area coverage of key biodiversity areas is less than 30%. Progress has been more positive in Northern America and Europe, Sub-Saharan Africa, Latin America and the Caribbean, and Australia and New Zealand, where over 40% of each key biodiversity area is now covered on average.

Target 15.5: Species extinction risk continues to worsen, as evidenced by a 12% deterioration in the aggregate Red List Index between 2024 and 1993 (and 4% since 2015). The extinction risk of the world's amphibian species was recently comprehensively re-assessed, revealing that for amphibians, climate change impacts, habitat conversion and alien invasive fungal disease are the most severe drivers of increasing extinction risk.

Target 15.6: Countries continue to make progress in ratifying and implementing access and benefit-sharing instruments. By the end of 2023, 75 countries (up from 6 countries in 2016) and 93 countries (up from 12 countries in 2015) had reported on their legislative, administrative or policy measures under the Nagoya Protocol and the International Treaty on Plant Genetic Resources for Food and Agriculture, respectively.

Target 15.7.1/15.c.1: Estimates available for the first time show that, globally, intercepted illegal wildlife trade as a proportion of all wildlife trade (legal and illegal) increased from 2017 onwards, reaching its highest levels during the COVID-19 pandemic in 2020–2021. It is estimated that wildlife seizures made up around 1.4 to 1.9% of global wildlife trade in 2020–2021.

Target 15.9: In 2023, 90 countries implemented the international statistical standard to measure the environment and ecosystems and their connection to the economy, an increase of 30% since 2017.[275]

Goal 16: Promote peaceful and inclusive societies for sustainable development, provide access to justice for all and build effective, accountable and inclusive institutions at all levels

Around the world, we need peace in every sense. Yet the road to global peace and security has become even more complex. Global forced displacement is at an all-time high, exceeding 110

[275] "Progress and info, 2024" Goal 15, Department of Economic and Social Affairs, United Nations, https://sdgs.un.org/goals/goal15#progress_and_info.

million people forced to flee from persecution, conflict, violence and human rights violations as of May 2023. Between 2022 and 2023, civilian casualties experienced the highest spike since the adoption of the 2030 Agenda. Persistent threats to human security across the globe underscore the breakdown of peaceful and inclusive societies, crucial for sustainable development and the need to restore trust and strengthen and renew global peace and security frameworks to heed the desperate pleas for peace from countless voices worldwide.

Just how does one "promote peaceful and inclusive societies"? You cannot drag tyrants and dictators to peace conferences. As a reference, how has the United Nations fared in this regard since its inception? As for "inclusive," the world has learned the Diversity, Equity, and Inclusion (DEI) is the road to ruin and meritocracy.

Target 16.1: The global homicide rate gradually decreased, falling from 5.9 victims per 100,000 population in 2015 to 5.5 in 2020. However, this trend was disrupted in 2021, with a sharp rise to 5.8 victims per 100,000 population, only slightly decreasing to 5.6 in 2022. High levels of violence linked to organized crime and gang activities in Latin America and the Caribbean, along with Africa's heightened vulnerability to homicide, continue to contribute to these regions having the highest homicide rates and numbers globally.

The number of civilian deaths in armed conflict skyrocketed in 2023. Between 2022 and 2023, civilian casualties increased by 72%, the highest increase since 2015. In 2023, seven out of ten recorded deaths occurred in the Occupied Palestinian Territory and Israel. Moreover, for the second consecutive year, the number of civilians killed in conflict has risen dramatically; reversing the downward trend between 2016 and 2019. By 2023, the number of civilian casualties had risen to over 33,400, almost matching the peak of 2015. By 2023, four out of every ten civilians killed in conflicts were women, and three in ten civilians killed were children, doubling and tripling, respectively, the previous year's proportion.

Data on experience of violence, remain limited outside of Europe and Northern America and Latin America and the Caribbean. Available data show women and men are not impacted by the same type of violence. The median prevalence of sexual violence in countries with data is 3.0% for women compared to just 0.8% for men. However, the median prevalence of physical violence is 3.0% for men compared to 2.1% for women.

Target 16.2: Violent discipline is the most common and widespread form of violence against children. In 82 (mostly low- and middle-income) countries with available data from 2015 to 2023, nearly 8 in 10 children from 1 to 14 years of age were subjected to some form of psychological aggression and/or physical punishment at home in the past month.

Target 16.3: Available data for 53 countries for the period 2010–2022 shows that the proportion of victims of physical assault and robbery in the previous 12 months that reported their victimization to competent authorities, shows a median proportion in countries with data of 36% and 45%, respectively. This is notably higher than the proportion of victims of sexual assault that reported their victimization, for which the median in countries with available data was of 17%.

Globally, the estimated number of persons in detention was 11.4 million in 2022, representing a prison-population rate of 142 prisoners per 100,000 population. In 2022, nearly a third (3.5 million) of the global prison population was being held in pre-trial detention and their share remained stable between 2015 and 2022 (around 30%).

Target 16.5: Based on data from 138 countries between 2015 and 2022, 19% of people who had contact with public officials in the last 12 months reported being asked to pay or paid a bribe to a public official. Regional differences range from an average of 32% in low-income countries to 9% in high-income countries.

Target 16.6: Budget reliability improved in 2021 and 2022, reaching an average of 13.5% compared with 15.3 % in 2020 but remained weaker than pre-pandemic levels with 10.6% on average. In part, this is due to the incidence of new international challenges including global political stresses, inflation and resource price volatility.

Target 16.7: The overall representation of people under the age of 45 or less in parliaments is increasing globally but with contrasting trends: a rise in developing countries and a decline in developed ones. Moreover, growth in women's share of parliamentary leadership posts continues to be slow-moving, albeit steady. As of 1 January 2024, women presided over 23.8% of parliaments as Speakers (an increase of 2.9 percentage points since 2021) and held 27.2% of committee chair posts.

Target 16.9: While a few regions like Northern America and Europe and Australia and New Zealand have achieved universal birth registration, only half of African children under five have had their births registered.

Target 16.10: The number of killings of human rights defenders, journalists, and trade unionists recorded by national human rights institutions and the United Nations decreased in 2023; to 320 cases in 40 countries, compared to 448 cases in 36 countries in 2022. In conflict zones, however, there was a sharp increase in journalists and media workers killed—40 lives lost—reversing the downward trend since 2017. Additionally, enforced disappearances have been nearly doubling for the second consecutive year, with at least 54 cases reported across 14 countries in 2023. Strong protection frameworks are therefore needed to stem this trend, particularly in countries where violent conflict or social unrest erupts or escalates.

In 2024, 140 countries had laws that specifically guaranteed the rights of citizens to access public information, up from 105 in 2015 and 14 in 1990.

Target 16.a: Between 2015 and 2023, the number of countries with independent national human rights institutions (NHRIs) meeting international standards increased by 23%. More than 40% of countries now have independent NHRIs.[276]

Goal 17: Strengthen the means of implementation and revitalize the global partnership for sustainable development

Global partnerships for sustainable development encompass key areas such as finance, technology, trade and data. There are mixed trends in mobilizing financial resources for development, expanding internet connectivity and strengthening statistical systems. However, a substantial $4 trillion annual investment gap for developing countries to achieve the SDGs, persistent and crippling issues such as unprecedentedly high external debt levels, and limited access to online connectivity in low-income countries underscore the need for sustained collaboration and enhanced cooperation and support in a landscape of worsening international cooperation and geopolitical tensions.

Calling an annual $4 trillion dollar investment shortfall a "gap" is akin to putting lipstick on a pig. This goal was ill-conceived, never

---

[276] "Progress and info, 2024," Goal 16, Department of Economic and Social Affairs, United Nations, https://sdgs.un.org/goals/goal16#progress_and_info.

attainable, and only created to maximize the amount of money that would be contributed to a lost cause.

Finance

Target 17.1: 2022 data from approximately 130 countries show that globally, government revenue accounts for approximately 33% of GDP. The average overall tax burden or revenue in the form of taxes is 26% of GDP among advanced economies and 18% of GDP among emerging market and developing economies. In 2019, the overall average of proportion government expenditure funded by taxes was about 66% among advanced economies and 61% among emerging market and developing economies. The overall average sharply declined following the pandemic to about 52% in 2020 but rebounded in 2021 and 2022 for both groups of economies (to 62% for advanced economies and 59% for emerging and developing countries), however, still lower than the pre-pandemic level.

Target 17.2: In 2023, ODA by member countries of the Development Assistance Committee (DAC) amounted to $223.7 billion, representing 0.37% of DAC members' combined GNI. Total ODA in 2023 rose by 1.8% in real terms compared to 2022 and by 47% compared to 2015. This was the fifth consecutive year ODA reached a new high. The increase was primarily due to aid for Ukraine, humanitarian aid and contributions to international organisations.

Target 17.3: In 2022, financial resources for developing countries from multiple sources reported by 101 bilateral and multilateral providers amounted to $276.6 billion in official resources, $55.3 billion mobilized from private finance and $10.2 billion from private grants for development. Sustainable development grants (both official and private) decreased in 2022, compared to 2021. However, sustainable concessional development loans increased by 6%, while non-concessional loans decreased and mobilized private finance increased by 21%, compensating the decrease of 2021.

Global Foreign Direct Investment (FDI) flows in 2023 amounted to an estimated $1.37 trillion, a marginal increase over 2022. However, the increase was due largely to higher values in a small number of conduit economies; excluding these conduits, global FDI flows were 18% lower. The number of international investment projects announced in developing countries in sectors relevant to the SDGs—including infrastructure, renewables, water and sanitation, food security, health and education—remained flat.

The annual SDG investment gap in developing countries is now about $4 trillion. If the SDG investment needs to 2030 are to be met, some $30 trillion of additional investment must be found over the next eight years. More than half of the gap, or $2.2 trillion, relates to the energy transition alone.

In the post-COVID period, remittances have proved to be resilient and become a premier source of external finance for developing countries. In 2022, remittance flows to low- and middle-income countries increased by 8%, to reach $647 billion. This increase is remarkable, given that it followed a 10.6% growth rate in 2021. The remittance growth rate is expected to moderate to about 4% in 2023.

Target 17.4: The external debt stock level of low- and middle-income countries decreased in 2022 for the first time since 2015, to $9.0 trillion in 2022 from $9.3 trillion in 2021. Despite the slight decrease in 2022, external debt stock levels remained unprecedentedly high following more than a decade of rapid debt accumulation. Moreover, going forward, interest costs both in nominal terms and in relation to GNI and export revenue are expected to increase given the aggressive rise in global interest rates to tame inflation and could become increasingly burdensome by crowding out spending on other priorities for many low- and middle-income countries.

Target 17.5: The number of countries that actively promote outward foreign direct investment to developing countries, including least developed countries, remains limited. In 2023, at least 50 countries, including 19 emerging or developing economies, had at least one type of investment promotion mechanism for outward foreign direct investment in place. However, out of those, only 23 countries have adopted an outward foreign direct investment promotion scheme specifically targeting developing countries, including least developed countries.

Information and communications technology

Target 17.6: Fixed-broadband subscriptions continue to grow steadily, at an average annual growth rate of 6.4% between 2015 and 2023, reaching 19 subscriptions per 100 inhabitants in 2023 globally. Nevertheless, while fixed connections are common among households in upper-middle-income and high income countries, they are nearly non-existent in low-income countries due to high prices and a lack of infrastructure.

Target 17.8: Approximately 67% of the world's population, or 5.4 billion people were online in 2023. This represents a growth of 4.7% since 2022, a higher increase than that recorded from 2021 to 2022 at 3.5%. While there was an uptick in the increase in the number of Internet users during the COVID-19 pandemic, in the last three years growth rates in the number of Internet users were back to pre-pandemic levels.

Data, monitoring and accountability

Target 17.18: One of the far-reaching effects of the COVID-19 pandemic was the limited ability of national statistical offices to collect recent data for the Sustainable Development Goals. This was reflected in a drop in average data coverage scores in the Open Data Inventory (ODIN). Despite the recent decrease in data production capabilities, a comparison of ODIN coverage scores from 2017 to 2022 shows that the scores of low- and middle-income countries have increased at the same pace as high-income countries.

Globally, scores on the Data Sources Performance Index (Statistical Performance Indicators Pillar 4) and Data Infrastructure Performance Index (Statistical Performance Indicators Pillar 5) have been improving since 2016. Data sources improved by only 3 points, held back in part because of COVID disruptions, while data infrastructure—meaning both the hard and soft infrastructure needed to produce data are available—has increased by around 14 points.

In 2023, 159 countries and territories reported having national statistical legislation in compliance with the Fundamental Principles of Official Statistics, representing a significant increase from 132 in 2019 and marking the fastest annual growth of 10 countries.

In 2023, a total of 163 countries and territories reported having implemented a national statistical plan, marking an increase from 143 in 2019 and 156 in 2022. Of these, 109 plans were fully funded, up from 91 in 2019 and 100 in 2022. These trends suggest a recovery from the long-term disruptions caused by the pandemic on the planning and execution of statistical activities.

Target 17.19: There has been a resurgence in international support for the development of data and statistics, reaching $799 million in 2021 and 26/26 representing a 14% increase from 2020 and a substantial 44% increase from 2015. Notably, 2021 marked the first time that multilateral aid providers emerged as the main source of funding.[277]

On July 10, 2023, the UN Department of Economic and Social Affairs published its most recent progress report regarding its unattainable SDGs and impending doom for the 2030 Agenda, thus saving mankind. As with the other progress reports, this one is equally "disappointing" (to the globalists), with similar missed goals, prompting another "powerful call to action."

> **10 July 2023:** The Sustainable Development Goals Report 2023: Special Edition provides a powerful call to action, presenting a candid assessment of the SDGs based on the latest data and estimates. While highlighting the existing gaps and urging the world to redouble its efforts, the report also emphasizes the immense potential for success through strong political will and the utilization of available technologies, resources, and knowledge. Together, the global community can reignite progress towards achieving the SDGs and create a brighter future for all.

According to the report, the impacts of the climate crisis, the war in Ukraine, a weak global economy, and the lingering effects of the COVID-19 pandemic have revealed weaknesses

---

[277] "Progress and info, 2024," Goal 17, Department of Economic and Social Affairs, United Nations, https://sdgs.un.org/goals/goal17#progress_and_info.

and hindered progress towards the Goals. The report further warns that while lack of progress is universal, it is the world's poorest and most vulnerable who are experiencing the worst effects of these unprecedented global challenges. It also points out areas that need urgent action to rescue the SDGs and deliver meaningful progress for people and the planet by 2030.

"Unless we act now, the 2030 Agenda will become an epitaph for a world that might have been."

António Guterres
Secretary-General, United Nations[278]

Secretary-General Guterres has issued but another in his long list of calls to action. Will his unending pleas for the bankrupt nations to gouge their citizens even more so they can shovel ever more money into the coffers of his organization that is led by terrorists and criminals finally go unanswered? One can only pray.

There is a direct link between sustainability initiatives and population control.[279] Bill Gates, in a moment of rare candor, announced in a TED Talk years ago (that has since been thrown down the internet memory hole) that the way to global prosperity begins with a 10 percent reduction in the world population. Do

---

[278] "The Sustainable Development Goals Report 2023: Special Edition," United Nations Statistics Division, https://unstats.un.org/sdgs/report/2023/.

[279] Robert Engelman, "Population and Sustainability: Can We Avoid Limiting the Number of People?" *Scientific American*, June 1, 2009, https://www.scientificamerican.com/article/population-and-sustainability/.

the math—take 10 percent of eight billion people, and the result is eight hundred million useless eaters to eliminate. The Owners are disappointed but resolute. Their high expectations for the bioweapon fell way short of that goal, but they have many more weapons in their arsenal.

The Centers for Disease Control and Prevention (CDC)'s Vaccine Adverse Events Reporting System[280] only captures a fraction of the real data, as most vaccine deaths are not reported or misreported as due to another cause. But the CDC assures us that the vaccines are safe.[281] What a relief. At first I thought that all of those young, strong athletes and others falling over dead for no "apparent" reason might have something to do with the shots, but alas, those deaths are not mentioned on the CDC website. Less than blessed assurance. But the CDC does report, "Some people have no side effects. Many people have reported side effects such as headache, fatigue, and soreness at the injection site that are generally mild to moderate and go away within a few days."[282] No worries, get your tenth booster today, and they will put you on a six-month reminder for your next one.

How do the sustainability goals relate to reproductive health? Well, *The Lancet*, the once renowned peer-reviewed weekly

---

[280] See "About the Vaccine Adverse Event Reporting System (VAERS)," Vaccine Safety Systems, US Centers for Disease Control and Prevention, August 7, 2024, https://www.cdc.gov/vaccine-safety-systems/vaers/index.html.

[281] See "Safety Information by Vaccine," Vaccine Safety, US Centers for Disease Control and Prevention, July 31, 2024, https://www.cdc.gov/vaccine-safety/vaccines/index.html.

[282] "Selected Adverse Events Reported after COVID-19 Vaccination," US Centers for Disease Control and Prevention Archive, May 31, 2023, https://archive.cdc.gov/www_cdc_gov/coronavirus/2019-ncov/vaccines/safety/adverse-events.html.

medical journal, has produced a road map for how to achieve the development goals while advancing sexual and reproductive health and rights.[283]

The Lancet was "once renowned?" *The Lancet* is the publication that had to retract a COVID-19 paper that warned people not to take hydroxychloroquine (HCQ).[284] I am sure, though, that the warning paper had nothing to do with President Trump stating in a news conference shortly before that he heard that HCQ might be helpful. Of course, Fauci immediately attacked such a wild and crazy notion.

After all, if people were to take well-known, inexpensive, and effective medications such as HCQ, ivermectin, and azithromycin, the "emergency use authorization" would not have been authorized. Fauci, as the highest paid federal government employee, is most likely just the tip of a pharma kickback iceberg. The buy-in of the European Union was critical for the production of vaccines under the guidance of Vice President Mike Pence's Operation Warp Speed and absolutely necessary for the profit margins of Big Pharma.

According to the National Center for Biotechnology Information, family planning is a vital "investment." This is so

---

[283] "SDG Target 3.7 Sexual and reproductive health," World Health Organization, https://www.who.int/data/gho/data/themes/topics/sdg-target -3_7-sexual-and-reproductive-health. See also: "Accelerate progress— sexual and reproductive health and rights for all: report of the Guttmacher–*Lancet* Commission," *The Lancet* 391, no. 10140 (June 30, 2018): P2642–2692, https://www.thelancet.com/journals/lancet/article/ PIIS0140-6736(18)30293-9/fulltext.

[284] Erika Edwards, "The Lancet retracts large study on hydroxychloroquine," NBC News, June 4, 2020, https://www.nbcnews.com/health/health-news/ lancet-retracts-large-study-hydroxychloroquine-n1225091.

that the Owners can achieve their SDGs. After all, we invest in the stock market and real estate; now we must also invest in our families by not having children. It makes perfect sense if you are Bill Gates—who is revered throughout the third world as their savior? *Not.* [285]

Resource management is another significant issue regarding SDGs. There are two kinds of resources: natural and human. So, human resources are unnatural? Just pondering, don't mind me.

Let us start with human resources—"green human resources management," or GHRM. Once again, we leave it up to Google artificial intelligence to provide the details. GHRM is:

> A strategic approach that incorporates environmental sustainability into human resource management practices. GHRM aims to create a sustainable workplace culture by encouraging environmentally responsible behavior from employees. It's an important part of organizational strategy as companies strive to embed sustainability into their core values. GHRM originated as an academic concept from debates about corporate and sustainable development.[286]

---

[285] Christine Ro, "Why African Groups Want Reparations From The Gates Foundation," *Forbes*, September 2, 2024, https://www.forbes.com/sites/christinero/2024/09/02/why-african-groups-want-reparations-from-the-gates-foundation/.

[286] Text generated by Google AI.

It sounds like a perfect way for companies to help the world achieve the Owners' SDGs. Or, are various woke HR departments just guiding their organizations down the primrose path?

As for natural resources and SDGs, the UN has proposed a way to manage nature worldwide through 2030. The UN introduced a global framework for managing nature (kinda like chemtrails?) on July 12, 2021, in Montreal, Canada.

> The UN Convention on Biological Diversity (CBD) Secretariat today released the first official draft of a new Global Biodiversity Framework to guide actions worldwide through 2030 to preserve and protect nature and its essential services to people.[287]

Continuing from the same 2021 press release:

> Still a work in progress, the Global Biodiversity Framework will ultimately advance to UN Convention on Biological Diversity's COP-15 for consideration by 196 member Parties
>
> 21 targets, 10 'milestones' proposed for 2030 en route to 'living in harmony with nature' by 2050;

---

[287] "A New Global Framework for Managing Nature Through 2030: 1st Detailed Draft Agreement Debuts," press release, UN Sustainable Development Goals, July 12, 2021, https://www.un.org/sustainabledevelopment/blog/2021/07/a-new-global-framework-for-managing-nature-through-2030-1st-detailed-draft-agreement-debuts/.

Include conserving and protecting at least 30% of Earth's lands and oceans.[288]

Several international organizations and nongovernmental organizations are now heavily involved in implementing the 2030 Agenda. Here are but a few according to Google artificial intelligence:

> Council of Europe: Promotes itself as a "guardian of rights." As it "Helps member states translate the 2030 Agenda into action at the national and local levels"

> Office of the High Commissioner for Human Rights (OHCHR): This UN organization "Works to ensure that the 2030 Agenda is human rights-based and that all people are included"

> United Nations Development Programme (UNDP): Another UN organization, and "A partner in the UN's sustainable development efforts"

> International Labour Organization (ILO): Another "specialized agency of the United Nations"

> International Organization for Migration (IOM): The opener of the flood gates of the movement of people to western nations, it "works with member

---

[288] "A New Global Framework."

states to protect the rights of migrants and help
them become part of their new societies"

Global Compact: Another one of the many UN
self-fulfilling ventures, the Global Compact is
building local networks in Africa to support
both businesses and multinational corporations
that support Agenda 2030.[289]

Many private sector actors are involved in promoting and
implementing the *2030 Agenda for Sustainable Development*,
with much of the guidance coming from UNDP. UNDP's Private
Sector Strategy promotes the integration of SDGs into private
sector operations and plans. UNDP also partners with private
sector actors to influence the adoption of sustainable business
practices.

Believe it or not, a feature on the UNDP website starts with
a visual set of appearing and disappearing eyes and the headline:
"Would I lie to you?" with a subheading, "How disinformation
is taking us through the looking glass."[290] I answer "Yes" to the
question and accept the statement as an admission of guilt. I don't
know whether to call for a "cyber exorcist" or reread *1984*. Here
are but a few of the private sector organizations suffering from a
severe case of "wokeitis":

The International Organisation of Employers (IOE), the
self-proclaimed "largest network of the private sector in the

---

[289] Text generated by Google AI.
[290] "Would I Lie to You?" United Nations Development Programme, https://
feature.undp.org/would-i-lie-to-you/.

world, with more than 150 business and employer organisation members."[291] It represents over 50 million companies.

As the "world's strongest law firm brand"[292] for twelve years running and boasting "solutions for a connected world,"[293] Baker & McKenzie "has organised 8 workshops…with local business, academics, and government officials to gather input [for the 2030 Agenda]."[294]

Private sector actors are the key players promoting and implementing the 2030 Agenda.

In conclusion, the implications of the 2030 Agenda for national sovereignty, economic development, and individual freedoms are ominous. The UN has created a giant web of supporting nongovernmental organizations, spreading the net so wide, no fly will escape. The Owners have flooded the zone with so many supporting tentacles that any opposition is drowned out through the sheer numbers of agenda-protection attack bots.

---

[291] "International Organisation of Employers (IOE)," profile, LinkedIn, https://www.linkedin.com/company/international-organisation-of-employers-ioe-/.

[292] "Baker McKenzie law firm honored with 'Friendly Workplace 2023' award," press release, Baker McKenzie, June 21, 2023, https://www.bakermckenzie.com/en/newsroom/2023/06/friendly-workplace-2023-award.

[293] "Solutions for a Connected World," Baker McKenzie, https://www.bakermckenzie.com/en/expertise/solutions-connected-world.

[294] *Overview: IOE Overview on Implementation of the 2030 Agenda for Sustainable Development*, International Organisation of Employers, 2016, 9, https://www.ioe-emp.org/fileadmin/ioe_documents/publications/Policy%20Areas/sustainability/EN/_2016-08-02__C-538_IOE_Overview_on_Implementing_Agenda_2030_the_role_of_business_ANNEX.pdf.

TODD S. CALLENDER, J.D., JEROME R. CORSI, PH.D.,
AND CRAIG D. CAMPBELL, PH.D.

Private sector employers are eager to compel their employees to become obedient slaves to the coming corporate zombie apocalypse. HR departments are now just DEI, CRT, SDG borg agents. The hive mind plantation is expanding and absorbing like the Blob.

CHAPTER 7

THE WORLD ECONOMIC FORUM: THE RISE OF THE TOTALITARIAN "GREAT RESET"

The World Economic Forum (WEF) was founded on January 24, 1971 by Klaus Schwab. The WEF is an international non-governmental organization funded primarily by the governments and organizations represented by its over one thousand members. The WEF's stated mission is "improving the state of the world by engaging business, political, academic, and other leaders of society to shape global, regional, and industry agendas."[295] In reality the WEF, in particular, has played a leading role in a worldwide coup. The WEF goes so far as to publicly admit its criminal plan and confessing—by the mouth of Klaus Schwab. That confession has infiltrated many nations and international institutions.

---

[295] "Terms of use," World Economic Forum, last updated April 8, 2024, https://digital-members.weforum.org/info/terms-policy.

Todd S. Callender, J.D., Jerome R. Corsi, Ph.D.,
and Craig D. Campbell, Ph.D.

Just scroll through the list of WEF members or members of the Young Global Leaders (the WEF's political economy school). It is a who's who of the widespread and ubiquitous presence of their emissaries. Analyze their institutional and political commitment to the WEF plan to recognize the level of obedience and subservience to the interests of these elite. Be afraid, very afraid.

The main threat concerns the very survival of mankind, which in the dystopian thinking of the WEF—steeped in delusional neo-Malthusianism—means that they would like to reduce humanity to five hundred million people (from seven billion), using for this purpose (as they themselves have repeatedly stated) vaccines, limited wars, pandemics, induced infertility, poverty, famines, earthquakes, tsunamis, and other seemingly natural but High-frequency Active Auroral Research Program[296] technology-induced calamities. The encouragement of abortion and euthanasia, along with gender transition, go in the same direction. These scourges, scientifically provoked by actions designed for the purpose of obtaining results in a short time, are presented as the effect of fictitious apparent causes, with the complicity of information and thanks to widespread censorship in the media and social platforms: again, recent news reports have confirmed a criminal disinformation network composed of large multinational corporations, information companies, government leaders, and secret services.

This subversive action, carried out with the complicity of governments (bought over the years with real streams of money)

---

[296] Fabien Deruelle, "Natural Disasters are Not All Natural," *Journal of Geography, Environment and Earth Science International* 27, no. 11 (2023): 74–94, https://journaljgeesi.com/index.php/JGEESI/article/view/727.

is so blatant that it has been denounced by political, cultural, and civil society figures.

On September 21, 2020, the WEF convened its virtual summit on Sustainable Development Impact Summit 2020. King Hussein of Jordan opened the proceedings by urging all nations to take drastic action to address the problems caused by the global response to the virus. He labeled that proposed action a "Great Reset."

One of the key components of the Great Reset is to create a different kind of capitalism.[297] Brian Balfour, senior vice president of research for the John Locke Foundation, clearly sees the Great Reset for what it really is: a frontal attack on national sovereignty and personal freedom. According to the WEF, the Great Reset will consist of three main components. The first involves efforts to "steer the market toward fairer outcomes." Achieving this component will require governments to make changes to tax, regulatory, and fiscal policy.

> The ultimate goal here is more "equitable outcomes" and would also include government policies punishing fossil-fuel companies and "new rules governing intellectual property, trade, and competition."

> The second component would "ensure that investments advance shared goals, such as equality and sustainability." Massive government

[297] Ira Basen, "Can the Great Reset really create a gentler, more equitable capitalism?" CBC, May 24, 2023, https://www.cbc.ca/radio/ideas/great-reset-equitable-capitalism-1.6851812.

"stimulus" and welfare spending, along with "green" energy mandates, are the preferred tools for this goal.

The third is to "harness the innovations of the Fourth Industrial Revolution to support the public good." The Fourth Industrial Revolution refers to the exponential growth of technology in fields such as artificial intelligence, robotics, nanotechnology, biotechnology, and energy storage. The WEF desires the "opportunity and power" to "shape" this technological revolution and "direct it toward a future that reflects our common objectives and values," with equity and sustainability being foremost among them.[298]

Regarding Balfour's first point, steering the market toward more equitable outcomes seems to at least have resonated with billionaire and CEO of Salesforce, Marc Benioff.

Ira Basen, in his 2023 article, "Can the Great Reset really create a gentler, more equitable capitalism?" answers that question from a position supportive of the WEF in this regard, through the thoughts of Benioff.

Benioff touts "enlightened stakeholder capitalism" as "the greatest platform for change."

---

[298] Brian Balfour, "The Great Reset: An Attack on Freedom and Sovereignty," The John Locke Foundation, June 6, 2023, https://www.johnlocke.org/the-great-reset-an-attack-on-freedom-and-sovereignty/.

He's also part of a growing number of the super rich who say the system that worked so well for them has led to environmental destruction, income inequality and social dysfunction.

That system has outlived its usefulness, according to Benioff, and needs to be replaced by a "new kind of capitalism that's not just about making money."[299] It is again fascinating to listen to the mega-yacht-and-private-jet class trash the very system that made them filthy rich. I guess when you have it made, you quickly forget it is the very system you used to get there.

Of course, it is increasingly clear that stakeholder capitalism is actually a misnomer. Advocates really only want to prioritize the views of stakeholders who agree with their activism on social and political issues. It is much more akin to crony capitalism than traditional shareholder capitalism.

Shareholder capitalism, the system under which Benioff benefited so greatly, is the construct of Milton Friedman, American economist and Nobel Prize winner. Friedman explained his "Friedman doctrine," oft coined as "Shareholder Theory," in his 1970 article, "The Social Responsibility of Business is to Increase its Profits."[300] Friedman disagreed with business leaders who altered the focus of their companies to "social responsibility." Putting your own money where your mouth is as a means of addressing issues like poverty and the environment is praise-

---

[299] Basen, "Can the Great Reset."

[300] Milton Friedman, "A Friedman doctrine — The Social Responsibility of Business Is to Increase Its Profits," *New York Times*, September 13, 1970, https://www.nytimes.com/1970/09/13/archives/a-friedman-doctrine-the-social-responsibility-of-business-is-to.html.

worthy. Using your company as a means to promote pet causes is merely self-serving.

Friedman applauded the virtues of "shareholder capitalism," in which the primary responsibility of corporations is to their shareholders. Period. Corporations are to focus on increasing profits, resulting in greater prosperity for all. Personal philanthropy is the way to address the problems of society.

The first part of Balfour's description of the WEF's second component, ensuring that "investments" advance shared goals, such as "equality" and "sustainability," exposes the soft underbelly of the entire scheme. Margaret Thatcher has something to say about that:

> The problem with socialism is that you eventually run out of other people's money.

Balfour is over the target as he correctly translates into clear English just what the term "investments" mean. Massive government "stimulus" and welfare spending, along with "green" energy mandates, are the preferred tools for this goal.

Perhaps the WEF should take heed of this advice from the former American president William Jefferson Clinton in his State of the Union address, on January 23, 1996:

> We know big government does not have all the answers. We know there's not a program for every problem. We have worked to give the American people a smaller, less bureaucratic government in

Washington. And we have to give the American
people one that lives within its means.[301]

Of course, in that paragraph, Clinton was only taking credit
for the highly popular positive results of the austerity measures he was forced to sign into law as Republican Speaker of
the House Newt Gingrich made good on his "Contract with
America" promises.

Clinton did, however, provide a right-handed pat on the back
to the Republicans. He then softened the blow to his teeth-grind-
ing supporters with an even stronger left-handed pat to his
own party.

> I compliment the Republican leadership and the
> membership for the energy and determination
> you have brought to this task of balancing the
> budget. And I thank the Democrats for passing
> the largest deficit reduction plan in history in
> 1993, which has already cut the deficit nearly in
> half in three years.[302]

The Dems had been dragged kicking and screaming to the
signing table due to inescapable public cries to make the country
great again after decades of Democrat legislative control. Today's
déjà vu again, Yogi?

---

[301] "President William Jefferson Clinton, State of the Union Address," The
White House (archived), January 23, 1996, https://clintonwhitehouse4.
archives.gov/WH/New/other/sotu.html.

[302] "President William Jefferson Clinton, State of the Union Address."

Any resemblance between Democrat priorities and Clinton's thoughts on government size and spending bring to memory a favorite line from Ralphie in the now classic Christmas tale, *A Christmas Story*:

> My old man's spare tires were actually only tires
> in the academic sense. They were round, they
> had once been made of rubber.[303]

Obviously, during times of significant challenge and unexpected change, corporations, like individuals, need to make course and priority corrections. But, it is possible for the forces of darkness to use such eventualities as opportunities to manipulate people into adapting their priorities.

For example, the WEF has used the adaptations people and organizations were forced to make as a result of the plandemic to paint a silver lining around that dark cloud through a "digital transformation."[304] According to the WEF, prior to 2020, many half-hearted, limited-focus actions to take advantage of advances in technology did not result in major global advances or failed outright. The time is right, based on the new circumstances, argues the WEF, to pool resources, create a synergistic approach, and implement global technology solutions. Such a

---

[303] "A Christmas Story, Jean Shepherd: Ralphie as an Adult," IMDb, https://www.imdb.com/title/tt0085334/characters/nm0791789.

[304] *Digital Transformation: Powering the Great Reset*, World Economic Forum, July 2020, https://www3.weforum.org/docs/WEF_Digital_Transformation_Powering_the_Great_Reset_2020.pdf.

digital transformation is key to the achievement of the sustainable development goals.[305]

The aftermath due to the release of the bioweapon from the Wuhan lab in Communist China enabled the Owners to sell the need for a path forward for the post-plandemic world. One small step backwards for man, one giant leap forward for the Owners.

As Balfour correctly states:

> For most, the Covid pandemic and subsequent lockdowns were terrifying both from a health standpoint and as an example of government tyranny run amok.
>
> But for one organization of substantial global influence, it represented an "extraordinary opportunity" to reset the global economy to be guided by a theory they've been advocating for fifty years.
>
> That organization is the World Economic Forum (WEF), and their desired transformation of the global economy is known as the "Great Reset."[306]

Yet, as grand and glorious all of the Owners' expectations for the Great Reset appear, translating lofty words and even loftier expectations into tangible and positive results is an immense

---

[305] Carolina Perez Diago, "How digitalisation contributes to the achievement of the SDGs?" Telefónica, April 30, 2024, https://www.telefonica.com/en/communication-room/blog/how-digitalisation-contributes-to-the-achievement-of-the-sdgs/.

[306] Balfour, "The Great Reset."

undertaking. An undertaking, which at its core, would undeniably result in a great loss of freedom and prosperity for the "owned," and great control, power, and wealth for the Owners.

Harken back to the presidential campaign of 2008, when first-term US Senator Barack Hussein Obama promised "hope and change" if he were to be elected. Many people envisioned that "hope" meant Americans moving forward together, hand in hand, realizing the dreams of Dr. Martin Luther King Jr. Those same supporters presumed that "change" meant unity and a positive future, resulting in uniform prosperity.

Now looking back, in the Obama/Biden era of strife at home, war abroad, and national descent into debt and division, all hope had been lost, and the changes were definitely not for the better.

Be careful what you wish for, and be even more careful to demand precise definitions of terms. I doubt if anyone today would define the 2008 campaign slogan as truthful in its intent. In fact, many results-oriented observers have reached an easily defendable conclusion that the Owners had once again rigged the game to achieve their dark goals.

We must be extremely careful today to not repeat the innocent mistakes of trust many voters made back then. The potential for the establishment of a totalitarian global order outweighs any altruistic hope and misunderstanding of the intentions of change with which we are faced today.

In that vein, the influence of the WEF's power elite and the organization's partners, including multinational corporations, political leaders, and "thought" leaders, must be closely scrutinized. The Owners do not intend to share or limit their power and wealth. To believe they intend to share and share in a fair way is pure folly.

Truly we are in a spiritual battle.

In his book, *The Anti-Globalist Manifesto: Ending the War on Humanity*, my coauthor, Dr. Jerome Corsi, clearly states that Satan's hands are all over what the WEF is attempting to implement by waging war against us with our own money.

> When we read in the writings of the medieval saints that money was considered Satan's dung, we are tempted to disagree because we believe that money is very much needed today, especially at a time when the Great Reset-induced economic crisis is forcing vast swaths of the population into poverty. Sometimes, we confuse money with its value—that piece of paper with what it represents in terms of work and experience, physical or intellectual labor, and the passion and expertise of someone whose effort has created value. Satan's dung is precisely represented by the colossal debt money fraud, with each of us indebted to a private bank that calls itself a Central Bank even though it is not a state-owned entity. Satan's dung is the indebtedness of the sovereign people to private bankers who demand that we pay interest on the money we guarantee them in government bonds. Under the thumb of Central Bank-created money, we find ourselves economically dependent on a potent

lobby that for centuries has crafted the economic policy of nations for decline, domestic policy to destroy the nuclear family, and the foreign policy of governments to engage in perpetual war.[307]

From the inception of his WEF, Schwab's intention was to reengineer society. The son of Eugen Wilhelm Schwab, who supplied munitions to the Nazi regime during World War II,[308] Klaus is merely carrying on the family tradition. Trained as a mechanical engineer, Klaus set about combining his education with his heritage in 1971. His unstated goal would be in essence to create a "Fourth Reich," or as he would later characterize it, the "Fourth Industrial Revolution."[309]

Make no mistake about this, the reference to a fourth revolution is Klaus's sly way of further pursuing the Führer's dream. Adolf Hitler dedicated his evil existence to the attainment of world domination. In the early '70s, Klaus began his own *Kampf*, a battle against humanity using economic munitions. Just as Hitler was obsessed with new and advanced weaponry, Klaus is also so disposed in our new digital age. Again, Dr. Corsi captures the essence.

---

[307] Corsi, *Anti-Globalist Manifesto*, 177.

[308] Text generated by Google AI (accessed January 30, 2025). "Eugen Wilhelm Schwab, the father of Klaus Schwab (founder of the World Economic Forum), was involved in supplying munitions during World War II, as he worked as a director at Escher Wyss AG, a German industrial company that acted as a contractor for the Nazi regime, producing armaments and machinery for military use."

[309] "The Fourth Industrial Revolution, by Klaus Schwab," World Economic Forum, https://www.weforum.org/about/the-fourth-industrial-revolution-by-klaus-schwab/.

Now, the globalist elite wants to see us subjugated when we agree to believe its supreme lie: that the physical and intellectual, the moral and cultural, and the political and religious energies of a people can be controlled by means of a virtual currency, a digital currency that physically resides on a server and to which nothing corresponds but an infinite series of 0s and 1s. With our labor, we create the good that gives us a living: not those who connect us to a (social) credit card and decide if, what, and when we can buy, where we can go, and if we can eat. The Chinese dictatorship has done in a short time what takes longer with us because of the "too little tyrannical" systems of Western countries and because of the partial failure of the psycho-pandemic operation. The admiration of Schwab, Soros, and other mad technocrats for Beijing shows that the Nazi blood of their fathers, unscrupulous speculators, and collaborators with Hitler still runs in their veins. That must be why so many World Economic Forum members are so indulgent of the Ukrainian regime, in which the neo-Nazi component is dangerously dominant.[310]

The lust for power and control is the quintessential characteristic of the Owners. The narcotic snorted at the top rung of the ladder does not satisfy a need. It merely leads to larger doses

---

[310] Corsi, *The Anti-Globalist Manifesto*, 153–154.

taken to reach the next high, followed by a desperate quest for ever more potent potions. Klaus, the engineer, immediately recognized the power that can be derived from the technological advances emerging on the scene. The WEF page about the Fourth Industrial Revolution captures the essence of its Klausian vision:

> Ubiquitous, mobile supercomputing. Intelligent robots. Self-driving cars. Neuro-technological brain enhancements. Genetic editing. The evidence of dramatic change is all around us and it's happening at exponential speed.[311]

As a mechanical, and now human, engineer Klaus has closely embraced the opportunities being presented by the rapid and revolutionary advances in science and technology.

> Professor Klaus Schwab, Founder and Executive Chairman of the World Economic Forum, has been at the centre of global affairs for over four decades. He is convinced that we are at the beginning of a revolution that is fundamentally changing the way we live, work and relate to one another, which he explores in his new book, *The Fourth Industrial Revolution.*[312]

Der Professor: "Ich bin ein Revolutionar!" Yes, Klaus has been at the epicenter of demonic global affairs for decades. His dark vision of how to fundamentally change the way the little people

---

[311] "The Fourth Industrial Revolution, by Klaus Schwab."
[312] "The Fourth Industrial Revolution, by Klaus Schwab."

live, work, and relate has been expressed in the ruling styles of many "Young Global Leaders" of government and industry that the WEF has cranked out like wurst—Justin Trudeau, Angela Merkel, Bill Gates, Mark Zuckerberg, Larry Page, and others.

In June of 2020, Klaus Schwab's WEF website posted, "Now is the time for a 'great reset.'"[313] Taking advantage of the fear and chaos that was created as the COVID-19 bioweapon was released from the Wuhan lab in Communist China, Schwab lifted the veil on a world domination plan that had been brewing for decades. It is no shock then that Klaus includes the "biological world" when describing what the WEF and by extension himself are all about in the WEF post about the Fourth Industrial Revolution.

> Previous industrial revolutions liberated humankind from animal power, made mass production possible and brought digital capabilities to billions of people. This Fourth Industrial Revolution is, however, fundamentally different. It is characterized by a range of new technologies that are fusing the physical, digital and biological worlds, impacting all disciplines, economies and industries, and even challenging ideas about what it means to be human.[314]

Interesting: "challenging ideas about what it means to be human." Since humans were made by God in his image, that

---

[313] Klaus Schwab, "Now is the time for a 'great reset,'" World Economic Forum, June 3, 2020, https://www.weforum.org/agenda/2020/06/now-is-the-time-for-a-great-reset/.

[314] "The Fourth Industrial Revolution, by Klaus Schwab."

challenge is to challenge God himself. Satan's minions take pride in snarling in the face of Christ followers. The minions then go about their dark business of destroying God's creation.

> The resulting shifts and disruptions mean that we live in a time of great promise and great peril. The world has the potential to connect billions more people to digital networks, dramatically improve the efficiency of organizations and even manage assets in ways that can help regenerate the natural environment, potentially undoing the damage of previous industrial revolutions.[315]

Yes, we do live in times of great peril and much of that peril has been purposely created by Obama/Biden, Biden/Harris, and other regimes worldwide bent on destroying the traditions that have been in place for centuries with their Satan-inspired false notions of "better." Yet, even Klaus has "grave concerns." Perhaps those concerns were heightened as he has yet failed to put us all in the grave.

> However, Schwab also has grave concerns: that organizations might be unable to adapt; governments could fail to employ and regulate new technologies to capture their benefits; shifting power will create important new security concerns; inequality may grow; and societies fragment.[316]

---

[315] "The Fourth Industrial Revolution, by Klaus Schwab."
[316] "The Fourth Industrial Revolution, by Klaus Schwab."

Thankfully, with the emergence of leaders who truly put the welfare of their people first, such as Donald Trump, Javier Milei, Nayib Bukele, and Giorgia Meloni, there is hope to push back against the "Klausinistas."

> Schwab puts the most recent changes into historical context, outlines the key technologies driving this revolution, discusses the major impacts on governments, businesses, civil society and individuals, and suggests ways to respond. At the heart of his analysis is the conviction that the Fourth Industrial Revolution is within the control of all of us as long as we are able to collaborate across geographies, sectors and disciplines to grasp the opportunities it presents.[317]

Klaus may put the "most recent changes" taking place in the world in a "historical context," but I prefer to put them in a biblical context.

2 Corinthians 4:4 (NLT)

Satan, who is the god of this world, has blinded the minds of those who don't believe. They are unable to see the glorious light of the Good News. They don't understand this message about the glory of Christ, who is the exact likeness of God.

---

[317] "The Fourth Industrial Revolution, by Klaus Schwab."

Klaus and his pack of wild dogs are blind, out of their minds, and hell-bent on destroying God's creation, both in the case of earth and mankind.

> In particular, Schwab calls for leaders and citizens to "together shape a future that works for all by putting people first, empowering them and constantly reminding ourselves that all of these new technologies are first and foremost tools made by people for people."[318]

Oh Klaus, poor, deluded Klaus. The rulers the WEF has trained in the dark arts never put themselves first and the people last. These evil minions suck the power, wealth, and resources from their underlings at all levels. The technologies the misguided ones design and implement are made by the Owners, for the Owners.

> Learning how humankind can benefit from this revolution while addressing its challenges is also the central aim of the World Economic Forum Annual Meeting 2016, which is being held under the theme "Mastering the Fourth Industrial Revolution."[319]

Ensuring humankind never learns what the masters are really doing to destroy our brothers and sisters and enslave the few survivors of their depopulationist antics is job number one of

---

[318] "The Fourth Industrial Revolution, by Klaus Schwab."
[319] "The Fourth Industrial Revolution, by Klaus Schwab."

the WEF. Klaus, Inc. is dedicated to using his "Fourth Industrial Revolution" to master the world.

> Crowdsourcing ideas, insights and wisdom from the World Economic Forum's global network of top leaders from business, government and civil society and young leaders, this new book looks deeply at the future that is unfolding today and how we might take collective responsibility to ensure it is a positive one for all of us.[320]

Joe Biden is a master at "crowdsourcing" insights and wisdom from anyone more intelligent than him, which means all of us. The Biden crime family has perfected ways to take ultimate personal advantage of business, government, and society. Biden has applied gain-of-function methods to "Make America Grovel Again" by ensuring we are last in all respects.

In his book, *The Truth about Neo-Marxism, Cultural Maoism, and Anarchy*, my coauthor, Dr. Jerome Corsi, describes the evil powers behind the New World Order and the direction they desire to take the planet.

> Fronted by the World Economic Forum, these New World Order globalist mobsters and their multinational corporate accomplices are preparing to be the ultimate masters of the world. In a wave of transgender transhumanism, the globalist demons believe they have the technology to

---

[320] "The Fourth Industrial Revolution, by Klaus Schwab."

create the final Nietzschean *Übermensch* to rule over an enslaved, vastly diminished, worldwide population of subservient mortals willing to obey just to receive their daily bread. At the end of their Reign of Terror, the woke generation may finally realize they have birthed their demise—a realization they will not experience until they are herded off to the gulag or walk up the steps with their hands bound behind their backs to face the guillotine.[321]

We must conclude that the implications of the Great Reset do not bode well for democracy, individual freedoms, and economic inequality. In fact, the reality we must all face is that the Owners are desperately trying, during the most important transitional phase in history, to use this period and their influence as their best chance to remove all hope by changing the world into their vision of a global one-world order. The order being one in which, following the great depopulation, the remnant of slaves obey and the handful of Owners rule.

---

[321] Jerome Corsi, *The Truth about Neo-Marxism, Cultural Maoism, and Anarchy* (Post Hill Press, 2023), xiii.

CONCLUSION

THE FINAL BATTLE TO VANQUISH SATAN: DEFEATING THE GLOBAL COUP D'ÉTAT'S NEO-MALTHUSIAN PLAN OF MASS EXTERMINATION

The international mass social rejection of all things United Nations/World Health Organization (WHO) is required. An immediate reappropriation of national sovereignty from the Owners must follow. After we have wrenched the planet from their demonic grip, the prosecution of the embezzlers, criminal conspirators, and their useful puppets in this global criminal enterprise is the next step.

The perpetrators of these crimes against humanity are to be judged, condemned, and publicly punished by the courts of the sovereign nations as already agreed and binding by international law. The appropriate process is already established in international military tribunals, such as those used by the Nuremberg and Kiev war crimes tribunals upon the conclusion of World War II. Those tribunals set a firm and just foundation of international

criminal law as the crimes of using humans involuntary as experimental laboratory animals were universally deemed abhorrent
and egregious.

The WHO was born of those trials, and ironically, used the
repugnant experimentation to highlight the need to universally
prevent a recurrence of the very weaponized diseases that the
"guinea pig" prisoners, disabled and disaffected, were given in
World War II by Germany and Japan. Surely, and even perhaps
on an even more ironic note, the US and Soviet Union had simultaneously launched similar development programs.

It is a perfect "rope-a-dope" maneuver to apply the long-prac-
ticed Hegelian dialectic—create a problem that results in a cry
from the masses for a solution. The Owners then ensure that a
"cure," more virulent than the disease, is provided to the willing public. In reality, the WHO and their global partners, who
are planning the democide now in progress, used the fear of an
enemy using bioweapons to maim and kill. Having spent decades
crafting a legal, financial, and scientific machine, the Owners have
unleashed their hell upon the unsuspecting earth.

The Owners always mitigate their risks, avoiding concen-
tration in one vector, pathogen, manufacturer, and even nation.
The Russians were perfectly siloed as the evil Soviet Union, an
ever-present danger to the US and half the world, against which
bioweapons and other weapons systems could be made secretly
and justifiably. The exact same paradigm was used in relation to
the US and its Western partners who employed the same psychological warfare on their citizens.

No one, not even the scientists making the bioweapon and
other weapons, would dare question the motivation behind

doomsday devices capable of eradicating all of humanity, quickly and efficiently. If it were not for the selfless whistleblowers, dedicated people-first physicians, and a cadre of other freedom fighters, the Owners would have succeeded.

To go back to my time in Poland and other socialist states—I wondered, while living under communist rule, how the true communist believers could possibly perceive the US as such a threat. Of course, a majority of the responsibility lay with the multi-layered propaganda machine and brainwashing of the youth.

I wondered even more how paradoxical and strange it was that our view as Americans was exactly the same and opposite—a non sequitur that only makes sense when you fully understand that the Owners actually do own both sides, almost all sides, and almost everything.

Today's reality is that a small group of people own almost all of the money-printing central banks of this world. They literally print money and fabricate digits out of thin air, regardless of the currency and country. They then lend those fabricated financial resources to their subsidiary governments in return for collateralized national assets, including their citizens.

Nothing is beyond their reach, power, and control. Imagine the temptation for abuse and disdain for the little people.

- If you were an Owner, would you support and own each side of a political party?
- Would you make sure you always had a bogeyman threatening and ensuring that every nation remains in a state of constant fear and working in response on their own doomsday weaponry?

- Would you poison the population to keep the vast majority of them dull, drugged, poisoned, and perpetually sick so they could never have the time, intellect, or resources to figure out the scheme?

- Would you murder scores of people in fantastical and very public ways to shape political perception to your liking?

- Would you groom, hire, promote, and exalt entertainers and athletes to provide some psychological carrot to distract people from their humdrum lives while simultaneously wielding a stick to their collective backsides?

- Would you grow and implant criminal conspirators and collaborators in every permanent bureaucracy in every government?

- Would you carefully select and contrast two candidates for the top executive job to execute the very same policies regardless of their party affiliation?

- Would you pervert God and His words while plotting heinous hypocrisy in the churches and spiritual leaders?

- Would you reward promiscuity and intoxicants to break the bonds of family and long-term relationships to keep people preoccupied and worried about their own circumstances?

- Would you own the media, sports teams, and all forms of entertainment to shape and drive public opinion and perceptions?

- Would you exchange all currencies for digital, programmable ones that could be used to track the products purchased and places visited by the underlings to control every aspect of their lives?

- Would you take the burden of all private property away from people through taxation or other means, such as restitution for failure to pay a debt, or otherwise so leverage everything to impoverish people?

- Would you reclaim vast areas of land from property holders by having environmental laws so strict that the smallest violation or contamination creates a legal and speedy means for the government to steal the property?

- Would you give yourself the power to expropriate peoples' pensions and lifelong savings with taxes and "I owe you" government annuities?

- Would you ensure everyone is implanted with SV-40 immortal cancer cells to ensure that the population is forever sick and forced into insolvency by paying hospitals and doctors you own?

- Would you harvest all the knowledge and intellectual output globally through ownership and control of the university systems?

- Would you specialize all those bright minds by siloing them in their fields of study so that the whole scientific and historical picture could never be discerned or discovered?

If you answered yes to any of the above questions, you have the moral equivalency of an Owner. Only Satan himself would smile and say, "Well done, my evil and faithful servant."

Killing seven to eight billion people is no small task, and medical martial law is frightening by itself. The extermination of that number of people is difficult to envision, much less contain and control. I have exposed in this book that in 1980, the US government made it official national policy to limit the number of people on this planet to not more than eight billion people. That US policy was merely the execution arm of what every other nation, permanent bureaucracy, and the public-private-partnership oligarch (some calling themselves the "Good Club") had already agreed upon.[322] Putting aside the moral question, how would you poison, kill, maim, eradicate, or transform nearly the whole of humanity—almost eight billion people?

- Would you unleash a man-made pathogen (SARS-CoV-1 or SARS-CoV-2 [patented and held by US Department of Health and Human Services]) in order to scare people who have been exposed to countless movies and television programs that are based upon bioweapons and plagues being released upon them so they comply with the "cure"?

- Would you use your owned media and entertainment resources to hype the plandemic?

- Would you reward hospitals and old folks' homes financially and otherwise to poison and kill the patients and residents in order to make the fear palpable?

- Would you tie the hands of humanity from having any rights or legal recourse during the execution of the democide?

- Would you demonize, demean, disengage (disemploy), and disenfranchise all independent thinkers?

---

[322] The Observer, "Secret 'Good Club' holds first meeting in New York," *Taipei Times*, June 1, 2009, https://www.taipeitimes.com/News/biz/archives/2009/06/01/2003445098.

- Would you ensure the pathogenic contents of a supposed vaccine were at least dual purpose so that victims not killed could be controlled through programming?
- Would you implant devices to harness the survivors' biorhythms and genomes as economic power sources and computing nodes?[323]
- Would you convince humanity that virtue requires the enthusiastic uptake of the bioweapons provided them?
- Would you make a "vaccine" program a *military operation*?

Why, many people ask me, would anyone do such a thing?

There are many reasons, including that technology is now so advanced that machines and genetically fabricated droids (not humans) would serve most any purpose an Owner could want. The only thing the Owners do not own is time itself. Yet, as this book has explained, they are even trying to overcome that obstacle by becoming immortal through transhumanism.

But as an Owner ages without the deed to eternity in hand, the motivation to reach that ultimate level creates an enormous driver to become a God. To succeed in building yourself back better or even best, you must upgrade your personal species while destroying the inferior species, the "un-Owners," before they figure out the true landscape of your brave new world and form a defense.

Would you ensure the existence of many vectors of eradication or transformation such that various unseen, unknown

---

[323] Dustin Abramson, Derrick Fu, and Joseph Edwin Johnson, Jr., "Cryptocurrency system using body activity data," US Patent, WO2020060606A1, filed June 20, 2019, published March 26, 2020, https://patents.google.com/patent/WO2020060606A1/en.

weapons systems could be deployed to surround your targets with an invisible electromagnetic field or directed-energy weapon transparent prison?

Would you implant people with the capability to remotely monitor, track, trace, and record all of their audio and visual experiences for intelligence purposes?

Would you hack us mere "hackable animals" as Noah Yuval Harari calls us?[324]

According to the demon Harari, our time has come to an end. We "useless eaters," along with our meaningless God, are destined for his ash can of history if he has his way. But the one true God has a different plan for us all.

Jeremiah 29:11 (NIV)

*"For I know the plans I have for you," declares the
LORD, "plans to prosper you and not to harm
you, plans to give you hope and a future."*

We stand on the proverbial precipice in the story of humanity. We are in the throes of a global coup d'état. Whether one considers it to be merely a "corporate takeover"[325] or the culmination

---

[324] "Commencement Speech 2020: Congratulations, You are Now Hackable Animals," video, Yuval Noah Harari, June 28, 2020, https://www.ynharari.com/commencement-speech-2020-congratulations-you-are-now-hackable-animals/.

[325] Nick Buxton and Lynn Fries, "Global Coup d'État: Mapping the Corporate Takeover of Global Governance," Transnational Institute, February 18, 2021, https://www.tni.org/en/article/global-coup-detat.

of the imposition of the New World Order[326] by the Owners, the result may be the same, or even the success of them both, as a coalition of evil. The multiplicity of globalist actions is a coordinated effort to impose upon the globe a neo-Malthusian plan of mass extermination.

We, the non-Owners, perhaps the lessees, have more than just a moral and ethical imperative to resist and denounce the globalist agenda.[327] It is every human's duty to stop the evil plan of the Owners, for if we do not, the story of humanity ends here. As freeborn human beings, we are all examples of God's creation. We cannot and must not allow the end of humanity to succeed.

The paradigm, the choice, and the proposition before us is literally the decision to survive by choosing God's path and fight like hell or Satan's side, in which the collective flame of life dies out and our species ends. I remain both haunted and encouraged by Matthew 13:38 (ESV):

> *The field is the world, and the good seed is the sons of the kingdom. The weeds are the sons of the evil one.*

As such, the role of faith, whoever you pray to for spiritual guidance, during this period of our ultimate resistance is

---

[326] Ian Martin, "The New World Order: Opportunity or Threat for Human Rights?" Human Rights Program, Harvard Law School, 1993, https://hrp. law.harvard.edu/wp-content/uploads/1993/06/The-New-World-Order_ Ian-Martin_1993.pdf.

[327] Joel H. Rosenthal, "Autocrats, Oligarchs, and Us: A Moment of Crisis for Responsible Internationalism," Carnegie Council for Ethics in International Affairs, September 23, 2022, https://www.carnegiecouncil.org/media/series/ presidents-desk/autocrats-oligarchs-crisis-responsible-internationalism.

paramount. We must exhibit the courage of lions and solidarity of an infantry platoon sweeping their lane while remaining foundationally family first.

This is the pathway to reclaiming our personal and national sovereignty, freedom of choice and life, and human dignity, including the reformation of our societies to demand personal responsibility and reforms, political activism, and community building.

Humanity has the only means of reacquiring the world we lost, the one God made. We are the children of God, and we have been given an opportunity to save ourselves. If we cannot be bothered to do that one all-lifesaving task, then why would our Creator waste his time saving us?

Therefore, this fight is for our collective and individual relationships with God. We must draw on His strength in this final struggle. It is a fight to the death. We have survived long enough to enter into this ultimate conversation. We have also been proven to possess the strength of individuals and small groups holding the last red line. There is no middle ground, no half measures, no two-state solution.

This book is a call for a humanity-wide, humanity-unified global effort to defeat the forces of tyranny.

In the words of President Trump after the attempt on his life in Pennsylvania this year (2024): "*Fight! Fight! Fight!*"

In the end, God always wins. Fear not, stand firm, trust in Jesus.

ABOUT THE AUTHORS

Todd S. Callender, Esq. is an international lawyer and has practiced law for thirty years primarily outside of the United States. He currently serves as the principal in the law firms of Disabled Rights Advocates PLLC and The Corporate Law Firm. Todd is the CEO of social media platform CloutHub and the Cotswold Group of Companies, a Caribbean-based, multi-national insurance group with worldwide subsidiaries and investments.

In 1997, Todd opened trade and commerce between the United States and Cuba by running a field trial of a needle-free mass vaccination device in collaboration with Cuba and the US State and Commerce Departments. He has become heavily experienced in the field of vaccines and vaccinations. In 2021, Todd filed the first lawsuit (*Robert v. Austin*) against the US Department of Defense, Dept. of Health and Human Services, and Food and Drug Administration to stop the "vaccine" mandates in the DOD. The mandates were halted, ensuring access and judicial oversight to exemption procedures for 400,000 service members.

In 2023, Todd filed the first writ of quo warranto with the US Attorney against the entire cabinet of the US executive branch for failure to provide required and perfected oaths of office. Since filing the writ, significant and voluminous evidence has come forward worldwide that fraudulent, nonexistent, or defective Oaths of Office are the norm throughout government in many countries.

Todd is now dedicated to revealing the truth through his writing, CloutHub channel, Vaxxchoice.com, interviews, and other ways to shed light on the darkness.

Jerome R. Corsi received his Ph.D. from Harvard University. He started his multifaceted career as a university professor, contractor for the US State Department, and worked in financial services. Since 2004, Dr. Corsi has written over thirty-five books on politics, economics, energy, culture, climate change, and other major topics. Several of his books became *New York Times* bestsellers, and two rose to the level of #1 bestsellers. In 2024, he co-authored *The Final*

Analysis: The Assassination of John F. Kennedy, and followed that with his most recent book, *The Antiglobalist Manifesto*. Dr. Corsi is co-authoring a book soon to be released regarding various evil intentions of globalist elites.

Dr. Corsi conducts weekday podcasts through his websites thetruthcentral.com and corsination.com. He is the founder and CEO of Corstet LLC, and cofounder of the 501(c)(3) God's Five Stones (godsfivestones.com), dedicated to ensuring election integrity. He is advancing various telemedicine companies, including one in development specifically designed to serve US military veterans.

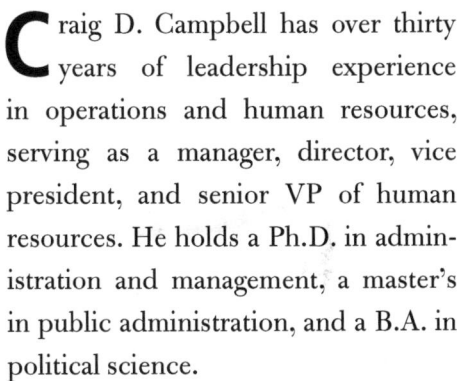

C raig D. Campbell has over thirty years of leadership experience in operations and human resources, serving as a manager, director, vice president, and senior VP of human resources. He holds a Ph.D. in administration and management, a master's in public administration, and a B.A. in political science.

His expertise spans the private, government, and nonprofit sectors, and he has worked across diverse industries including manufacturing, healthcare, transportation, pharmaceuticals, and biotechnology. Dedicated to service, he volunteers in veterans' support programs and church administration.

Made in the USA
Middletown, DE
17 January 2026

27210152R00199